RAND

The Decline of the U.S. Machine-Tool Industry and Prospects for Its Sustainable Recovery

Volume 2, Appendices

Edited by David Finegold

Prepared for the
Office of Science and Technology Policy

Critical Technologies Institute

Preface

This is the companion volume to a report describing the findings of the Machine Tool Study, a Congressionally mandated research project examining the competitive position of the U.S. machine-tool industry. This volume presents supporting material in the form of nine appendices. The study was sponsored by the White House Office of Science and Technology Policy (OSTP) and is being conducted by the Critical Technologies Institute (CTI).

The broad approach we have taken to the analysis of the machine-tool industry should make this report of interest to a wide audience. Federal and state policymakers interested in questions of industrial competitiveness, technology development and transfer, and the adequacy of the U.S. skill base will find the review of existing policies in Chapter Six of the main report very relevant.[1] Researchers working on the machine-tool industry in particular, or manufacturing more generally, can make use of the large amount of data presented in the main report, as well as the supporting appendices in this volume. And machine-tool makers themselves may benefit from the descriptions of successful corporate strategies in Chapter Five and the identification of key future technology trends in Appendix F.

CTI was created by an act of Congress in 1991. It is a federally funded research and development center (FFRDC) within RAND. CTI's mission is to

- provide analytical support to the Executive Office of the President of the United States;
- help decisionmakers understand the likely consequences of their decisions and choose among alternative policies;
- improve understanding in both the public and private sectors of the ways in which technological efforts can better serve national objectives.

Inquiries regarding CTI or this document may be directed to:

Stephen Drezner
Director
Critical Technologies Institute
RAND
2100 M Street, N.W.
Washington, DC 20037-1270

[1]The body of this report is in a companion volume (Finegold et al., 1994).

Contents

Figures

Tables

Appendix A
The Japanese Machine-Tool Industry

Brent Boultinghouse, RAND

Overview

This appendix will examine the development and structure of the Japanese machine-tool industry, with specific attention to the forces shaping the industry in the 1980s. Developments in the Japanese machine-tool industry stand in sharp contrast to circumstances in the United States. In Volume 1 of this study, we identified various factors as keys to competitive success in the machine-tool industry. We discussed how the relative lack of these factors had a strong impact on the current state of the U.S. machine-tool industry. The U.S. weaknesses are

- failure to obtain economies of scale and scope through large companies or cooperation among small firms
- low productivity, resulting from slow adoption of new manufacturing processes
- inadequate access to human capital
- inadequate capital investment by the makers and users of machine tools
- poor government-industry relations
- lags in adjusting to new market demands
- a poor export infrastructure.

Trends in the Japanese machine-tool industry provide a virtual mirror image of circumstances in the United States. The role of government policy, rather than market forces, in shaping economic development in Japan is often questioned. The results of the marriage of these two forces are less disputed. The Japanese machine-tool industry's rise must be viewed in the context of Japan's dramatic postwar economic successes.[1] Many highly integrated, export-oriented firms in

[1]Mitsubishi, Mitsui, and Sumitomo are examples of *Zaibatsu*—prewar industrial conglomerates that combined financing from banking operations, markets through trading operations, intragroup transactions, and equity cross-holding. These international relationships were the precursors of the modern *keiretsu*. *Keiretsu* refers to a variety of business relationships: Vertical *keiretsu* are integrative relationships between suppliers and principals or producers and users; horizontal *keiretsu* involve integration of less structurally linked enterprises, such as between producers and trading companies.

Japan moved prominently into global markets in automobiles, precision machinery, construction machinery, and aerospace—all major customers of machine tools.

Japanese policymakers targeted machine tools as a key industrial sector in the mid-1950s and devised plans for shaping the industry's future. The resulting policies coddled the industry throughout the 1960s, and officials of the Ministry of International Trade and Industry (MITI) kept close watch in the latter part of the decade as capital restrictions began to be relaxed. The currency and oil shocks of the early 1970s interrupted more than a decade of double-digit economic growth. During this period, MITI began again to push for consolidation and specialization in the machine-tool industry. Economic growth and expansion of the machine-tool industry's output resumed at a brisk pace in the late 1970s, peaking in 1980. Much of the growth in the latter period was in the newly emerging market segments for computer numerical control (CNC) commodity machines—a market that the Japanese effectively created.

In the 1980s, an enormous surge in private investment pushed machine-tool demand to an all-time high as fiercely competitive user industries invested heavily. After the rapid appreciation of the yen following the Plaza Accord, firms intensified automation as a way to reduce costs and remain competitive in foreign markets. These firms bought new, more efficient machines to capture incremental improvements in productivity and to alleviate production constraints created by a tight domestic labor market. Competition among machine-tool builders to meet consumer demand spurred constant technological improvements. As the industry strove to enhance demand by creating lines of commodity tools with CNC applications, users sought more versatile tools for use in flexible manufacturing operations. This trend was strengthened by long-standing relationships between machine-tool builders and other members of the same business *keiretsu*, which helped to shore up demand and encourage investment in product innovation.

Throughout most of the postwar period, the presence of a highly skilled work force with little worker mobility between firms provided both machine-tool makers and users alike with an easily trained labor force. Yet while workers were well trained, they were increasingly scarce, and the most talented were often drawn into careers in more lucrative sectors, such as financial services, and away from manufacturing jobs. These trends were acute in technical and engineering fields, and the pattern was even more pronounced among

The formality of these relationships can vary significantly in terms of cross-holding of equity, representation on boards, and extent of intra-*keiretsu* trade.

subcontractors and smaller firms (International Institute for Global Peace, 1991). Such pressures created further incentives for a variety of manufacturers to automate processes whenever possible and to shift labor intensive production abroad.

This appendix first examines the phases of government policy toward the machine-tool industry. We next look at broader structural features of the Japanese market and economy that drove the Japanese to the top of the world machine-tool industry in the last decade. Lastly we examine the prospects for the industry's future and the role of Japan in global machine-tool markets.

A Sheltered Childhood

In the postwar period, the Japanese pursued infant industry policies in a number of sectors. The machine-tool industry led a rather sheltered childhood, during which the government blocked direct foreign investment and encouraged Japanese firms to license and diffuse foreign-developed technologies. Postwar policymakers' first major attempt to shape the machine-tool industry came in the form of the Machinery Promotion Law of 1956.[2] This legislation established investment, production and export goals, as well as promoting standardization of parts and reductions in production costs. In an effort to produce tools in what policymakers considered to be appropriate lot sizes, firms were encouraged to specialize in certain machine types and consolidate operations with other producers.

Zysman (forthcoming) argues that this type of Japanese interventionism produced a distinct pattern of responses in various industries. The government acted as a technology gatekeeper, promoting intense managed competition in the Japanese market. Under this regime, pursuit of market share was the best way to ensure profits. Firms were encouraged to specialize in certain markets in which they could seize a significant share and achieve economies of scale in production. To the extent that "excessive competition" could not be dissuaded, firms built up capacity to achieve market share and used this to sell at the margin in export markets. Zysman's argument of result certainly seems to be borne out in the Japanese example: Production innovation in the firm combined with a global search for technology and waves of increasing capacity translated into intense pressure to export.

---

[2]The Machinery Promotion Law, reenacted in the postwar period in 1956, was one of the tools used by officials to attempt to shape the machine-tool industry's development. Friedman (1988) and Vogel (1985) offer detailed accounts of government involvement in the early stages of the industry's development.

Pressures from the United States and other Organization for Economic Cooperation and Development (OECD) members forced the gradual liberalization of foreign direct-investment controls in place in Japan during the late 1960s. During this period, the machine-tool industry received close attention from MITI. In the mid-1960s, MITI, working with the Japan Machine-Tool Builders' Association (JMTBA) strengthened efforts to "rationalize" the industry through mergers and cooperation. MITI set up a rationalization cartel to increase specialization and upgrade products. They also adopted a product approval scheme, whereby MITI had to give permission for new products. If the new product fell within the firm's designated sphere of products, approval was automatic; if not, approval was almost always denied (Vogel, 1985, pp. 71–72). In 1968, MITI established the Basic Promotional Plan for the Metal Cutting Machine-Tool Manufacturing Industry. This plan set up a 5- to 20-percent goal for production consolidation. Firms that produced less than 5 percent of industry association output in a specific tool type, when that tool accounted for less than 20 percent of their product mix, were to move out of production in that tool. Results appear to have not often matched stated goals, and firms resisted pressures to move out of markets (Friedman, 1988, p. 94). Vogel (1985) argues, however, that while these programs may not have been wholly successful, they did have a positive cumulative impact on the industry.

A Rebellious Youth?

The currency and oil price shocks of the early 1970s briefly disrupted an era of extraordinary economic development in Japan. The new policy push for the machine-tool industry during this period was movement toward more sophisticated machines using CNC technology and tie-ups with the country's growing electronics industry.[3] The Electrical Machinery Law (1971) attempted to hasten the incorporation of CNC technology into Japanese machines and to focus firms on specializing in specific market segments through production restraints.

During this same period, government officials also worked to counterbalance low-cost foreign credit terms as part of a program of import substitution. MITI worked with the Japan Long-Term Credit Bank and the Industrial Bank of Japan to get loans for domestically produced machines. Vogel (1985, pp. 73–74) summarizes the results of these efforts as follows: Once Japanese companies

[3]Japanese data do not distinguish between numerical control (NC) and CNC production. Industry and government officials concur that the vast majority of Japanese production represented in NC data involves CNC technologies and applications. For a more detailed treatment of controllers, please refer to Appendix D.

could produce acceptable machines of a given type, imports of that machine basically ended, even if foreign machines were competitive in quality and price.

Given the dramatic global recession early in the decade, it might not be surprising that none of the production targets established under the Electrical Machinery Law were met (Friedman, 1988, p. 95). Friedman offers an elaborate argument that the industry association (*gyokai)*, rather than MITI regulators, was more effective in establishing and enforcing production restraints. But because it had no control over nonmembers, who often held substantial market shares, the *gyokai's* ability to regulate production was also limited.[4]

While the industry failed to meet MITI's goals for CNC production as a share of overall output, the growth of this ratio over the period is nonetheless impressive. Japanese CNC production accounted for only 7.8 percent of total production in 1970; the share had grown to almost 30 percent by 1978 and reached 50 percent in 1980. (MITI's target for 1978 was 50 percent.) MIT's study of the Japanese machine-tool industry notes the connection between MITI's push for the development of small, standardized NC and CNC machines and its efforts to see this technology diffused to small lot, large variety, just-in-time (JIT) suppliers throughout Japanese manufacturing industries (March et al., 1989, p. 35).

By 1980, 64 percent of machine purchases by small firms (firm size less than 300 employees) involved CNC applications. The trend in the United States was not nearly as pronounced. The U.S. share of CNC machines to small firms reached roughly the same point in 1983, but firm size was defined as less than 500 employees, rather than 300 as in Japan (Edquist and Jacobsson, 1988, pp. 41–42). Furthermore, although the low level of import penetration of machine tools into Japan allows us to assume that most of this market was met by Japanese producers, the surge of Japanese tools into the U.S. market during the same time frame argues against such an assumption in the U.S. case. In fact, much of this new U.S. market appears to have been filled by rapidly expanding Japanese machine-tool lines.

The rapid advances of Japanese machine-tool makers in CNC tool markets are due in no small part to the emergence of Fujitsu Automatic Numerical Control (FANUC), the global leader in CNC equipment production. FANUC started as an internal division of electronics giant Fujitsu. The organization worked jointly

---

[4]Friedman, like most scholars with challenging hypotheses, has drawn his share of detractors. The issue of whether MITI engineered the development of the industry, or rather the industry association engineered MITI into doing its bidding, will continue to be debated. This argument is presented here to illustrate the level of interaction between government actors and firms whose client bases were overwhelmingly commercial (Friedman, 1988, pp. 95–105).

with Japanese tool makers to develop and refine controller applications while at the same time keeping a close watch on technology developments in the United States. In 1974, FANUC entered into an agreement with Gettys to license servomotor production, giving up on one of its founder's own technologies. Within five months of receiving the license, FANUC had mastered production and had a system on display at the International Machine-Tool Show that autumn. Within seven years, FANUC had replaced these motors with its own similarly designed models. Between 1975 and 1977, FANUC produced 12,000 CNC units, the equivalent of all production from the firm's inception through 1974 (Vogel, 1985, p. 82). By 1993, FANUC was producing 6,500 controls per month, far more than the annual production of any U.S. CNC maker.

Through the Extraordinary Measures Law for the Promotion of Specific Electronic Industries and Specific Machinery Industries, MITI undertook a "CNC rationalization," setting performance and quality standards for a variety of machines, and stipulating 50-percent CNC content by 1977. Developers of conventional tools ran into trouble with MITI product approvals, while such approvals were easy if tools had CNC. Firms were also encouraged to specialize in certain types of machines. Machine tools with CNC were excluded from capital liberalization; thus foreign firms could not invest but could only sell their technology. Further, these machines were classified as computers when imported and subjected to higher duties (Vogel, 1985, p. 83).

The role that MITI played in establishing FANUC as an industry leader is hotly debated. But it is the efficacy, not the existence, of policy that is questioned. What is clear is that FANUC shot to the top of the market for high-volume commercial application of CNC controllers using solid-state technology and microprocessors. FANUC's success may initially have come from its ability to license American technology, but it improved upon this and developed its own technology by the mid 1980s. It captured not only the lion's share of the fast-growing Japanese market but also 50 to 70 percent of the global controller market by the mid 1980s.[5]

A Coming of Age

By the start of the 1980s, the Japanese machine-tool industry had taken its seat at the table with other global producers. By the end of the decade, it would open a gulf between itself and its nearest competitors. MITI continued to pull policy levers during the period. For example, it worked with the JMTBA to establish tax

---

[5]Appendix D; also see March et al. (1989), p. 36.

incentives for businesses to invest in energy-saving equipment. Yet, increasing scrutiny of MITI's involvement with the industry, and a decline in the relevance of its policy tools relative to larger economic forces at work, led to a shift in policy focus.

As market penetration from Japanese competitors raised concerns in Europe and the United States, MITI became increasingly involved in managing the flow of Japanese trade. The ministry negotiated formal restraints on exports to the United States and became intimately involved in EC efforts to "monitor" Japanese exports to that market. After a doubling of the yen's value failed to produce a significant increase in import penetration or a noticeable decline in exports, MITI became even more actively involved in encouraging machine-tool imports. MITI officials are quick to point out that no policies are currently in place designed specifically to assist the machine-tool industry and that the tariff rate for machine tools is zero. In the early 1990s, MITI went so far as to establish a system of tax credits for businesses importing machinery. MITI is still reeling from business criticism for agreeing to market-share goals for foreign semiconductor producers. For machine tools, there are no stated import targets, but market shares for most major machine-tool exporters to Japan have remained extraordinarily low and stagnant. Between 1980 and 1992, imports always accounted for 6 to 8 percent of consumption, with the United States, Germany, and Switzerland each accounting for roughly one quarter of the total in any given year. (See Volume 1, Chapter Four.)

Yet, in the areas of capital investment and human capital, there are programs encompassing all manufacturing industries that have a direct positive impact on the machine-tool industry. The first of these is low-cost loans to small businesses for capital investments. Operated at both the national and prefectural (and sometimes municipal) levels, these loans make it possible for small firms, which often have the hardest time raising funds for investments, to gain access to low-cost capital. While interviews with MITI officials failed to produce data on the uses of such funds, officials confirmed that one of the most likely uses is the purchase of equipment, such as machine tools (RAND interviews).

Another key policy tool involves wage subsidies from the Ministry of Labor to manufacturing industries during recessionary periods. Upon designation by the government that the country has entered a period of recession, firms in manufacturing industries can apply to the government for up to 50 percent of the wages of their full-time workers. In exchange for these subsidies, firms agree not to lay off any workers and agree to offer training to workers in proportion to the size of the subsidy. Thus, if a firm accepts a 50-percent subsidy, it is obliged to train workers half time during the period that it is receiving the payments. In addition to the obvious benefits from this increased training, firms benefit substantially from not losing workers in whom they have already made significant training investments. Furthermore, as business begins to pick up again, firms do not have to rehire and train workers to take advantage of what one industry participant termed "the short, sweet spring" during which the ability to produce machines rapidly in response to increased customer demand can yield the windfalls necessary to ride out tougher times ahead.

While the JMTBA has pushed for several years to shorten depreciation schedules for machine tools, their efforts appear to have produced few results. Depreciation schedules are typically set according to the user industry, rather than the type of machine. Thus, for example, most machines used in the automobile industry fall under a 10-year depreciation schedule. JMTBA officials report that the Ministry of Finance's tax bureau has been less than receptive to the idea of lowering depreciation schedules in light of the fact that surveys show most machines are used well beyond the end of their schedules (RAND interviews).[6]

Yet the factors driving Japanese machine-tool industry development were largely the result of market rather than policy forces. The market forces consisted of a mix of demand, technology, and human capital components, and benefited from the existence of industrial organizations unique to Japan. These factors were put forward in the overview to this chapter and will be taken up individually below.

The Invisible Hand: Market Forces and Machine Tools

A major stimulus for demand during the period was an enormous investment boom. The Japanese machine-tool industry benefited greatly from a surge in investment that took place in the 1980s. Figure A.1 shows trends in private sector investment plotted against machine-tool orders. Machine-tool orders increased rapidly after a brief shock following the yen's appreciation (1985–1987). The reasons for Japan's investment boom are numerous and the subject of considerable debate. Although official lending rates as reported by the International Monetary Fund ranged between 6 and 8 percent over the decade, the real interest rate was much lower, and the real cost of capital was actually negative during parts of the peak investment period.[7]

---

[6]Rapid improvements in machine productivity and flexibility mean that older machines are often moved off into dedicated uses as newer machines are added to principal production lines.

[7]Many blue-chip Japanese firms were able to sell convertible bonds at a premium during this period, because investors felt certain that the stocks received upon conversion would more than cover the premium.

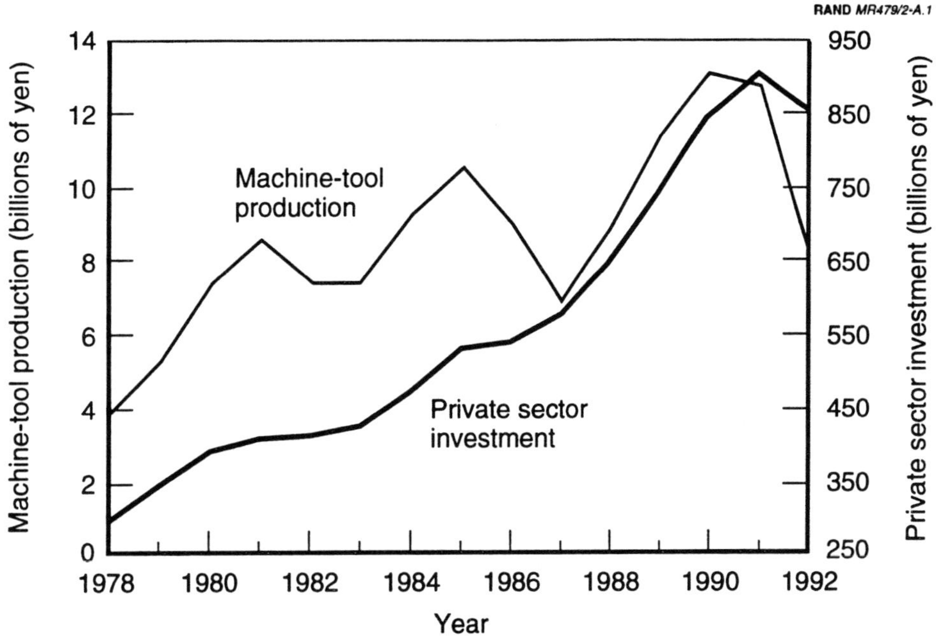

Figure A.1—Machine-Tool Production and Private Sector Investment

The benefits of this investment boom for the machine-tool industry are clear. The metal-processing machinery industry, which includes machine tools, grew by 15 percent in establishments, while its labor force grew by 7.5 percent between 1986 and 1991. Machine-tool orders virtually doubled during the same period. These orders were across a broad range of products and customer industries, though the ratio of CNC machinery continued to increase throughout the decade.

Demand was also spurred by constant innovation. Much has been written about the process of *Kaizen*—iterative improvement—in Japanese manufacturing enterprises. This term is used to characterize both product and process innovation. Its importance here is in illustrating a management philosophy that emphasizes constant incremental improvements that are acquired through training, quality circle activities, and the addition of marginally more productive equipment.

Debate raged in Japan following the yen's rapid appreciation as to what Japanese firms could do to remain competitive in global markets. Exemplary of their long-term perspective, machine-tool firms maintained prices in real terms to keep their market share and thus put a pinch on profits. This trend is evident in movements of export price indexes for various machine tools during that period (see Figures A.2 and A.3). In fact, while export prices should be expected to rise with the value of the yen to maintain receipts, they actually fell dramatically.

Similar pressures in many export-driven industries to hold foreign market prices (and shares) in the face of the rising yen created an enormous demand for cost-cutting measures and rationalization of production processes.[8] Once it became evident that the revaluation of the yen would not cause the demise of Japanese industry, investments in plant and equipment, and specifically in machine tools, began to shoot upward.

Customers also demanded innovation. For example, the push for flexible manufacturing capabilities in the automobile industry created the need for more flexible machine tools, which could be quickly transformed to perform a variety of tasks. The expansion of these manufacturing process technologies to other sectors of the economy, such as electronics and general machinery, boosted demand for more flexible machine tools from principal manufacturers down to minor suppliers. As noted earlier, MITI was also active in promoting the diffusion of flexible tools throughout supplier industries. The push for flexible production in other sectors created a demand for mass production in the machine-tool sector, allowing makers to capitalize on economies of scale in tool production.

Pressure to innovate was further heightened by the severe labor shortages that began to appear in Japan during economic booms. Quarterly surveys from the Bank of Japan attest to the growing sense of tightness in the labor market, especially in manufacturing sectors, as firms began to emerge from the slump of the mid-eighties (International Institute for Global Peace, 1991). This trend created a further boost for firms to increase automation levels through investment in equipment.

A combination of worker scarcity and companies' commitments to the Japanese system of lifetime employment created an environment in which workers embraced rather than resisted automation. Firms hired full-time employees on the basis of long-term growth projections, rotated workers between a variety of occupational classifications, and trained them to use new technologies as they came on line. During economic slumps, government wage subsidies to enterprises throughout the manufacturing sector allowed firms to retain workers in whom they had made training investments.

[8]For a more detailed analysis of price movements in the wake of yen-dollar exchange rate fluctuations, see Lowell and Yager (1994) and Knetter (1992).

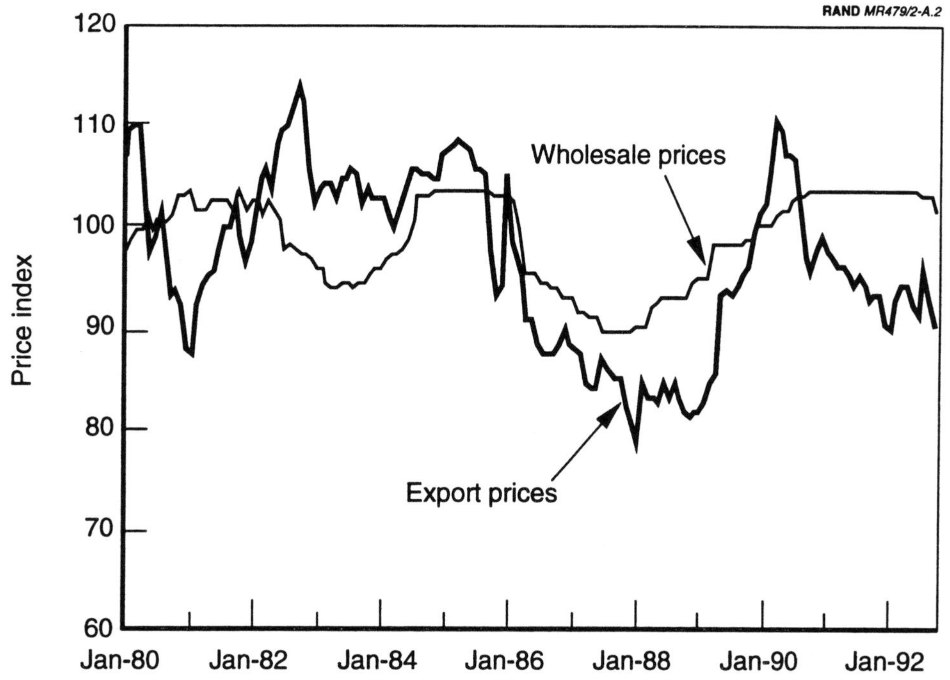

Figure A.2—Machining Centers: Wholesale and Export Prices

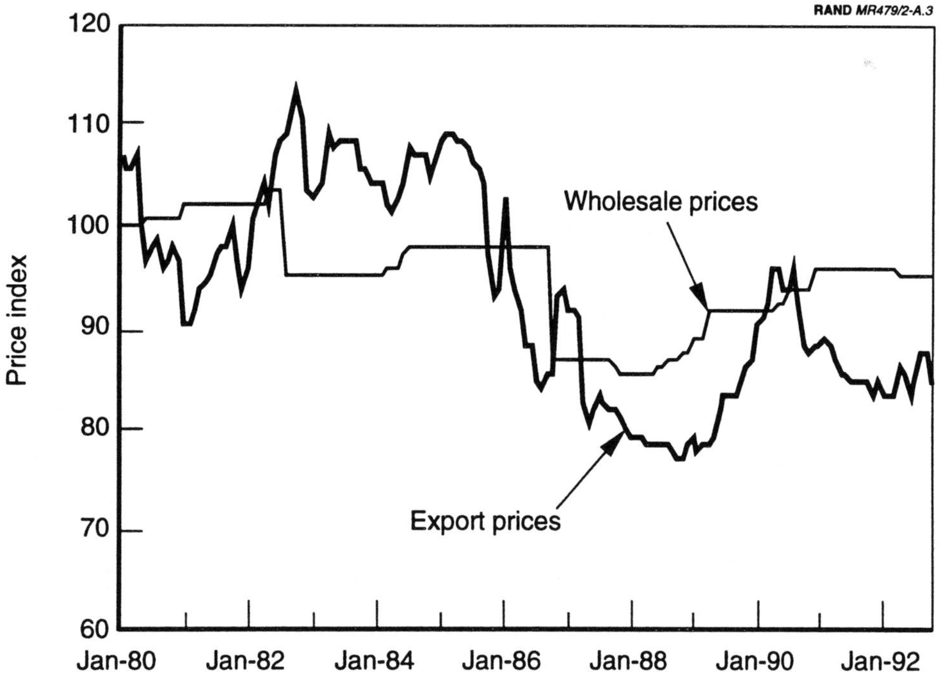

Figure A.3—NC Lathes: Wholesale and Export Prices

Japan Creates an Industry Standard

Japanese machine-tool makers introduced several innovations that, in effect, created a new international standard for the industry in the 1980s. Through the increasing use of controllers, modular design, and flexible production, these firms created a market for relatively cheap commodity tools that could be produced en masse using JIT and flexible manufacturing techniques.

CNC technology became increasingly important throughout the decade.[9] Figure A.4 demonstrates not only the increasing importance of CNC tools within Japanese production but also the dramatic difference between Japanese and American application of the technology. By 1991, almost three-quarters of Japanese production, in terms of value, involved CNC application. Conversely, U.S. production of CNC tools had yet to reach the level of the Japanese from more than a decade earlier. While U.S. machine-tool builders appear to have emphasized application of CNC technology in larger systems, the Japanese

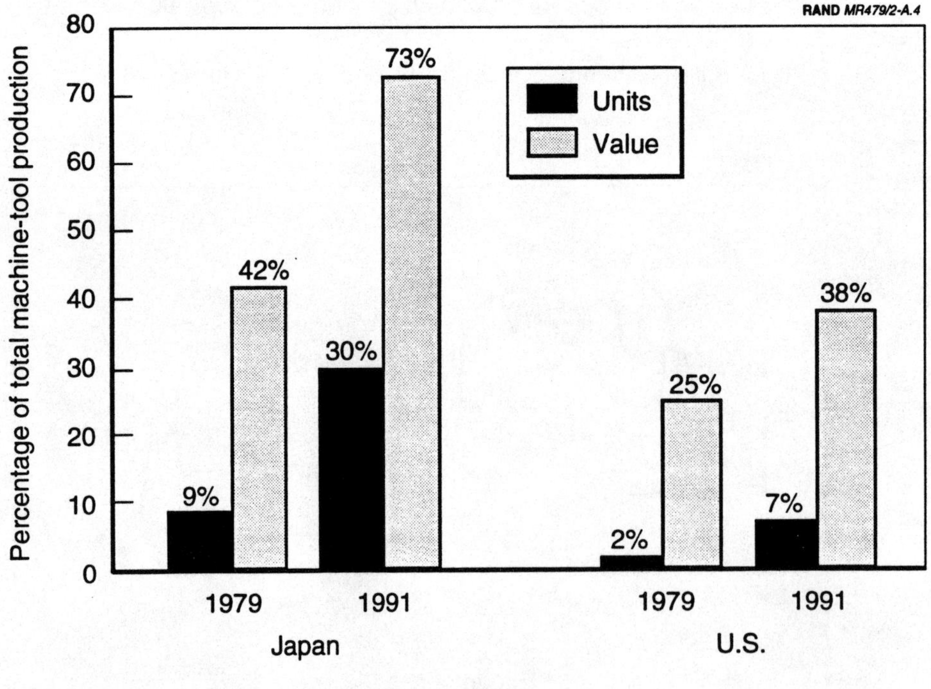

Figure A.4—Numerically Controlled Tools as a Percent of Total Machine-Tool Production

---

[9]Friedman (1988) concludes that Japanese success in application of CNC technology came about not as the result of effective policy on the part of MITI but rather as a result of the willingness of foreign firms, especially American, to license technology to Japanese producers as a way of breaking into the Japanese market. For example, FANUC's market share had fallen to 50 percent by 1983 as many firms established their own technology tie-ups to gain access to foreign technology.

concentrated initially on the small, job-shop CNC market, which had been largely ignored by U.S. producers (March et al., 1989; Friedman, 1988, p. 124).

Yet the application of CNC technology was only one component of Japan's technological success story. Advances in modular production also pushed the industry forward. Japanese machine-tool builders focused efforts on modularized production to create economies of scale while still allowing for the ability to "customize" ("optionize") machines to meet customer demands. Traditional practice often required machine-tool builders to re-create the wheel with each new order. This not only increased costs but also lengthened the amount of time required for delivery. Japanese firms began to approach this problem by creating modular design components, which were interchangeable between machines. This allowed for the design of a base machine with a set of standard options (optional modules) that could be added to accommodate customer demands. When possible, modules were also designed to be used on several base machines, further enhancing economies of scale. Using these techniques, production costs and part counts were reduced at the same time that significant design overlaps were achieved (RAND interviews; also see March et al., 1989).

This revolution in machine design was illustrated in a story related by the president of one of Japan's successful international machine-tool firms, who told how he made his engineering staff aware of the need always to consider design standardization (RAND interviews). In the late 1970s, he gathered his engineering staff into an area of the factory in which he had the firm's top-selling machines disassembled down to the bolts and laid out side by side across the floor. He then walked down the line with the staff pointing to similar components and quizzing the staff about the need for differences in their design specifications. "Why does this mounting require a 4.5-mm bore, while a similar component on a different machine uses a 5.5-mm bore?" "Is it not possible to design a tool changer for one machine that can be used on a variety of other machines as well?" These and similar questions were brought up to raise the engineering staff's appreciation of the need to standardize design wherever possible.

Total quality management (TQM) and JIT production processes were also incorporated into most machine-tool builders' production strategies much earlier than in the West. As in many other product sectors, utilization of these techniques allowed for constant improvements in product quality and design as information about product shortfalls and suggestions from production workers were fed back into the production process. Machine-tool makers built and utilized machines and, more importantly, integrated systems of machines for their own production processes and used the knowledge gained through this process to do the same for customers.

With competition among machine-tool builders revolving around rapid incremental improvements in machine capabilities, the life-cycle of machines declined. While long-term reliability of machines remained a key concern, technological innovation began to make machines obsolete long before they wore out. Both data on the average age of machines and interviews with industry participants suggest that it is cost-effective to replace machines with newer models in as little as five years.

Assigning employees more responsibility in the production process and fostering competition among quality control (QC) circles within the firm also enhanced overall efficiency in the production process by allowing employees to design their production activities more efficiently, while at the same time assuring sufficient attention to quality maintenance. Quality competitions are often elaborate international operations, with teams giving presentations on their suggested improvements and various incentives offered to top performers (RAND interviews).

Investing in Human Capital

Japanese firms derive a great source of competitive strength from the country's well-educated populace. Functional literacy and numeracy are almost universal in Japan. Up to 90 percent of Japanese high school graduates have been exposed to basic calculus by graduation. There are vocational high schools which have been established to feed high school graduates directly into certain occupations, but interviews suggest that few machine-tool builders see these vocational programs as a key element in training their workforces with specific skills. Instead, most firms consider the high level of general education to be an important factor in their ability to train their workforce. There are also national standards of proficiency in machining which benefit not only machine-tool builders but also a variety of user industries. In fact, metalworking is one of the most popular occupations for individuals to obtain further qualifications after leaving school (RAND interviews).

Japan's manufacturing workforce is still overwhelmingly male. This is especially true when considering full-time permanent staff—those most likely to receive significant training.[10] Japanese firms' training practices exemplify what has been

[10]An interesting fact to emerge from labor statistics from the machinery-processing industry is the statistic that women employees increased by 21.5 percent between 1986 and 1991, while total

described earlier in this report as a virtuous circle (see Volume 1, Chapter Four). Buttressed by the still-strong lifetime employment system, which guards against poaching, and policy incentives, which allow firms to keep and train workers during economic downturns, firms continue to invest heavily in training full-time workers. Machine-tool industry participants testified that the first year of employment is spent almost exclusively in training, both in specific job skills and in the firm's philosophy of quality management and maintenance. During this period, and in fact throughout their careers, workers are shifted through various departments so that they may master a number of skills and become familiar with the various operations of the firm.

This practice allows the firm flexibility in adjusting to changes in demand. Several firms noted that, during the current slump, they had moved a number of staff members from production to sales positions in hopes of further reducing pressures on inventories. In fact, firms appear to have very few job classifications, and there is little evidence that company-based unions press for stratification of the workforce into set occupational roles. Virtually all staff members are salaried, rather than hourly workers—a factor that some firms consider important in increasing the sense of professionalism among line workers.

However, a distinction must be drawn between workers who fall under the lifetime employment system—the firm's core labor force—and part-time or temporary workers who are brought in and released on an as-needed basis. In an effort to achieve more flexibility in the face of cyclical demand, firms have moved more and more toward the use of part-time line staff, using them in much the same way as they do the services of subcontractors (RAND interviews).

For workers, job security and wage levels appear to be directly proportional to the size of the firm and its place in the production "food chain." The smaller the firm, the less likely it will be able to offer lifetime job security. Furthermore, anecdotal evidence strongly supports the thesis that firms lower down the "food chain" are not willing to offer wages higher than those offered by the firms to which they contract. One interviewee put it this way: "If I can pay my workers more than the firm to whom I am selling my parts, then by definition my costs are too high. Workers understand this difference. That's why, when they enter the job market, they apply first to the contractor, then if unsuccessful, to the subcontractor" (RAND interviews).

---

employment in the industry grew by 7.5 percent. This certainly offers support to the thesis that Japanese firms can draw upon female laborers during peak production periods. Without adequate data, we can only surmise about how much training these workers receive, as their tenure is typically not guaranteed.

Industrial Structure and Machine-Tool Markets

The existence and importance of long-standing relationships between builders and their customers and suppliers have been alluded to earlier. These relationships are important not only in shaping demand for machine tools but also in shaping production relationships. The previous sections of this appendix focused on the forces shaping demand and development in the machine-tool industry. In the following sections, attention will shift to the structure of the present-day industry, its location, and markets.

Firm Structure

The Japanese machine-tool industry is composed overwhelmingly (97.5 percent) of firms with less than 500 employees, but the large majority of production and exports comes from the largest firms. In firms with 500 to 999 employees (1.7 percent), there is an average of 683 employees, but the average number of employees jumps to 2,272 for firms with over 1,000 employees. Association for Manufacturing Technology (AMT) figures suggest that Japan's top 15 firms accounted for roughly 79 percent of industry production in 1991. The JMTBA represents 114 of the approximately 200 firms active in the industry,[11] but the organization claims that its members represent well over 90 percent of the industry's total output. A breakdown of JMTBA member firms by number of employees is shown in Table A.1. In total, JMTBA members employed approximately 38,000 persons in 1991.

Table A.1

Number of Establishments by Employees in the JMTBA

Number of Employees	Number of Firms	Percentage of Total
Less than 49	18	15.8
50 to 99	17	14.9
100 to 299	47	41.2
300 to 499	11	9.7
500 to 999	13	11.4
More than 1000	8	7.0

SOURCE: JMTBA.

[11]Small-scale and low-end machine-tool makers are often engaged in production of products not classified as machine tools as well. MITI and industry association officials estimate over 200 active industry participants. The JMTBA compiles national data on machine-tool orders and assists MITI in compilation of data on production and inventories according to association members.

Builder-User and Builder-Supplier Relations

While a detailed discussion of *keiretsu* structures within Japan is beyond the scope of this analysis,[12] they bear mention here as they impact the machine-tool industry and its development. Several machine-tool builders are tied to both users and suppliers through both cross holdings of equity and long-established trading relationships. For example, Toyoda Machinery has long-standing ties to its former parent Toyota, and produces a significant share of tools specialized for the auto industry. Another example is Toshiba Machinery, related to the highly diversified Toshiba Corporation. Toshiba Machinery's machine-tool operations actually account for only 30 to 40 percent of the firm's total machinery sales, but the demand from this and other Toshiba operations provides a strong internal market for machine tools.

Such tie-ups within *keiretsu* provide a strong context for technology transfer and development, often on a partnership basis. Firms exchange engineers with major customers and may codevelop new machines with the understanding that the customer will have a voice in the diffusion of the technology to competitors, at least in the short term.

Similar relationships can be found between machine-tool builders and their suppliers. These relationships are a key to Japan's high productivity, as machine-tool firms outsource a greater percentage of value-added (52 percent) than their U.S. or German rivals (40 percent) (McKinsey Global Institute, 1993, p. 5). Again, much has been written about the buffer to economic hard times that small suppliers provide to major Japanese manufacturers in a variety of industries (Sakai, 1990).[13] MITI's *Vision of the 21st Century Machinery Industry* (1989), developed in cooperation with the JMTBA, cites over 5,500 first-tier suppliers to machine-tool makers. While many of these involve basic assembly or parts-processing relationships, numerous key suppliers work interactively with machine-tool builders in development of components. Where relationships with suppliers are long-standing, makers often exchange and train the staff of suppliers. They may also transfer certain technologies to suppliers to enhance their skills, increasing the quality of components while reducing their cost over time. Some firms also force their internal divisions to compete with suppliers for contracts. One firm noted that it always sources at least 20 percent of any given

---

[12]For more information on the structure and interworkings of *keiretsu* in the Japanese economy, see Lawrence (1991). Also see Cutts (1992).

[13]Majors often use suppliers to fill in during peak production periods, and then reduce subcontracting and internalize these operations during downturns.

component through outside sources as a means of providing a scale against which to measure internal competitiveness (RAND interviews).

Makers may also work with suppliers to facilitate the smooth flow of components into the production process, in effect shifting some of this burden onto suppliers. For instance, some Mazak suppliers both in the United States and Japan deliver prepackaged parts kits to Mazak's production facilities. These kits are stored on pallets by the firm's computerized inventory management system, which can mechanically deliver all requisite parts for the day's production to assembly stations at night while production crews are off duty.

Suppliers also face strong competitive incentives to keep their operations equipped with state-of-the-art technology. Machine-tool builders often survey operations of competing suppliers to assess their relative positions. Industry insiders explain that firms with more-modern equipment are thought to be more able to gradually lower prices for components, thus improving the builder's long-term competitive position. This same practice occurs across a broad range of industries and is cited as a key factor behind the strong demand for machine tools among the supplier tiers of manufacturing enterprises.

Location

The Japanese machine-tool industry is concentrated on the main island of Honshu, with a few establishments scattered across northern Kyushu and Shikoku. While some of the industry has developed along the Japan Sea side of the island, the majority of firms are to be found along the industrial corridor between Tokyo and Osaka, with a strong concentration around the Nagoya metropolitan area. Along with being the center of operations for Japan's largest automobile producer, Toyota, this region has a long history of excellence in the general machinery industry.

Japanese machine-tool firms have also moved abroad rapidly to establish transplant operations. By far the oldest in the United States is the Mazak Corporation, established in 1974 in Florence, Kentucky (see Volume 1, Chapter Four). Hitachi Seiki established operations in the United States in 1979; like Mazak, it concentrates on production of CNC lathes and machining centers. These firms were followed in 1983 by Mitsubishi Electric, which set up operations outside Chicago to produce CNC controllers for the U.S. market.

It is interesting to note that most Japanese machine-tool makers in the United States established operations contemporaneously with the enactment of the voluntary restraint agreement on the import of machining centers and CNC lathes. Furthermore, with the exception of Okamoto's surface grinders and GE-FANUC's and Mitsubishi's CNC operations, all transplants are involved in the production and/or assembly of machining centers and CNC lathes. The latter point bears further attention. While not wanting to be identified with specific remarks, a number of Japanese industry spokesmen concurred that some transplants are largely political operations, offering little economic benefit for producers and little technological diffusion and skill development for domestic workers (RAND interviews).

Japanese transplants have also been active in Europe and Asia. While operations in Europe appear designed to serve the European market, many operations in Asia have a high emphasis on exports and appear to be part of a broader long-term strategy to move low-end production offshore. Yamazaki-Mazak recently opened a facility in Singapore to produce machine-tool components, which are shipped to its factories in the United States, Japan, and Europe. Okamoto Machine produces conventional tools in both Singapore and Thailand that are destined largely for the U.S. market—60 percent and 100 percent, respectively. According to company spokesmen, there is virtually no domestic market for these simple tools in Japan, and the cost of producing the tools in Japan would make them uncompetitive on the global market (RAND interviews).

Client Structure

Table A.2 illustrates the consumption of machine tools broken down by user industry for the period between 1982 and 1991. Machinery manufacturing accounted for the lion's share of total demand (domestic) for machine tools, registering between 50 and 60 percent of total orders. General machinery producers accounted for between 25 and 30 percent of demand for tools during the period. Automobile makers also weighed in heavily, accounting for 16 to 20 percent of machine-tool demand. The electronic industry was also a significant consumer of machine tools during the period, accounting for approximately 5 percent of demand.

An interesting factor to note is the declining importance of trading companies and distributors in machine-tool demand. While these companies are not direct users of machines, they have traditionally been involved in facilitating purchases by smaller firms. The JMTBA cites the increased complexity of user needs in the creation of flexible manufacturing systems as a major reason for increased direct contact between users and makers, circumventing more traditional distribution networks. To meet this challenge, a growing number of trading firms have moved to establish special skills as systems integration specialists. The Japan

Table A.2

Machine-Tool Demand by User Industry (percent)

	1982	1983	1984	1985	1986	1987	1988	1989	1990	1991
Metal processing	1.9	1.3	1.3	0.9	0.5	1.0	0.8	0.9	1.0	1.0
Metal products	2.6	3.7	3.2	3.0	2.0	2.9	2.1	2.5	2.5	2.0
Machinery										
General	51.5	50.4	51.6	51.4	50.9	48.2	52.7	52.2	51.3	51.0
Electrical	6.7	10.8	9.8	7.7	6.3	7.0	7.0	6.6	7.2	8.3
Automotive	33.9	30.1	28.8	32.7	33.7	34.8	30.9	33.9	35.2	33.9
Shipbuilding/ transport	3.3	2.5	2.3	1.9	2.3	2.1	2.5	2.3	2.0	2.7
Total	61.8	53.0	55.3	54.6	50.4	53.1	58.1	60.1	60.1	60.1
Precision	4.6	6.2	7.5	6.4	6.8	7.9	6.8	4.9	4.3	4.1
Other manu-facturing	0.9	1.9	1.8	1.5	1.6	2.1	2.8	3.1	3.1	3.4
Public sector, schools	0.4	0.4	0.3	0.2	0.3	0.5	0.5	0.3	0.3	0.3
Other demand	0.5	0.8	0.9	0.5	0.7	0.4	0.7	1.0	0.9	1.0
Trading companies	9.7	10.6	8.7	8.3	8.5	8.2	6.7	5.5	5.7	6.4
Domestic demand (total)	77.9	71.1	71.3	69.1	64.0	68.3	71.7	73.4	73.6	74.3
Foreign demand (total)	22.1	28.3	28.7	30.9	36.0	31.7	28.3	26.6	26.4	25.7

SOURCE: JMTBA.

Machine-Tool Distributor's Association also established a system engineering training program in the fall of 1991 to assist in training personnel in the field of systems integration (JMTBA, 1992).

Leasing firms have also become common in the industry. While production of machine tools grew 1.8 times between 1982 and 1990, total leasing contracts increased threefold during the same period. The share of leased machines as a percentage of overall industry production grew from just over 20 percent in 1982 to over 40 percent in 1988 before declining to approximately 35 percent in 1990. In addition to the attractiveness of leasing to smaller firms, which may have more difficulty raising capital for investments in machinery, rapid technological change makes leasing an attractive option for firms seeking to avoid technological obsolescence of machinery prior to the end of depreciation schedules.

Prospects

The Japanese machine-tool industry has been hard hit by the collapse of the "bubble economy" (see Volume 1, Chapter Five). For the last two years, the Japanese business and economic press has engaged in a debate over the future of Japan's economic performance in the "post-bubble" era. Much of the unresolved debate revolves around the extent to which Japanese manufacturers may have "overinvested" in plant and equipment, specifically in automation, during the last investment boom. The seeming evaporation of huge pools of capital generated through real estate and equity investment suggests that even when investment picks up again, the intensity may be less pronounced.

The implications of this debate for the machine-tool industry are self-evident. Machine-tool demand in recent periods is less than one-half its 1990 peak, and some industry participants suggest that slower growth will push off a rebound until the end of this decade.

Yet the picture may not be this bleak. Although a high-priced yen will continue to squeeze export profits, Japanese machine tools show little sign of losing their competitive edge either domestically or abroad. Many of the factors that drove the industry remain strong. Given the overcapacity that now exists in the Japanese industry, strong incentives for production and exports will continue and intensify. Recent trends in European markets suggest that the Japanese are poised to move more forcefully into markets that have heretofore been left largely to the Germans and Italians.[14] Japanese companies are responding to the high yen by increasing their investments in the Pacific Rim, the most rapidly growing market for machine tools now and in the future.

Bibliography

Cutts, Robert L., "Capitalism in Japan: Cartels and Keiretsu," *Harvard Business Review*, July–August 1992, pp. 48–55.

Edquist, Charles, and Steffan Jacobsson, *Flexible Automation: The Global Diffusion of New Technology in the Engineering Industry*, Oxford: Basil Blackwell, 1988.

Friedman, David, *The Misunderstood Miracle: Industrial Development and Political Change in Japan*, Ithaca, N.Y.: Cornell University Press, 1988.

International Institute for Global Peace, *Nihon no Sangyo Kyosoryoku no Tenbo ni Kansuru Chosakenkyu [Survey Research on Japan's Industrial Competitiveness: The Effects of Labor Demand on Industrial Manufacturing]*, a report commissioned by the Sangyo Kenkyusho, Tokyo, March 1991, circulation limited.

Japan Machine Tool Builders' Association, *Seicho, Henkaku—Junen no Kiroku [Growth, Innovation—A 10-Year Record]*, Tokyo, 1992.

[14]RAND interviews with industry participants in Europe suggest that Japanese marketing practices in the EU market have become very competitive, with reports of two-for-one deals and significant inventory pile-ups.

Knetter, Michael M., *Exchange Rates and Corporate Pricing Strategies*, Cambridge, Mass.: National Bureau for Economic Research, Working Paper No. 4151, 1992.

Lawrence, Robert Z., "Efficient or Exclusionist: The Import Behavior of Japanese Corporate Groups," *Brookings Papers on Economic Activity 11*, Washington, D.C.: The Brookings Institution, 1991.

Lowell, J., and L. Yager, *Pricing and Markets: U.S. and Japanese Responses to Currency Fluctuations*, Santa Monica, Calif.: RAND, MR-438-CAPP, 1994.

March, Artemis, *The U.S. Machine Tool Industry and its Foreign Competitors*, working paper prepared for the Commission Working Group on the Machine Tools Industry, MIT Commission on Industrial Productivity, 1988.

McKinsey Global Institute, *Manufacturing Productivity*, Washington, D.C.: McKinsey and Co., Inc., October 1993.

MITI, *Vision of the 21st Century Machinery Industry*, Tokyo, 1989.

Sakai, Kuniyasu, "The Feudal World of Japanese Manufacturing," *Harvard Business Review*, November-December 1990, pp. 38–49.

Vogel, Ezra F., *Comeback, Case by Case: Building the Resurgents of American Business*, New York: Simon and Schuster, 1985.

Zysman, John, "Dynamic Diversity: Institutions and Economic Development in the Advanced Countries," in Robert Delorme, ed., *The Political Economy of Diversity*, London: Edward Elgar Publishing, forthcoming, pp. 126–146.

Appendix B
The German Machine-Tool Industry

Prof. Frank C. Englmann, Christian Heyd, Daniel Köstler, Peter Paustian, with the assistance of Susanne Baur and Peter Bergmann, University of Stuttgart

The Geographical Distribution of Machine-Tool Firms in the Federal Republic of Germany

The German machine-tool industry is mainly concentrated in Baden-Württemberg and North Rhine-Westphalia. Both regions together account for approximately 75 percent of German machine-tool production. The locations of machine-tool firms in Germany are detailed in Figure B.1.

RAND MR479/2-B.1

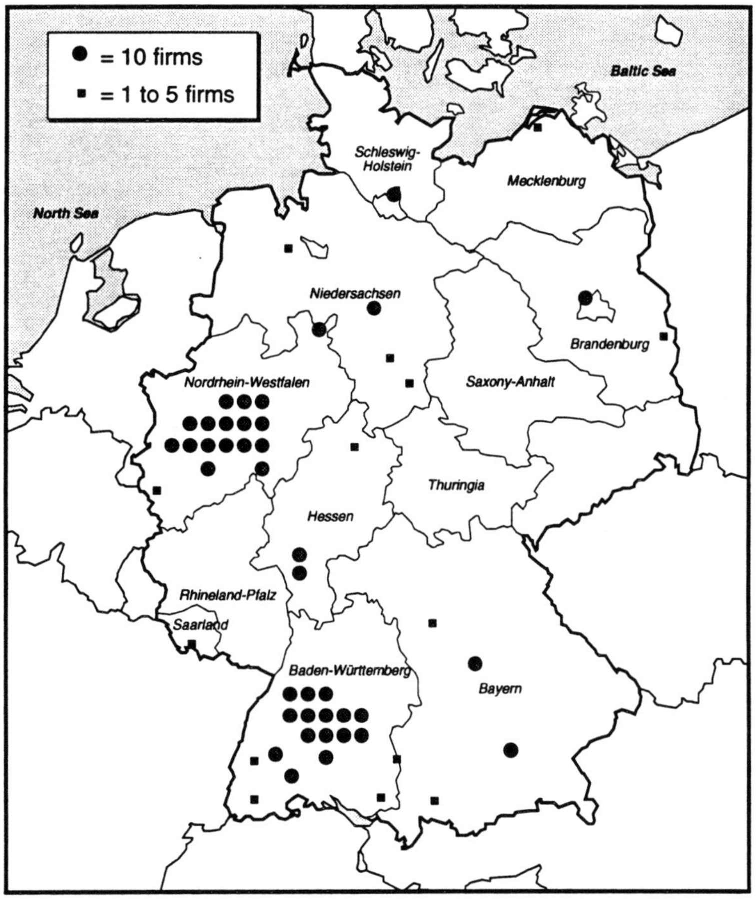

Figure B.1—The Regional Concentration of the German Machine-Tool Industry

Historically, the scarcity of raw materials forced firms to seek more skill-intensive manufacturing markets, leading to a high concentration of machine-tool makers in Baden-Württemberg. Extensive heavy industry in North Rhine-Westphalia accounts for the high concentration of machine-tool firms in this area. The process of concentration is self-reinforcing, because most of the main clients of machine-tool producers are manufacturers (machines, automobiles, metals) who are based in Baden-Württemberg and North Rhine-Westphalia. This domestic client structure has been consolidated during the past five years (see Figure B.2).

This geographical concentration creates a chain of machine-tool producers, metal-processing firms, automakers, and electrical engineering businesses that influence each other's development.[1] Such influence must not be confused with institutionalized interfirm relationships, since most of the connections are informal. The strong regionalism of the machine-tool industry also means that Baden-Württemberg has been very hard hit by the current economic crisis.

RAND MR479/2-B.2

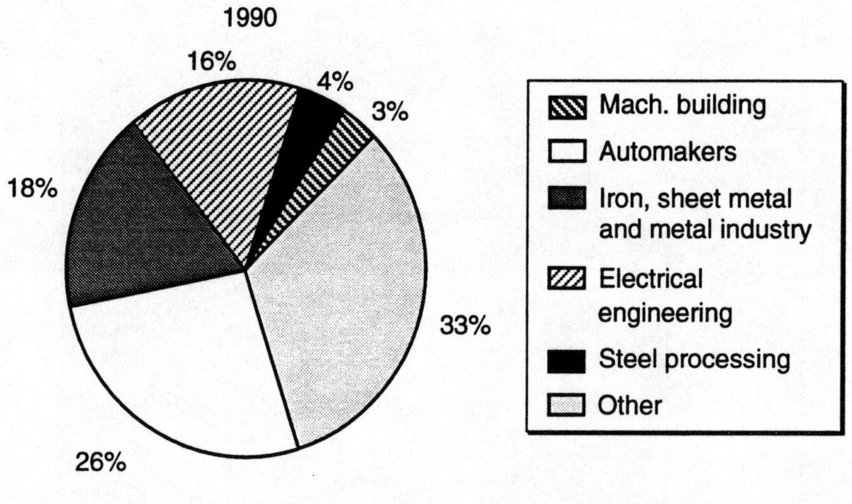

SOURCE: Organization of German Machine-Tool Enterprises (VDW).

Figure B.2—Client Structure of Machine-Tool Industry

---

[1]See W. Kelch, VDMA manager Baden-Württemberg, cited in *Stuttgarter Zeitung*, April 22, 1993.

The Importance of the Machine-Tool Industry for the German Economy

From a quantitative point of view, the machine-tool industry is not a large part of the German economy. In 1991, it employed about 100,000 people, i.e., 1.37 percent of the employees in the total manufacturing industry, and produced an output of 16 DM, i.e., 0.95 percent of the manufacturing industry's turnover. Rather, the industry's importance for the whole economy is grounded on its key technological position. Machine tools are essential to industrial production and, thus, have a far-reaching effect on the production process. The diffusion of innovations in the capital-goods industry is strongly related to the innovativeness of the machine-tool producers. Technical change in machine tools often stems from close but (at least until recently) individual relations between producers and customers. Thus, the machine-tool sector is strategically important for increasing productivity in German industry (see Rendeiro, 1985).

The machine-tool industry supplies investment-goods industries, so its business is more variable than overall business cycles (see Figure B.3). In view of this, the current crisis in the German machine-tool industry is often interpreted as one of the "regular" downturns. A closer look at the problems, however, casts doubt on this assumption.

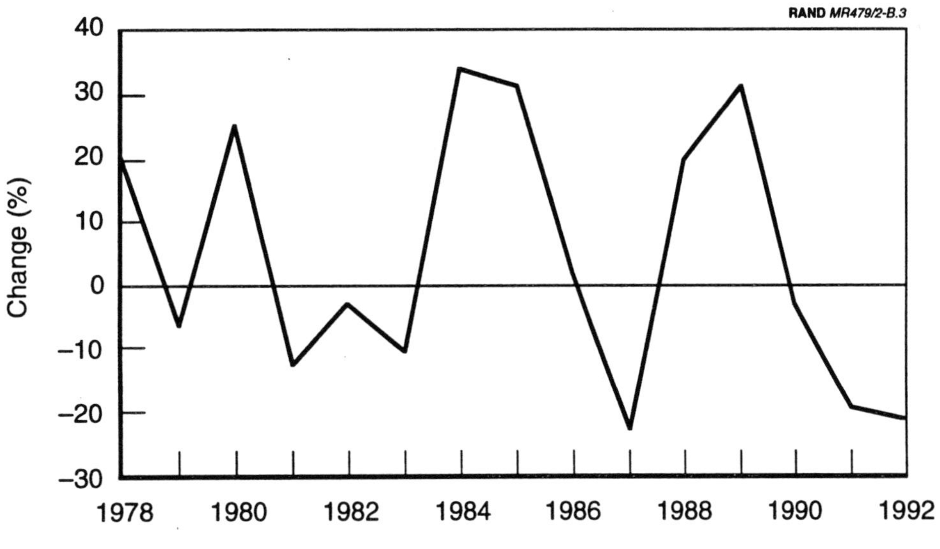

SOURCE: VDW and author calculations.

Figure B.3—Percentage Change in Incoming Orders

The Structure of the German Machine-Tool Industry

One characteristic feature of the German economy is the preponderance of small- and medium-sized enterprises (SMEs). About 95 percent of German enterprises are SMEs. Roughly three-quarters of all workers are employed in them (see, for example, the manufacturing sector, Table B.1) where two-thirds of all sales are realized.

The machine-tool industry, with roughly 400 firms, is also composed predominantly of SMEs. In 1991, only 5.1 percent of machine-tool producers had more than 1,000 employees, but they engaged 27.6 percent of all employees in the industry. Of the 20 largest German machine-tool producers in 1990, Trumpf held first place, with realized sales of 726 million DM. Tenth-placed Böhringer had sales just under 400 million DM. A complete classification by number of employees is given in Table B.2. These proportions have varied little over the past ten years. The number of small firms has decreased in favor of firm sizes from 250 to 1,000 employees, a trend that probably can be explained by expansion efforts during these prosperous years. However, firms with fewer than 100 employees still represent the majority of machine-tool enterprises.

A survey revealed the most important types of production and the product types, as shown in Figures B.4 and B.5.[2] Small series or even single orders account for 88 percent of production, as expected given the firm-size structure. Small lot sizes vary slightly according to firm size, but mass production remains negligible (the maximum fraction accounts for 1.15 percent).

Table B.1

The Distribution of Employment by Firm Size for the Manufacturing Sector in Germany

Size Class (employees)	Percentage (cumulative)
0–4	0.3
5–9	7.6
10–19	8.7
20–49	10.2
50–90	7.6
100–199	8.0
200–499	10.6
500–999	7.1
>1,000	35.0

SOURCE: Fritsch (1990), p. 4.

[2]Type of production and products related to all manufactured products and product groups; 136 respondents.

Customized products dominate the product slate, with a share of 70 percent in small firms, decreasing to 44 percent in firms with fewer than 1,000 employees. Still, customized products dominate in these size classes. Only in enterprises with more than 1,000 employees does the basic product type change, and specialized machines get priority in the production slate. Moreover, in large firms, standardized machines—"catalogue articles"—prevail over customized machines.

Table B.2

Classification of the Machine-Tool Industry by Number of Employees per Firm (percent)

	Up to 50		50 to 100		101 to 250		251 to 500		501 to 1000		> 1000	
Year	Firms	Empl.	Firms	Empl.	Firms	Empl.	Firms	Empl.	Firms	Empl.	Firms	Empl.
1982	35.0	2.5	16.0	5.4	21.9	15.3	12.7	19.5	8.8	26.3	5.6	31.3
1984	38.4	2.5	18.4	6.7	19.0	15.0	10.7	19.0	9.7	32.0	3.8	24.8
1986	36.2	2.3	14.3	4.6	22.2	15.0	12.2	18.9	11.1	32.6	4.0	26.6
1988	27.4	2.1	18.3	5.0	23.2	14.4	14.1	18.8	12.4	31.4	4.6	28.3
1990	28.1	1.9	12.9	3.2	25.0	14.0	14.3	17.6	13.4	29.8	6.3	33.5
1991	26.1	1.7	15.1	3.7	23.4	12.8	17.0	22.2	13.3	32.0	5.1	27.6

SOURCE: Organization of German Machinery and Plant Manufacturers (VDMA). Evaluation: *Stat. Abt. der Fachgemeinschaft Werkzeugmaschinen und Fertigungssysteme im VDMA.*

RAND *MR479/2-B.4*

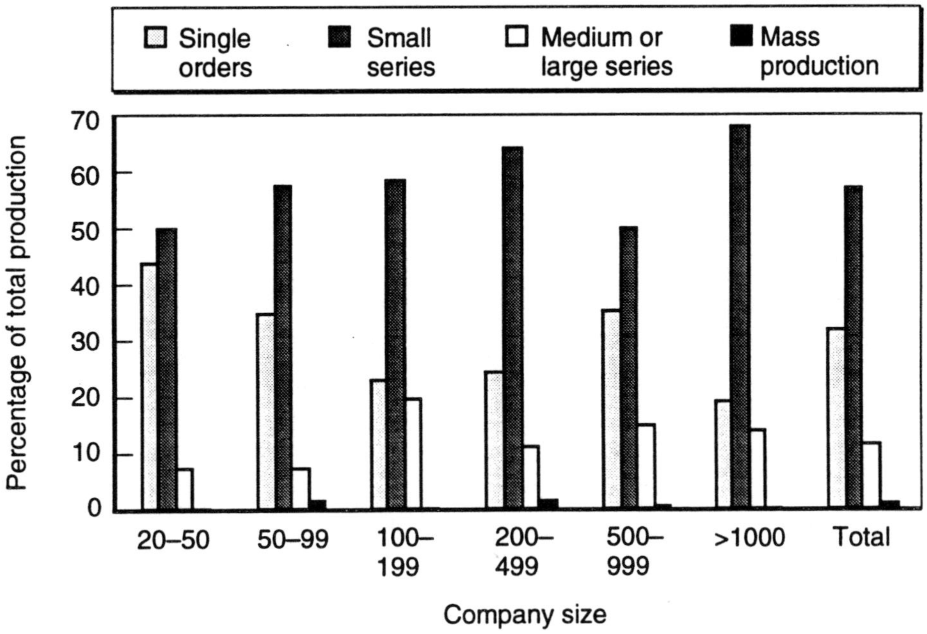

SOURCE: University Bochum, NIFA Panel, and author calculations.

Figure B.4—Types of Production in 1990

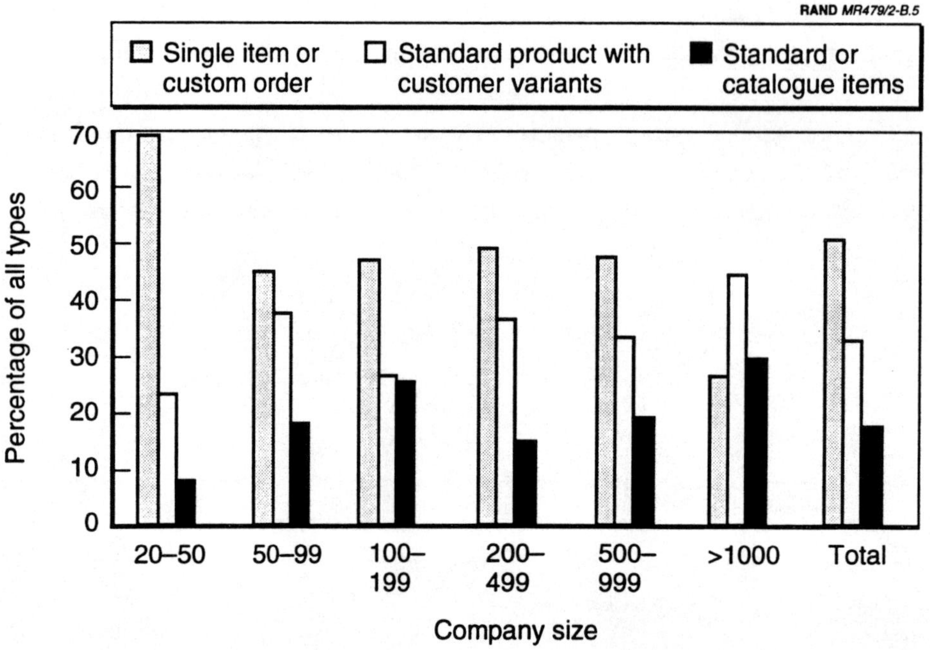

SOURCE: University Bochum, NIFA Panel, and author calculations.

Figure B.5—Product Types in 1990

For the whole industry, customized and specialized machines predominate (83 percent), but the share of standardized machines is also significant.

Human Capital

The fast technological development in recent years has made new demands on employees to innovate, and thus the quality of human capital is a key factor in firms' competitiveness. The quality of manpower is judged to be favorable in Germany, particularly in capital goods industries (Nerb, 1992, p. 20). The manpower development system consists of a well-built infrastructure of educational institutions and the dual system of apprenticeships.

The dual system offers specialized practical training in the firm or a training institution outside the firm, combined with special general training in a vocational school. Its main function is to support vocational training in SMEs. Unfortunately, because of their size and specialization, SMEs often have difficulty providing complete vocational training. They therefore use advanced training offered by private and government institutions.

In September 1987, a reorganized system of training in the metal industry vocations was launched. The impulse for this reorganization was the development and application of modern technologies. The ratio of numerically controlled machine tools to all machine tools used in the metal industry has doubled between 1985 and 1990 (Zedler, 1992, pp. 10–11), forcing workers to cope with a rapid integration of new technology. The special training for the new metallic vocations will teach students to act in complex production systems. Five years after the reorganization of the metallic vocations, young workers have proven to be more self-reliant, more capable of teamwork, and more flexible (Buresch, 1992, p. 30).

By including modern controlling technologies in initial training, the international competitiveness of the German metal industry could be enhanced. In the old "metal" vocational sector, many special vocations existed, and the qualifications for each worker were consequently quite narrow. The new vocations are more homogeneous. Therefore, the trainees in these vocations are distributed more evenly. For example, a remarkable change has been noted in the metal-cutting vocations. The "old" vocations, such as "lathe operator," "universal milling machine operator," "automatic tool setter," "boring mill turner," and "universal cutter" taken together comprised only 9.5 percent of the trainees in the metal sector. By contrast, the single "new" vocation "cutting engineer" comprises 13.6 percent of the trainees. The vocations "lathing technicians" and "cutting technicians" also have more trainees than in the former vocations.

Compared with international standards, the level of qualifications in the German metal sector is very high: 80 percent of the employees have passed vocational training (Werner, 1992, pp. 4ff). For most of the firms, vocational training is an important instrument for attracting qualified employees for two reasons: First, firms often have problems attracting people in the labor market who can adequately be employed; second, employees who are trained in the firm itself generally show a more positive attitude toward their job, and identify themselves with their firm to a higher degree. The *apprenticeship quota* (the ratio of apprentices to total employees) and the costs show how important education is for German firms (Gawlik, 1993, pp. 33ff); Table B.3 presents the training quota and the costs for initial training as a percentage of the total wages and salaries, in different sectors.

The apprenticeship quota in the machine-tool industry is 9.8 percent, and is thus well above average. In addition to apprenticeships, firms are attaching greater importance to advanced training. From 1981 to 1990, costs for advanced training

Table B.3

Apprenticeships in German Industry

Costs for the First Training as a Percentage of the Total of Sector-Specific Apprenticeship Quota			Training Costs as a Percentage of Wages and Salaries		
Industry	1987[a]	1990[b]	Industry	1985	1990
Banking, insurance	6.7	9.0	Banking, insurance	2.8	3.5
Electrical industry	4.7	4.0	Electrical industry	2.6	3.9
Chemical industry	4.8	5.6	Chemical industry	1.9	3.0
Automobile industry	3.7	4.3	Automobile industry	2.7	2.7
Metal industry	6.5	5.5	Metal industry	1.7	2.2
Public utilities and transportation	5.4	6.0	Public utilities and transportation	1.7	1.9
Trade	7.0	7.0	Trade	0.9	1.8
Total	5.6	5.3	Total	2.0	2.8

SOURCE: Gawlik (1993), pp. 33–34.

[a]Job counting.

[b]Counting of the Federal Institute for Professional Education.

in German industry have nearly tripled (average costs per employee: 1981, 370 DM; 1985, 680 DM; 1990, 978 DM[3]). In 1991, 21 percent of the 19- to 64-year-old employees had participated in at least one internal or external course of advanced training (*Bundesministerium für Bildung und Wissenschaft*, 1993).

In the machine-tool industry, expenditures for advanced training are below average (see Tables B.4 and B.5). More weight was put on the advanced training of management (see Table B.6) than of other employees. Almost 85 percent of the courses were conducted during regular working hours, and 72 percent of the training was external. Nevertheless, 42 percent of the respondents have their own education departments.

Many more advanced training courses are being offered. From November 1989 to January 1993, the total number of courses offered in Germany has increased from 24,300 to 110,000; 20,000 of the latter were in East Germany. Of these advanced training courses, 18 percent were in data processing and information technology, with another 8 percent in specific applications of data processing; 2.8 percent are courses in production, statistical process control (SPC), and computer integrated manufacturing (CIM) (*Institut der deutschen Wirtschaft*, 1993).

---

[3]The "Berufsakademie" institution has existed in Baden-Württemberg for several years. Recently, more were founded in Berlin and Sassonia.

Table B.4

Average Costs for Advanced Training per Employee in 1990 by Sectors of the Economy

Industry	Cost (DM)
Banking, insurance	1,855
Electrical industry	1,154
Chemical industry	1,015
Automobile industry	870
Metal industry	900
Public utilities and transportation	750
Trade	605
Total	987

SOURCE: Gawlik (1993), p. 34.

Table B.5

Relationship Between Costs of Training and the Total of Wages and Salaries

Industry	1981	1985	1990
Banking, insurance	1.3	1.8	2.7
Electrical industry	1.2	1.4	1.7
Chemical industry	—	—	1.8
Automobile industry	0.6	0.8	1.5
Metal industry	0.5	1.6	1.6
Public utilities and transportation	0.2	0.2	1.7
Trade	0.5	1.2	1.6
Total	0.9	1.4	1.9

SOURCE: Gawlik (1993), p. 35.

Table B.6

Advanced Training of Employees in the German Machine-Tool Industry, 1990

Task	Average Number of Days Per Person Per Year
Training of industrial workers	1.5
Training of salaried employees	1.7
Training of salaried employees in management positions	2.8
External training (percentage)	72.2
Internal training (percentage)	27.8
During working hours (percentage)	84.7
Out of working hours (percentage)	15.3
Expenditures for continuous training per person in one year (DM)	249
Internal organization divisional education and continuous training	42

SOURCES: VDW, VDMA.

Numerous private and public institutions offer advanced training; these include universities, professional schools, adult evening classes, professional associations, and the so-called *Berufsakademien.* Special mention must be made of the Steinbeis Foundation in Baden-Württemberg, whose original aim was the "education of the human being for the industry," that is, vocational training. The Steinbeis Foundation supports the vocational and advanced training in SMEs up to the level of foreman.[4]

Another important institution, the *Berufsakademie* (BA) in Baden-Württemberg, is an alternative to the university for students who have passed the *Abitur* (the university entrance exam). The BA is a combination of study and practical training in firms that allows graduates to forgo the initial training period for joining a firm. Students in Stuttgart, among them students in the machine-tool industry, are trained in production engineering, construction, or *Feinwerktechnik.* Most of the students are from SMEs. Their number has increased in recent years, as Table B.7 illustrates.

For technicians, foremen, and engineers, as well as commercial clerks and *Abiturients,* it is possible to study in the evening at the so-called *Verwaltungs- und Wirtschaftsakademie* (VWA) in Baden-Württemberg while having a job. The diploma is called "business economist (VWA)" and has the same rank as the "business economist (BA)" of the *Berufsakademie.* In the 1991–1992 winter term, 2,221 persons were enrolled at the VWA, including 228 technicians, foremen, and engineers; in the 1993 summer term, 2,143 persons were enrolled, including another 228 technicians, foremen, and engineers.[5]

Numerous courses are also offered by the Chamber of Industry and Commerce, the Chamber of Handicrafts, the trade unions, and firms. The following courses exemplify those relating to the machine-tool industry:

- *CNC-controlling of machine tools and programming I—basic course,* offered by the Berufsfortbildungswerk-Gemeinnuetzige Einrichtung des DGB
- *CNC-techniques—lathing,* offered by the Chamber of Industry and Commerce, Stuttgart
- *CNC-techniques—continuation course,* offered by the International Union for Social Work

---

[4]Speech of Dr. G. Meister at the diploma celebration at the Business Institute of the University of Stuttgart: "The importance of the SMEs for Baden-Württemberg—Professional Chances for the Academic Young Talents."

[5]Information from the VWA Stuttgart.

Table B.7

Number of Machine-Building Graduates at the *Berufsakademie*, Stuttgart, from 1986 to 1993

1986	1987	1988	1989	1990	1991	1992	1993
50	57	64	79	82	89	120	ca. 120

SOURCE: *Berufsakademie*, Stuttgart.

- *Handicraft sheet-metal working for beginners*, offered by the Chamber of Handicrafts, Stuttgart[6]

Firms' interest in advanced training corresponds to the economic situation. In an upswing, as in the second half of the 1980s, the demand for advanced training is stronger than during a downswing.[7]

Because mass production is of minor importance, the German machine-tool industry needs highly skilled employees. Despite having highly skilled workers who can be flexibly employed in various tasks, labor is much more highly specialized in Germany than in Japan, according to a recent comparison with the Japanese machine-tool industry (Brödner and Schultetus, 1992). Such practices as lean production and group work are very limited in Germany, owing to employee resistance and poor management training. Still, for German producers, a high skill level is one of the main factors of competitiveness (Puvogel, 1992). Tables B.8, B.9, and B.10 contain more information on human capital in the German machine-tool industry. The data were obtained by the industry association, VDW, through a survey of selected member firms. Between 1985 and 1990, staffing increased in development and construction (comparable to research and development). In 1990, 25 percent of the employees in this department were engineers (see Table B.9). The production staff, which also increased, consisted of over 80 percent skilled workers.

Summing up, the machine-tool industry in Germany, with its SME structure, regional concentration, and specialized, but flexible production, can be characterized as a variation of flexible specialization. In relation to the international machine-tool industry, we can conclude that the skill level of German employees is high. In a sectoral comparison within Germany, the apprenticeship quota in the machine-tool industry is above average, but the expenditures for advanced training are below average.

---

[6]See Arbeitsgemeinschaft für berufliche Fortbildung Stuttgart (1992).

[7]Conversation with Mr. Aur, Steinbeis Foundation.

Table B.8

Personnel Structure in the German Machine-Tool Industry (without apprentices)

	1985 (on average)	1990 (on average)
Development and construction		14.2
Industrial workers	12.8	0.5
Salaried employees	0.4	13.2
Employees on temporary loan	12.4	0.1
Material management		5.2
Industrial workers	4.9	2.0
Salaried employees	1.6	3.1
Employees on temporary loan	3.3	0.7
Production		60.7
Industrial workers	62.4	49.8
Salaried employees	51.7	10.1
Employees on temporary loan	10.7	2.2
Sales		11.2
Industrial workers	10.3	1.1
Salaried employees	1.0	9.8
Employees on temporary loan	9.3	0.0
Administration, including personnel and Social Division		8.3
Industrial workers	8.8	1.2
Salaried employees	2.0	6.9
Employees on temporary loan	6.8	0.0
Apprenticeship and education		0.7
Industrial workers	0.6	0.1
Salaried employees	0.1	0.6
Employees on temporary loan	0.5	0.0

SOURCES: VDW, VDMA.

Table B.9

Employee Qualification Structure in the German Machine-Tool Industry, 1990

		Range	
	Average	Low	High
Share of engineers in labor force			
Development and construction	24.7	4	45.0
Material management	0.4	0	0.3
Production	3.8	0	4.0
Sales	11.0	0	21.4
Skilled workers as share of industrial workers in production	82.2	70	95.3

SOURCES: VDW, VDMA.

Table B.10

Investments of German Machine-Tool Producers

	1980	1981	1982	1983	1984	1985	1986	1987	1988	1989	1990	1991
Investment per employee (DM)	5,203	5,779	4,131	3,962	4,281	6,354	8,533	7,425	9,466	9,787	9,428	—
Investment goal (%)[a]												
Extension of capacity	12	17	14	16	21	15	29	31	28	39	19	26
Rationalization	69	66	67	58	55	69	46	46	44	44	33	42
Introduction of new production methods	39	41	35	31	43	57	67	43	41	35	43	32
Replacement	19	17	19	26	24	16	25	23	28	17	48	32

SOURCE: IFO-Investment report.

[a]Percentage of respondents.

The 1980s and 1990s

Long Upswing from 1983 to 1990

Machine-tool manufacturers experienced a long and strong upswing from 1983 to 1990, with a 74-percent increase in production, from 9.4 billion DM in 1983 to 16.4 billion DM in 1990. The number of employees also followed this trend, reaching its absolute maximum in 1990, as indicated in Figure B.6.

The upswing can be explained by a worldwide increased demand for investment goods. The decline in the early 1980s was partly a consequence of the technological lead of the Japanese in control systems. Concentrated investments in new production methods were crucial to overcoming this crisis. The continuous increase of NC machine-tool output (see Figure B.7), even in the crisis years of 1982 and 1983, reflects the process of catching up.

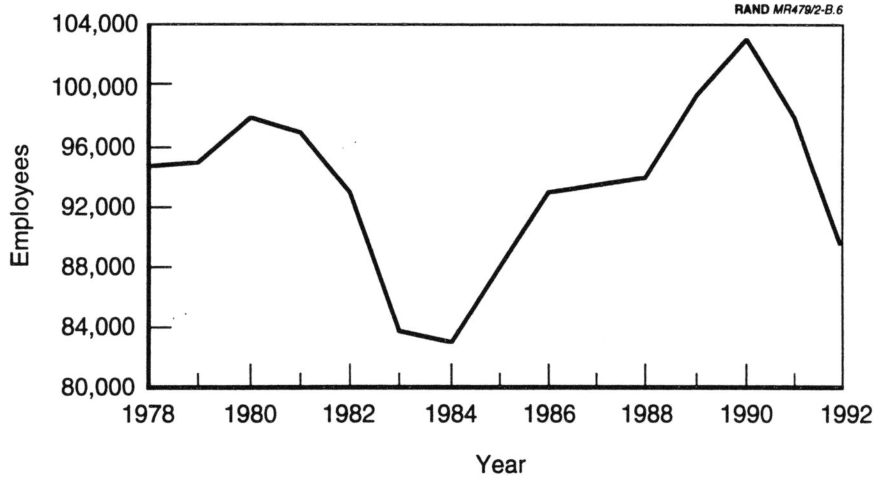

SOURCE: VDMA.

Figure B.6—Number of Employees in the German Machine-Tool Industry

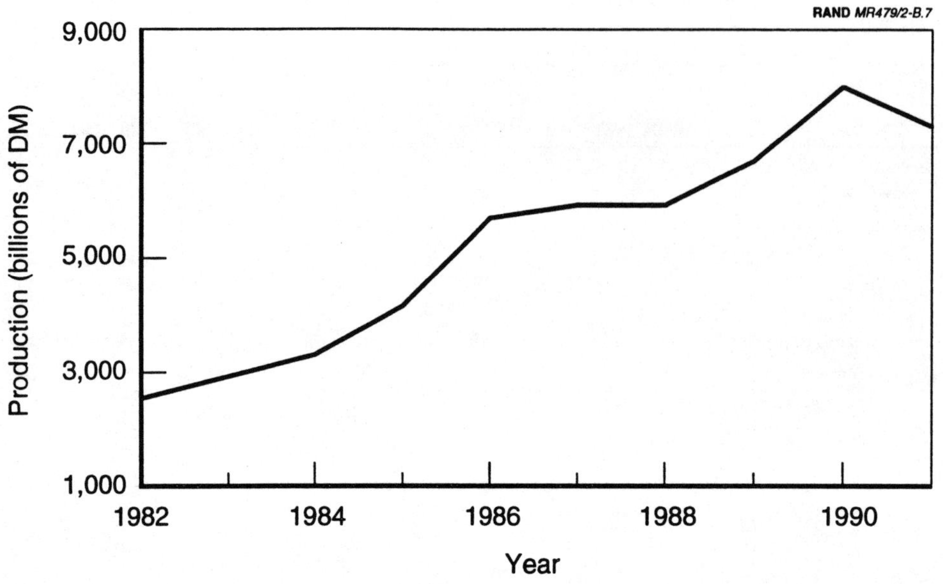

SOURCE: VDW.

Figure B.7—Production of NC Machine Tools

During the 1980s, German machine-tool producers failed to build up a standard control in conjunction with either the domestic or European microelectronic industries. Today, many different control systems (among them systems developed by single machine-tool producers) have been installed that are not compatible with each other. Such incompatibility causes a competitive disadvantage on world and domestic markets. The problem seems to have been recognized, and an initiative is under way to create a so-called open European control by the end of 1995.

Looking at the situation at the firm level, it is striking that profits and labor productivity (value added per employee) could not keep pace with the increase in output (see Table B.11). The growth of the value added was dampened by rising inputs, which can be interpreted as a decrease of the traditionally high percentage of in-house manufacturing due to a slow growth in subcontracting. The share of value added per employee, however, was much higher in Japan than in Germany. A comparison with equivalent Japanese data shows a wide productivity gap between the two machine-tool producers (see Tables B.11 and B.12). In 1989, for example, each Japanese employee added over twice the value that his or her German counterpart did. The main reasons for Japan´s productivity edge are a longer working day and work year, economies of scale in producing standardized machines, and the system of subcontracting.

Table B.11

Performance and Costs of German Machine-Tool Enterprises

Indicator	1980	1985	1989	Share of Sales (%) 1980	Share of Sales (%) 1989
Sales (millions of DM)	118	134	183	100.0	100.0
Material consumption	59	73	102	50.0	55.9
Total value added (millions of DM)	59	61	81	50.0	44.1
Depreciation	4	4	7	3.1	3.7
Staff expenditure	48	53	67	40.8	36.7
Other costs	3	3	4	2.8	2.5
Profit (before taxes)	4	1	2	3.3	1.3
Total employees	1,081	971	1,053		
Per employee (thousands of DM)					
Sales	109	138	174		
Staff expenditure	45	55	64		
Value added	55	63	77		

SOURCE: IFO, Statistisches Bundesamt.
NOTE: Average values for firms with more than 500 employees.

Table B.12

Performance and Costs of Japanese Machine-Tool Enterprises

Indicator	1980	1985	1989	Share of Sales (%) 1980	Share of Sales (%) 1989
Sales (millions of DM)	298	458	514	100.0	100.0
Material consumption	186	285	323	62.4	62.7
Total value added (millions of DM)	112	173	192	37.6	37.3
Depreciation	7	13	16	2.3	3.2
Staff expenditure	45	69	77	15.2	15.0
Other costs	23	38	34	7.7	6.5
Profit (before taxes)	37	53	64	12.4	12.5
Total employees	945	1,171	1,152		
Per employee (thousands of DM)					
Sales	315.4	390.7	446.6		
Staff expenditure	48.0	59.0	67.0		
Value added	118.6	147.3	166.4		

SOURCE: IFO, Japan Development Bank, Ministry of International Trade and Industry (MITI).
NOTE: Converted with the rate of exchange of 1989; average values for firms with more than 500 employees.

Also striking, especially in relation to the Japanese producers, is the very low profit margin, which shrank between 1980 and 1989. Thus, German machine-tool producers experience difficulty when demand and prices fall. For the near future, raising the profit margin is one of the most important aims, and it can be achieved only by better cost management. Such a goal was not very popular in the era of high demand and capacity utilization, and it became even more difficult in the depression of 1992 through 1994.

Severe Crisis After 1990

A sharp drop in production and employment followed the "fat" years between 1984 and 1990. Dr. B. Leibinger, chairman of Trumpf and member of the VDMA executive board, is forecasting that the number of employees in the industry will shrink by more than 50 percent by mid-1994 (*Stuttgarter Zeitung,* May 26, 1993). He extrapolates from a 31-percent downturn of incoming orders in 1992, a 48-percent downturn from January to March 1993, and a 29-percent decrease in production in the same period.[8] Even if his expectations overstate the real situation, there can be no doubt that many machine-tool producers are in distress. One response of firms has been to propose transferring production either completely or partially to low-wage countries. Thus, the crisis is not only within individual firms, but also threatens the regionalized network of this sector.

Right now, the producers of standard machines face the biggest problems as a result of direct competition from Japanese and Southeast Asian machine-tool builders. Since the worldwide recession has hit the Pacific Rim as well, strong price competition is taking place. But, as shown in Tables B.11 and B.12, the scope for price reductions is very limited for German machine-tool producers, who suffer from low profit margins. The technological qualities, which hitherto defined the competitive advantage of German machine tools, might no longer outweigh their relatively high prices. Also, because they are relatively small, the German machine-tool producers cannot realize economies of scale, which are necessary to bring down the cost of producing standardized machines. Their problems are aggravated by the fact that the Japanese suppliers have better chances to survive in cut-throat competition, because of their higher profits in the boom years.

---

[8]The data proclaimed by Dr. Leibinger are exaggerating the VDW data for income orders: −21 percent for 1992, −42 percent for Jan.–Mar. 1993.

More recently, the highly specialized niche suppliers have also begun to face difficulties. Because of the use of advanced control systems, more and more standardized machines with customer-specific variations are being developed. These machines may not offer the same range of services as customized machines, but they are much cheaper. Recently, demand has shifted away from high-tech and, in some cases, overengineered machines toward more standardized machine tools. Despite these problems, high technology machine-tool builders are much more stable than volume producers.

Germany remains a world leader in the export of machine tools, thanks, in part, to the regional concentration of the industry. According to Krugman (1991), in the presence of scale economies, three conditions are conducive to regional agglomerations:

1. Labor pooling
2. Intermediate inputs
3. Knowledge spillovers.

All three conditions are fulfilled for the machine-tool industry. Thus, regional concentration leads to higher levels of efficiency, and hence to strong international competitiveness and high export shares. From 1980 to 1990, Germany exported roughly 60 percent of its production, with the largest portion of exports going to Western Europe (see Figure B.8a). Accordingly, the German machine-tool industry suffers from the revaluation of the deutschemark within the European Monetary System that has taken place since September 1992, especially with respect to the Italian lira.

Germany has failed to shift its exports toward the opening and developing markets in southeast Asia. The firm size of German machine-tool builders is again a disadvantage, because their individual sales and profit margins are too small for the necessary investments. The European concentration of exports explains part of the current crisis.

Lack of demand in western European mass markets caused the orders for capital goods to decline. Other important clients were the states in eastern Europe and the Soviet Union. Their political changes have caused those markets to break away, resulting in another big loss in demand. The collapse of these markets hit Germany particularly hard because demand there tended to be countercyclical, making up for lost sales during western European recessions, and because Germany had such a high market share in eastern Europe.

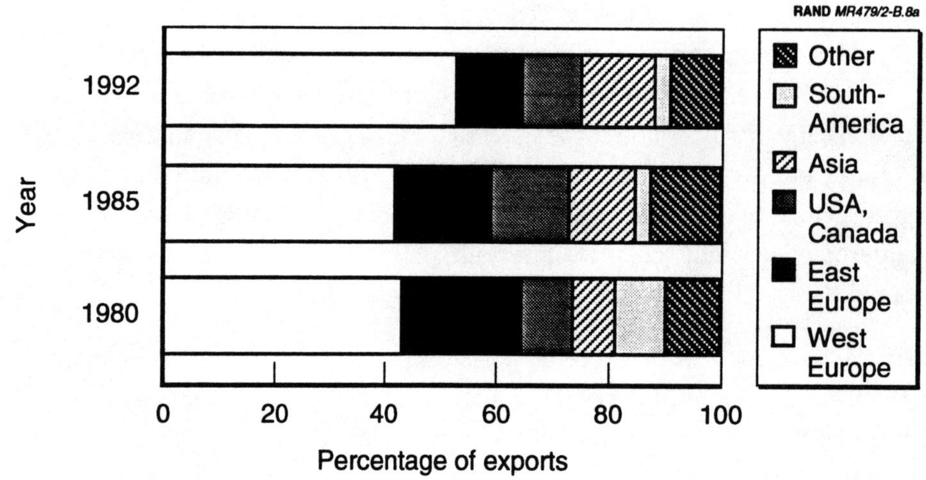

SOURCE: VDW.

Figure B.8a—Structure of Exports

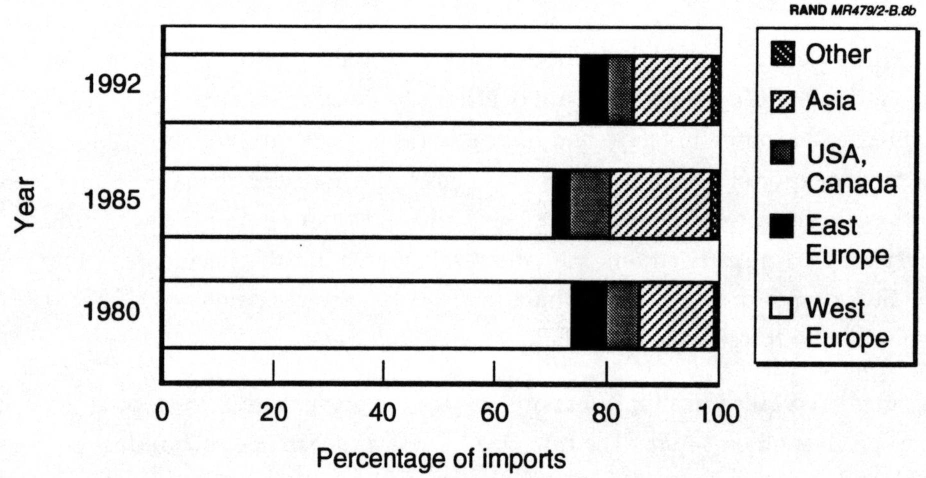

SOURCE: VDW.

Figure B.8b—Structure of Imports

Summing up, the crisis is to some extent a structural one, posing great challenges for the small- and medium-sized machine-tool producers. Their most important tasks are to decrease costs and to improve the efficiency of the development and construction of new machines. Some consolidation of the industry may occur, along with greater collaborations among firms, e.g., to enter the southeast Asian markets. The president of VDMA, J. Kleinewefers, is of the opinion that the small- and medium-sized structure will survive.[9] He argues that these small firms benefit from quick decisions and a high degree of flexibility.

Interfirm Relationships: Supplier–Producer

The 1980s. While producing a wide range of highly sophisticated machines, machine-tool makers normally conducted most of the R&D and made most of the parts they needed in-house. Consequently, they had to buy only small numbers of parts from suppliers, thus increasing the cost per order. This is the reason why no very intensive and efficient connections developed between producers and suppliers.

The 1990s. Suppliers and machine-tool makers are now working together more closely to achieve lower costs. Several activities are under way:

- Many firms (both suppliers and producers) have begun to *standardize* the highest possible number of parts and components. High standardization enables faster and cheaper production.
- Machine-tool makers are striving to reduce the costs of supplier parts through *long-term contracts.*
- Machine-tool makers normally do not have just-in-time production. They are not supplied "just in time" by their suppliers because of the small number of parts needed per year. To further reduce the costs per piece, e.g., ordering and transportation costs, they are tending to make *fewer but larger orders.*
- In addition to these activities, there is a trend toward strong cooperation between suppliers and machine-tool makers to ensure the quality of supplier parts. They are collaborating on *quality control* within the supplier firms; thus, machine-tool makers no longer need a separate quality-control function once the parts arrive.

Machine-tool producers have recognized that an internationally competitive supplier industry is necessary for survival in the long run, so they are working to build closer connections in R&D. They want to strengthen teamwork for inventing and improving new technologies and new machines. In the distant future, it is possible that machine-tool makers will relegate parts of their R&D to suppliers. Thus, suppliers would conduct the research for and develop products that would be sold to several machine-tool makers. The suppliers can thereby

---

[9]Interview in *Wirtschaftswoche,* January 1993.

achieve larger production numbers and reduce costs. Currently, German machine-tool makers do not buy components off the shelf; they prefer to participate in the development and layout of components.

At the low technology end, machine-tool makers are buying increasing numbers of basic parts from cheap suppliers in eastern European countries.

Interfirm Relationships

The 1980s. The 1980s were a boom time for machine-tool makers; hence, they could sell all the machines they produced. There was no need for cooperation, so most of the machine-tool makers stayed independent. Strategic alliances or even long-term plans for cooperation were unknown, and there were few capital exchanges between machine-tool makers.

Machine-tool makers were engaged in a wide range of R&D activities but remained competitors and did not cooperate even in fundamental technologies, such as CNC. Machine-tool producers developed some individual contacts with research institutions and universities to solve firm-specific problems. Cooperation with other machine-tool makers, even when promoted by government agencies, was an exception.

The 1990s. This is a time of crisis for machine-tool makers. Cooperation between machine-tool producers has become more attractive, enabling firms to become more competitive in terms of cost and technology. The extent of cooperation depends on the outlook of individual machine-tool makers. The range of possibilities is as follows:

- Cooperation in buying, selling, production or development
- Foundation of joint ventures to do buying, selling, production or development
- Foundation of joint ventures for special product lines
- Merger of two or more companies.

Machine-tool makers tend to proceed cautiously. They may start working together in small areas, e.g., common buying of supplier parts or common selling of certain machines. Later on, the activities may expand to cooperating in production or even in R&D. Only a small number of medium-sized machine-tool makers have set up common networks for worldwide selling of their products. In a few cases, the exchange of capital or even a merger is intended for the following aims:

- Building up bigger units that are competitive on the world market, even when compared with those of Japanese firms
- Cutting down per-unit costs of production by increasing production
- Increasing the firm's own capital and thus achieving objectives comparable to those of big enterprises.

Banks, which often own a part of the firms' stock or are the firms' creditors, are reputed to favor close cooperation or even mergers of machine-tool producers to attain a competitive size (*Stuttgarter Zeitung*, June 24, 1992). One stated possibility is to merge the four largest machine-tool producers into a "*Deutsche Werkzeugmaschinen-Holding* (DWM)[10] *GmbH*," as planned by Mr. Eder.[11]

Talks are currently proceeding about cooperation or mergers between the following firms:

- *Traub AG and Berthold Hermle AG:* Cooperation in worldwide selling. Both are using the marketing system of Traub AG to optimize their capacities.
- *MAHO AG and Deckel AG:* Merging into a new firm (*Stuttgarter Zeitung*, July 3, 1993). Although the final plant sites are not fixed, part of the production of Deckel is to be moved to existing MAHO plants, to concentrate the production capacities (*Stuttgarter Zeitung*, June 6, 1993). In the next four years, the fusion will incur costs of 120 million DM, but at the same time will save 342 million DM (*Stuttgarter Zeitung*, July 14, 1993, p. 11).
- *Deckel AG and Gildemeister AG:* Currently running a common company for selling the machines of both firms. In the future, common buying, production, or even R&D may occur.

It is difficult to know to what extent the single firms are working together in buying or in R&D. Normally, machine-tool firms do not publish news of their cooperative agreements. Small firms try especially hard to keep such agreements secret.

Several machine-tool makers are cooperating with CNC makers to develop a single standard for a European control. These firms initiated the European Open Control conference, which was convened without government support. Machine-tool makers have recognized that such cooperation and dialogue are crucial to remaining competitive (RAND interviews).

---

[10]In English, "German machine-tool holding."

[11]See *Stuttgarter Zeitung*, September 22, 1992; *Automobil-Industrie*, Vol. 38, No. 1, February 1993, pp. 50–51.

Outlook. In the long run, machine-tool makers can survive only through partnerships with other producers, creating a current trend toward more cooperation. Such cooperation normally starts with selling and proceeds to common buying; shared production and R&D are then possible. Final mergers will remain exceptions.

German machine-tool makers will need to diversify from the European market and to compete globally (most importantly in the United States and Japan). This will require the development of lower-cost, less technically advanced machines. The expansion to overseas markets will be done through partnerships of machine-tool makers. Such partnerships will play a very important role in the future of the German machine-tool industry.

Interfirm Relationships: Producer–User

The 1980s. In the German machine-tool industry, R&D has been technology-oriented, realizing technologically feasible machines and processes. Ideas for general improvement of machines or the use of new technologies rarely came from users. Few contacts are made between producers and customers when developing new machines or new techniques for processes. Niche producers had more contact than mass-producers, but far too little.

Because R&D was done by the machine-tool makers themselves, improvements normally stemmed from their highly skilled engineers. As a result, the machines were often overengineered, and most buyers were unable to use all the specific possibilities of the new machines: Either it was too difficult to learn how to operate them, or the users did not need all the functions that the expensive machines had.

For mass production machines, only "normal" business contacts were made between producers and users. No real connections developed between machine-tool makers and their clients. Only a few firms offered after-sales services to their clients.

Machine-tool producers in niches were small- and medium-sized firms. They responded to customers, developing special solutions for customers' needs. In addition to this customer-specific R&D, they conducted a wide range of other R&D activities. In general, German firms produce in a more customer-specific way than firms in other countries, which requires higher expenditures on R&D and leads to higher final-product prices.

The 1990s. German machine-tool makers lead the world in product innovations, but their advantage in high technology has eroded. Competitors have achieved similar performance in many areas, such as CNC and quality control.

Machine-tool producers have come to recognize that their proximity to customers is important. Customer contacts are most important in highly innovative markets, such as Japan (according to Trumpf).[12] Machine-tool makers will have to produce what the market requires and at an acceptable price ("target costing"). Normally, proximity to customers is ensured through a firm's sales network, which is a problem for SMEs, because they lack such a worldwide network.

In the meantime, machine-tool makers have recognized that users want higher productivity with every new machine they buy. A machine-tool producer must, therefore, understand the client's entire production system. Machine-tool makers and users are starting to become partners, which includes exchanging more information from the start of the development of a new product.[13]

Some niche producers are discussing future needs with important customers ("lead users"),[14] recognizing that overengineering hinders marketability. Since new products must be even more tailored to clients' wishes, there is likely to be more and earlier coordination between machine-tool producers and users in the development process. Unnecessary attributes can then be dropped (downsizing), resulting in less complex and cheaper machines.

Outlook. Firms want to improve their services to their clients through[15]

- On-site training of clients' machine operators
- Fast and reliable maintenance
- Early coordination between producers and users on machine requirements.

Both machine-tool makers and machine-tool users recognize that reliable partnerships ensure their international competitiveness. Thus, they intend to deepen their connections in many ways, such as increased information exchanges and more R&D coordination.

---

[12]See *Absatzwirtschaft*, No. 3, 1993, p. 20.

[13]See *Absatzwirtschaft*, No. 3, 1993, p. 22.

[14]See *Absatzwirtschaft*, No. 3, 1993, p. 20.

[15]See Ministry of Economic Affairs, February 5, 1993, p. 6.

The services of the employers' organizations (see discussion in next subsection) will become more important for SMEs, enabling them to have better contacts with clients abroad. Here, the establishment of trade centers in foreign countries is required to compensate for the lack of a global marketing system.

Intermediate Organizations' Roles in Firm Coordination

We first examine employers' organizations, then trade organizations, and finally, give an outlook on likely future developments.

Employers' Organizations

Employers' organizations either have obligatory membership or voluntary membership. Membership in the *Industrie und Handelskammer (IHK)* (Chamber of Industry and Commerce) is obligatory; that in the *Verband Deutscher Maschinen– und Anlagenbau (VDMA)* [Organization of German Machinery and Plant Manufacturers] and in the *Verein Deutscher Werkzeugmaschinenfabriken (VDW)* [Organization of German Machine-Tool Enterprises] is voluntary. Since there are no great differences in tasks and actions between these two groups, they will be analyzed together.

The most important organization for machine-tool makers is the VDMA and its special department for the machine-tool industry, the VDW. The main task of such organizations as the IHK and VDMA is to provide services to their members, such as marketing, legal advice, and information about foreign trade.[16] Such services are important to most machine-tool producers, which are small- or medium-sized and can ill afford their own service departments.

Employers' organizations also collect information, and each member has the right to access that information. Information is collected on the wide range of problems and questions that firms have about, for example, labor markets, foreign countries, firm-internal figures, traveling salesmen abroad, further education for the labor force, help in solving firm-specific management problems, the latest results of scientific research, economic information, and standardization guidelines.

Given the general lack of cooperation among firms, the organizations' most important function is to bring the heaviest competitors together to promote

---

[16]See *Handelsblatt*, October 14, 1992, p. 25.

cooperation in solving common problems[17] and, sometimes, to discuss market segregation. Employers' organizations are also involved in administering government programs, such as the "production technology" program sponsored by the federal government (see below). The organizations often establish special departments for a special mission, such as solving one particular common problem. Even here, there are certain limits to cooperation between competitors. Whereas they would never exchange the latest firm-specific experiences and information, it is often possible to set up common rules and guidelines.[18]

Finally, employers' organizations try to interpose between bigger and smaller member firms and their interests. This kind of adjustment of different interests is an advantage German machine-tool producers have over their competitors, even Japanese machine-tool firms.

Trade Organizations

Trade organizations offer their services to anyone who is interested in them, in contrast to employers' organizations, which offer their services to member firms only. They function as normal market-based firms, which means they have to compete for clients to earn money and survive in the long run.

There are many different trade organizations—sometimes specialized, sometimes all-round advisors. These organizations act in different ways and present themselves in different ways to the public. Cooperation between these organizations is negligible.

Trade organizations are indirectly supported by the (regional) government. The government subsidizes SMEs to enable them to pay for advice from some of the organizations, for example, *Rationalisierungs-Kuratorium der Deutschen Wirtschaft (RKW)* [Board of Trustees for Rationalization in the German Industry] or the Steinbeis Foundation.

The Steinbeis Foundation's services range from providing information about state-of-the-art technology and problem analysis to technology and market studies, from project management to conducting development projects. The foundation has about 130 centers (mostly located at the polytechnics) for technology transfer. The centers concentrate on flexible automation, manufacturing and process engineering, electronics and microelectronics,

---

[17]See *Handelsblatt*, October 14, 1992, p. 25.

[18]See *Handelsblatt*, March 31, 1993, p. 5.

software engineering, and introduction into computer-aided design and manufacturing (CAD/CAM).

RKW analyzes productivity improvement and industrial and economic trends. RKW focuses on technique and production, material management, and personnel and labor relations. RKW is included in the network of Task Force SME, a commission of the EU, and, via an on-line database service, informs enterprises on the European market and rules of trade.

No specific trade organization coordinates contacts between machine-tool suppliers, producers, and customers. Several experts from trade organizations interviewed said that two or more firms never worked together to solve their problems. Such reported behavior shows that the readiness to cooperate is not very high.

Outlook

Within employers' organizations, there is a trend to establish information centers abroad, especially for machine-tool makers. Employers' organizations will also establish more common service societies abroad, which service and maintain members' machine tools. Such societies especially benefit SMEs.

The Role of Government

Regional Government

Economic Policy for SMEs. The regional government of Baden-Württemberg provides a stable legal framework and the necessary infrastructure for private business. Especially in Baden-Württemberg, an essential part of this infrastructure is the universities and research institutes. Because R&D has positive external effects, special R&D incentives are also offered to private firms. Another essential part of the infrastructure is the various government agencies that support SMEs. Within this framework, however, single firms have to struggle for their survival on their own. Only in exceptional situations, such as the current general business downswing, are specific helpful measures taken by the regional government.

The following programs are available to all firms, regardless of size or sector:

1. The *Landesgewerbeamt (LGA)* [Department for Industry], which is part of the administration of the state, is in charge of promoting cooperation between

SMEs. It establishes "working groups" and "experience exchange groups." If two or more SMEs want to participate in an exposition abroad, the LGA gives them subsidies. It also gives money if firms want to enroll in courses of instruction or education or if they want to carry out projects together with other firms.

2. The government has put the RKW in charge of consulting with firms on all problems concerning cooperation. The consultations inform the firms about advantages and possible gains, but also about risks and possible costs, of cooperation with other firms. To make these consultations available to SMEs, the government pays part of the costs to participating firms.
3. The government promotes cooperation between suppliers and producers, and subsidizes joint R&D or joint quality assurance projects.

Furthermore, the government makes special efforts to help SMEs in all industries in Baden-Württemberg to withstand economic downturns. The Ministry of Economic Affairs has launched several special programs, as follows:

1. Program "ASEAN" (see Ministry of Economic Affairs, September 7, 1992, pp. 7–10)—In this program interested firms are provided expert advice free of charge to export to the Association of South East Asian Nations (ASEAN). RKW is the agency in charge.
2. Program "Japan" (see Ministry of Economic Affairs, September 7, 1992, pp. 10–13)—The Ministry of Economic Affairs has developed a special program to facilitate entry of SMEs of Baden-Württemberg to the Japanese market. This program provides information about the Japanese market, e.g., about customers and competitors. Consultation is available to firms to find partners and to solve individual marketing problems. To run this program, the government has put several institutions and organizations in charge, such as the *Gesellschaft für internationale wirtschaftliche Zusammenarbeit (GWZ)* [Company for International Economic Cooperation], the *Arbeitsgemeinschaft der Industrie- und Handelskammern Baden-Württemberg* [Working Pool of Chambers of Commerce of Baden-Württemberg], and the *LGA*. The program contains the following measures:
   - *Information for firms interested in Japan.* With the help of a textbook by the GWZ, SMEs are given information on important aspects of Japanese business practices and the Japanese market.
   - *Japan Information Center, Stuttgart.* Since fall 1992, a specialist on Japan is available to industry in Baden-Württemberg. He counsels firms that intend to export to Japan on how to enter the Japanese market and arranges contacts to corresponding German or Japanese organizations.

The Ministry of Economic Affairs and the Chambers of Commerce of Baden-Württemberg finance this information center.

- *GWZ office, Tokyo.* The existing GWZ office in Tokyo provides consulting services regarding distribution, cooperative ventures, plant transplants, mediation of licenses, etc. The GWZ pays for up to two man-days of consultation.
- *Miscellaneous.* Various fact-finding trips to Japan by government and business leaders were arranged. The Ministry of Economic Affairs sponsored the spring 1993 symposium, "Ways to the Japanese Market."

3. Joint job training initiative for the metal industry (see Ministry of Economic Affairs, September 17, 1992, pp. 1–10)—The Ministry of Economic Affairs, the employers' organization, and the trade union of the metal industry, as well as the representatives of the Working Pool of Chambers of Commerce of Baden-Württemberg, agreed that a well-educated labor force is a strategic factor ensuring the competitiveness and, therefore, strengthening the industrial sector of Baden-Württemberg. The participants agreed that an entirely integrated concept is necessary to ensure effective job training, calling for the following measures:
   - *Lobbying for advanced job training.* Baden-Württemberg offers a good infrastructure for advanced education. The initiative participants appealed to both the employers and the employees to regard job-oriented training as an essential instrument for ensuring competitiveness, jobs, possibilities in business and private life, prosperity, and quality of life.
   - *Increasing visibility of successful projects.* Many enterprises have difficulties recognizing the need for ongoing job training. The Ministry of Economic Affairs, the employers' organization and the trade union of the metal industry, and the Working Pool of Chambers of Commerce of Baden-Württemberg want to present successful projects of firms that developed and implemented concepts of employee training concurrently with plans for new investments, new production, or new organization methods. One focus will be the introduction of working in teams.
   - *Job-training pilot projects.* These projects started in early 1993. The first two years are supported financially by the Ministry of Economic Affairs. The projects inform employees about existing job education opportunities and motivate them to participate. They also inform employers how to identify skill needs and how to link training programs with business plans.

- *Training unskilled and semiskilled workers.* Unskilled and semiskilled workers must become qualified on the job so that they can join working groups in new factories. The Ministry of Economic Affairs wants to support projects for developing programs on how to educate these persons adequately.

4. Joint initiative to improve the automotive industry suppliers—To facilitate the information transfer between automobile producers and their suppliers, the government has asked that special roundtables with representatives of all firms involved be established. The government awarded the Steinbeis Foundation a 4.5 million DM, three-year contract to arrange the roundtables and help firms find experts for their specific problems.
5. Government-backed securities for financing trade centers in important export markets—Presently, SMEs in Baden-Württemberg have one trade center in Yokohama, Japan. A second will be built in Singapore in the near future. Other centers are planned for Seoul (South Korea), South China, Vietnam, Taiwan, Chile, Argentina, and Mexico.
6. Direct government loans—The regional government of Baden-Württemberg helps firms to withstand short-term liquidity crises. For this special program, the government provides a total of 235 million DM.

In general, the government keeps in constant contact with firms, trade organizations, labor unions, customers, and scientists through intermittent meetings. In these conferences, the problems of the economy and possible solutions are discussed.

Research and Technology Policy. Baden-Württemberg is a region with few raw materials. Since the onset of general industrialization, it has been essential for firms to manufacture high-quality products. This ability requires advanced technology which, in turn, requires strong efforts in research and the ability to rapidly translate new technologies into feasible production methods and sellable products. The government realizes the importance of a well-run research infrastructure and supports the establishment of institutes and organizations. Because of this background, a highly diversified technological infrastructure has grown up, consisting of a wide range of industry-oriented research facilities that want to be partners with industry and offer services that are based on the needs of industry.

All existing research facilities can be divided into five groups:

1. Contract research institutes at universities
2. Institutes of industrial joint research

3. Institutes of the Fraunhofer Society
4. Large-scale research establishments
5. Steinbeis Foundation for Economic Promotion.

The Fraunhofer Society is considered to be the leading applied research organization in Germany. Of special importance for the machine-tool industry in the region are its two institutes, *Institut für Arbeitswirtschaft und Organisation* (IAO) [Institute for Labor Management and Organization], and Institut für Produktionstechnik und Automatisierung (IPA) [Institute for Production Technology and Automization] (both located in Stuttgart), which pursue research in such areas as computer-aided engineering, industrial engineering, automation and corporate planning, and control. A single Fraunhofer Institute may conduct more than $12 million in applied research annually.

Even if a special program does not exist to support the R&D activities of machine-tool makers at the regional level, the close contacts between the researchers at those largely publicly financed institutions and the engineers in machine-tool firms are very helpful for the R&D process in the machine-tool firms. Because engineers dominate this process, there is a risk that R&D may be too technology driven rather than demand oriented. Furthermore, necessary organizational innovations are not emphasized. In general, the regional government does not promote special branches; it promotes R&D activities and knowledge transfer to firms, as well as cooperation, concentrating on SMEs.

Federal Government

Economic and Research and Technology Policy for SMEs. At the level of federal government, two ministries are of special importance for the machine-tool industry:

1. The Ministry of Economic Affairs, which pursues restrained interventionist economic policy
2. The Ministry of Research and Technology, which pursues a more interventionist kind of policy, targeting special areas for research and development.

Since the 1970s, national R&D policy has been characterized by changes in emphasis that took account of the often untapped innovation potential of SMEs (Becher et al., 1990, p. 119). Before then, R&D projects were promoted and fostered in large research establishments (Hornschild and Meyer-Krahmer, 1990,

p. 11). In 1978, a shift occurred toward national R&D programs (the Concept for Research and Technology in SMEs program created by the Federal Ministry of Research and Technology) geared mainly toward the improvement of SMEs' innovation potential, because they often faced difficulties in finding the necessary capital and personnel for research (*Bundesbericht Forschung*, 1979, p. 29).

The most important programs were the startup promotions of new-technology-based firms (NTBF) (219 NTBFs received 240.2 million DM in the 1983–1991 period), the R&D-Personnel-Expenditure Grants (*FuE-Personalkosten-Zuschuß-Programm*) (PEG) by the Federal Ministry of Economic Affairs (BMWi), and the supporting promotion of the R&D-Personnel-Growth (*FuE-Personalzuwachsförderung*) (PI) by the Federal Ministry of Research and Technology (BMFT) that was initiated in 1985.

The PEG program promoted SMEs from 1979 through 1987 by subsidizing their personnel expenses. This was the first time that subsidies were applied to promote human capital as opposed to normal capital expenditures for R&D. Nearly 20,000 enterprises were helped by this program from 1977 to 1988, and the total appropriation was 3.14 billion DM (Hornschild, 1989, p. 603).

Whereas the PEG program could be characterized as a subsidy of existing SME R&D activities, the PI program required new recruits, leading to an increase of capacity (Edler and Hornschild, 1992, p. 49). The participating enterprises recruited R&D personnel from 1984 to 1987. More than 6,000 enterprises were subsidized for a total appropriation of about 250 million DM (Becher et al., 1990, p. 119). The available appropriations are shown in Table B.13.

There is no general answer to the question of whether the programs were effective in realizing the SME´s innovation potential. The German Institute for Economic Research (DIW) and the Fraunhofer Institute for System Techniques and Innovation Research (ISI), which evaluated both programs, concluded that, although the deadweight losses of the subsidies were considerable, a significant number of SMEs participated in the programs. In terms of deutschemarks, such promotions were the most important R&D advancement activities geared to SMEs. Their cancellation created a gap in the field of SME R&D promotion (Hornschild, 1989, p. 607) and the trend of accelerated SME innovation may reverse (Becher et al., 1990, p. 122).

The previous governmental technology policy was aimed at promoting cooperation between business and research institutions (Kunze, 1992, p. 63). Inspired by the industrial network models evolved primarily in the Scandinavian countries (Lundvall, 1992) and northern Italy, the BMFT recently concentrated

Table B.13

The Development of Direct and Indirect Project Promotions

	Number of Projects in a Given Year						
	1982	1983	1984	1985	1986	1987	1988
Direct project promotion	6319.6	5768.5	5923.5	6636.9	6304.8	6743.1	6707.7
among which							
Enterprises with less than 1,000 employees	237.9	185.7	168.5	172.0	200.6	229.4	226.9
Indirect and indirect specific promotion	589.3	640.6	615.6	707.7	764.5	929.4	609.4
among which							
Promotion of R&D–personnel (PI and PEG)	390.0	375.0	320.0	381.7	408.3	249.2	201.7
Contract research and development	13.0	13.1	21.2	40.0	50.6	49.1	63.3
Technology transfer and research cooperation	8.9	8.6	8.3	8.8	14.2	18.0	20.2
Indirect specific measures	75.3	130.1	139.9	105.7	116.6	97.1	57.2

SOURCE: Hornschild (1989), p. 606.

subsidy programs on R&D cooperation both among SMEs and between SMEs and large enterprises.

What all these programs have in common is that they are not tailored to a specific industry or technology. Instead, SMEs in any industry get equal support, independent of whether the industry or the technology in use is "strategic."

The Production Technology Program. The Federal Ministry of Research and Technology supports many different research projects in technological fields that are judged "strategic." One field that is especially important for the machine-tool industry is production technology. Since the production technology program was established in 1980, more than 1 billion DM have been provided by the federal government. In the following pages, this program is described in detail, especially the extent to which the machine-tool industry participated in it.

The program was started by the Schmidt administration in 1980. Since 1982, it has been carried on by the Kohl administration with minor modifications. The *Kernforschungszentrum Karlsruhe* (KFK) was put in charge of implementing the program. Table B.14 shows the main areas provided with money in 1982 and 1983. Mostly joint research projects were funded. For SMEs, simplified procedures were created for filing applications.

Table B.14

Main Areas in Production Technology Program

	Projects (number)	Value (million DM)
CAD/CAM	89.0	38.0
Handling systems	37.0	17.0
Quality control	27.0	6.6
Machine control	65.0	14.0
Flexible manufacturing systems	160.0	67.7
Accompanying research in the social sciences	11.0	2.9

Results and Impacts of Label Program, 1980–1983. From 1980 to 1983, the Ministry of Research and Technology provided 161 million DM. Firms received 55 percent of the money; research institutes, 36 percent. Of the money provided to firms, 75 percent flowed to SMEs in general and 21.2 percent to machine-tool producers. In the machine-tool industry, the BMFT funded 57 projects with 18.5 million DM. On average, firms matched government project expenditures.

Special emphasis was put on technology transfer, because the aim of the program was not to subsidize specific firms but to increase the overall technological level in German industry. To this end the following measures were taken:

1. Project results were required to be transferable to other firms.
2. Results of single projects were published immediately.
3. Seminars were given on production technology with timely material.
4. A CAD/CAM laboratory and other projects were established for demonstration purposes.

The effects of the program were multiplied by the dissemination of the results in the trade media. The identification of industrial development deficiencies by KFK and employers' organizations fostered unsubsidized R&D. The participation of employers increased over time, with the number of working groups growing from 12 to 46, thus speeding up the diffusion of research results. The program was judged positively; at the end of 1983, the BMFT decided to fund a second Production Technology Program for 1984 through 1988.

The Production Technology Program, 1984–1988. The second stage of the program was originally budgeted at 510 million DM, but as a result of high demand by firms, the BMFT eventually provided 610 million DM. The policy instruments underwent fundamental change. Most projects were funded by means of indirect-specific promotions, meaning that not every project was checked and that parallel development projects were no longer excluded from funding. The goal was to further the introduction of CAD/CAM in general and especially in SMEs. Thus the promotion is *specific* because certain industries are targeted. It is *indirect* because the firms decide which specific projects are to be funded. A condition for funding was that the projects be carried out in Germany.

The projects had three components:

1. Indirect-specific promotion
   1.1. Introduction of CAD/CAM
   1.2. Development of industrial robots
2. Promotion of joint research projects
3. Technology transfer, technology assessment

- ***Component 1: Indirect-Specific Promotion***

— ***Component 1.1: Promotion of the Introduction of CAD/CAM***

The BMFT funded a total of 1,286 projects in 1,193 enterprises with 326 million DM. The total amount of money invested in the projects was 1.2 billion DM. About 170 machine-tool producers were granted 53.6 million DM for 193 projects. A high percentage of the subsidized firms were located in Baden-Württemberg. The firms received 40 percent of the cost for staff, hardware, software, outsourced (subcontracted) R&D, consulting, and training. The maximum amount per firm was 400,000 DM. The structure of the project costs is depicted in Figure B.9.

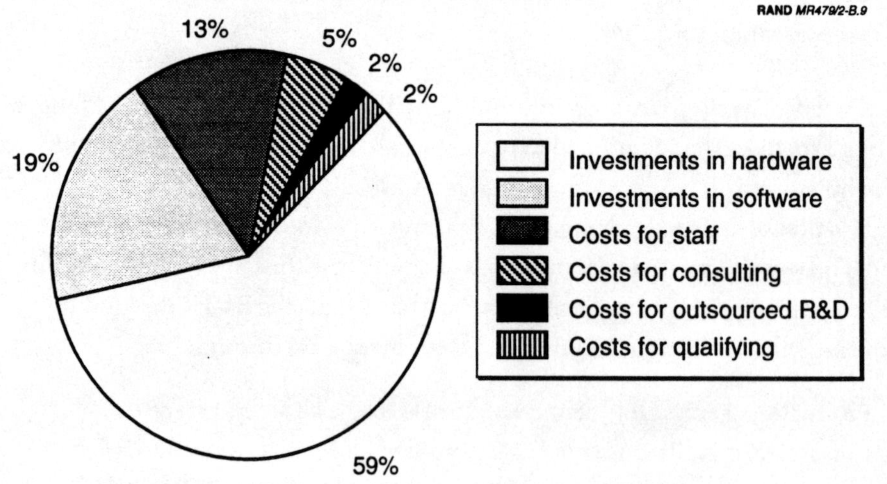

SOURCE: ISI.

Figure B.9—Structure of Costs in Promoted CAD/CAM Projects

The investments in hardware include the purchase of CNC. From 1984 to 1988, the percentage of those using CAD rose from 11 to 33 percent, and for those using CAD/CAM, from 25 to 50 percent. These increases in new technology led to a productivity increase of about 25 percent and cut production time by about 30 percent.

— ***Component 1.2: Development of Industrial Robots***

In total, 140 projects in 140 firms were funded; 21 firms in the machine-tool industry were granted money. Of the developed industrial robots, 38 percent were designed to be used in the production of machine tools. Again, Baden-Württemberg had the highest percentage of funded projects.

The indirect-specific promotion was judged a success, because the diffusion of new production methods could be sped up in firms that usually did not participate in prespecified government R&D. The effects of the Production Technology Program, 1984–1988, were also judged positively. According to an evaluation study (KfK reports 147 and 150), the program had the effects listed in Table B.15.

In view of these results, the BMFT decided to fund a third program for 1988 through 1992.

The Production Technology Program, 1988–1992. The areas of promotion were the following:

1. Computer integrated manufacturing (CIM)
    1.1. CIM technology transfer
    1.2. Standardization of CIM
    1.3. Indirect-specific promotion of CIM
2. New production technologies

Table B.15

Effects of the Production Technology Program, 1984–1986

Effect	Industrial Robots and Handling Systems (%)	CAD/CAM (%)
Catalyst	20	10
Widening of scope and shortening of project time	40	15
Earlier implementation of projects	14	50
Free-rider effect	26	25

SOURCE: KfK.

- ***Component 1: Computer Integrated Manufacturing***

— ***Component 1.1: CIM Technology Transfer***

Sixteen CIM transfer centers were installed at universities all over the Federal Republic of Germany. Their tasks were to

- gather information on the state of the art in CIM
- conduct seminars on CIM components, organization forms, introduction strategies, social compatibility
- demonstrate sample solutions
- consult with CIM users and accompany projects
- exchange experiences and organize regional working groups
- conduct public relations.

IHKs, the RKW, the VDMA, the association of German engineers (VDI), and other associations were involved in organizing the activities of the various CIM technology transfer centers, thus creating regional networks. The BMFT granted 3,786 million DM for the CIM technology transfer.

— ***Component 1.2: Standardization of CIM***

Twenty million DM were granted in this area.

— ***Component 1.3: Indirect-Specific Promotion of CIM***

The goal of indirect-specific promotion was to strengthen the enterprises' self-starting of CIM introduction, concentrating on SMEs. As with CAD/CAM, the firms received 40 percent of the cost for staff and software, outsourced R&D, consulting, and training. The BMFT granted about 300 million DM. The total cost of the projects was about 820 million DM. Again, a high percentage of the grants flowed to Baden-Württemberg. Furthermore, about one-third of the machine-tool producers participated in the program. In general, and this most probably holds true for the machine-tool industry as well, the firms granted funds in the CIM program were others than those granted in the CAD/CAM program. One explanation for this might be that the CAD and the production-controlling systems were important components of CIM. This indicates that latecomers now participated in the CIM program. Thus, if we add up the machine-tool producers subsidized by the two production-technology programs, 1984 to 1988 and 1988 to 1992, we see that about 70 percent of the machine-tool producers were granted money.

The first results of the program evaluation show that the program succeeded in speeding up the diffusion of CIM. Thus, in 1993, about one-third of the machine-tool producers implemented some form of CIM. (See the diffusion curves of CIM components in Figure B.10.)

However, expectations regarding the impact of CIM turned out to be overly optimistic. Furthermore, the projects were too oriented toward technological solutions and neglected organizational requirements. An ISI evaluation of the program came up with the results tabulated in Table B.16.

- *Component 2: New Production Technologies, Mounting*

Table B.17 shows projects in which the machine-tool industry was involved in creating flexible automatic mounting systems [FAMOS]. (The sums in this table show money granted by the BMFT; no EU money flows to German machine-tool producers within the context of these programs.) Here, we see a sizable connection to the EU level. Research and technology policy at the EU level will play an even more important role in the future.

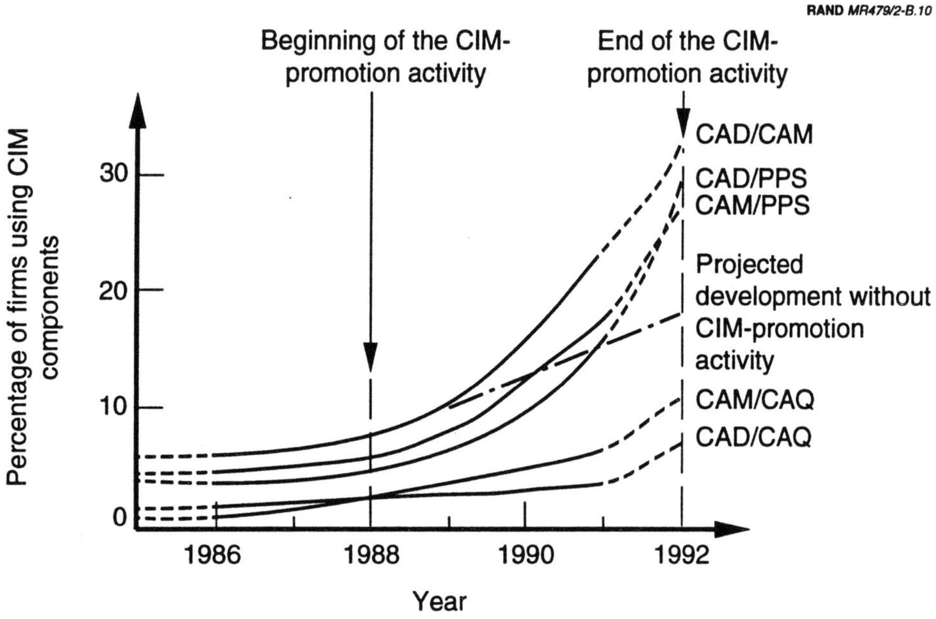

SOURCE: Institut für System- und Innovationsforschung (ISI), Karlsruhe.

Figure B.10—Diffusion Curves of CIM Components

Table B.16

Effects of the Indirect-Specific Promotion of CIM, 1988–1992

Effect	Percentage
Initializing effects	5
Widening of scope and shortening of project time	20
Bringing forward of projects	40
Free-rider effect	35

SOURCE: KfK.

Table B.17

Promotional Projects of the Machine-Tool Industry in the European Community

Project	Description	Duration	Promotion of the Machine-Tool Industry (in DM)
FAMOS–HIFAS (EU 288)	Eureka integrated project setup of job lots and middle-scale production, developmental stage	1988–1992	3,286,750
FAMOS–PRISMA (EU 293)	Setup in the machine-tool industry, realization stage	1988–1992	2,897,900
FAMOS–MOCIM (EU 203)	CIM-oriented setup—partial plan: setup of robot components	1988–1992	4,257,900
FAMOS–IMOLOS (EU 412)	Integrated logistical systems for small and middle setup units, research stage	1989–1993	3,005,350
FAMOS–CIRCUIT (EU 397)	Circuit-board tipping with special elements	1990–1991	782,600
Projects matched to setup problems		1991–1992	49,998
High-precision cutting with geometrically determined cutting edge		1990–1993	3,212,353
Sheet-metalworking		1990–1994	3,979,826
Grinding of high-performance ceramics		1990–1994	1,221,647
Total:			22,694,324

SOURCE: BMFT-promotion catalogue, pp. 459–476.

Summing up, the Production Technology Program helped the German machine-tool producers to introduce CNC and CAD/CAM into the production process. A drawback of indirect-specific promotion may be that individual machine-tool producers introduced CNC and CAD/CAM at too many production stages, thus preventing the machine-tool industry from establishing an efficient division of labor.

European Union

The Single European Act was the basis for the first comprehensive political strategy on technology. It contained the first instance of a formulated research and technology development policy. The Community Framework Program in the field of technological development and research is both the basis and instrument of European research and technology policy.

The first Framework Program (1984–1987) was followed in September 1987 by the second Framework Program (1987–1991), which was a clarification of a research and technology strategy. The new Framework Program (1990–1994) covers three high-priority areas:

1. Research on enabling technologies
2. Management of natural resources
3. Management of intellectual resources.

Every natural or legally naturalized (under public or private law) person who lives in an EU member state is allowed to participate in the programs. The basic principles of cross-border research cooperation are as follows:

- One other partner from another EU member state must participate.
- New products or processes must be precompetitive.
- The person must be able to raise the self-financing contribution (50 percent).

The first high-priority area, enabling technology, is of particular interest to the machine-tool industry.[19] It is subdivided into the two following lines of action:

- Information and communication technologies (areas of research are microelectronics, information processing systems and software, peripherals, computer integrated manufacturing and engineering, basic research)
- Industrial and material technologies (areas of research are materials and raw materials, design and manufacturing, aeronautics).

The new EU information system, the Community Research and Development Information System (CORDIS), provides relevant information on community activities in the field of research and technological development; this system reveals that, EU-wide in 1992, machine-tool makers were involved in 50 projects

---

[19]In the case of information and communication technologies (ESPRIT) and industrial and material technologies (BRITE), roughly 20 percent of the applications were funded.

within the enabling technology area. German machine-tool makers were partners in only six of these projects.

The following reasons are given by entrepreneurs for the small participation in EU R&D programs by German machine-tool enterprises:[20]

- A disproportionately high bureaucratic expenditure at the EU level
- Difficulties in seeking and choosing suitable partners for international cooperation
- Very time-consuming coordination between the various project partners
- Nine different languages
- Twelve different traditions and cultures.

The EU Commission reacted to these problems by creating a new program, Cooperative Research Action for Technology (CRAFT), which is addressed specifically to SMEs that do not have a research capability of their own. As yet, no data are available on the German machine-tool industry's participation in this program.

Concluding Remarks

After the long upswing during the 1980s, the German machine-tool industry entered a severe crisis in the 1990s, the exact nature of which is not yet clear. Certainly, the downswing has a very strong cyclical component. Nonetheless, the following factors signal that the crisis is structural as well:

1. During the upswing, German machine-tool makers were not able to generate large profits, and thus had little in reserve to deal with the sharp drop in demand. Hence, many firms that are operating at the technological frontier now run the risk of going bankrupt. This risk jeopardizes many of the well-established business connections of the past, and, consequently, the advantages of the regionalized, flexible production system constituted by a large number of closely clustered SMEs. In any case, SMEs in the German machine-tool industry need to become more specialized and develop closer cooperative networks to increase profits. Here, prolongation of the upswing in German industry after German reunification, which led to overoptimistic demand expectations and hence to a substantial buildup of productive

---

[20]In general, and for a variety of reasons, German participation in EU R&D programs is low. This is also true of German research institutions.

capacities, has turned into a disadvantage. The earlier downswing in other countries has forced their machine-tool industries to restructure well ahead of Germany.

2. Another reason for low profitability is high labor costs. Compared with Japan, wages are not the culprit, but rather the high indirect costs and the lower number of hours actually worked in the German machine-tool industry. The risk that the high hourly costs of German labor will lead to a loss of manufacturing jobs has increased since the fall of the Berlin wall; low-wage-paying countries with a skilled labor force are now located just beyond the eastern border of Germany.
3. The internal structure of many German machine-tool producers does not seem to be flexible enough because of employee resistance to new structures and lack of management training.

The crisis has forced several firms at risk to start cooperating with each other. Still, most of the SMEs are not keen to do so. Cooperation usually takes place in the precompetitive field, through employers' organizations that are promoted and moderated by the state. Furthermore, firms are usually only willing to cooperate in marketing and servicing in new foreign markets.

A continuing advantage of the German machine-tool industry is the high skill level of the labor force, which is supported by the dual apprenticeship system and many public education institutions. But even here, the crisis has led to substantial cuts in expenditures, especially for advanced training at the firm level, thus endangering future competitiveness. The regional government of Baden-Württemberg has recognized this danger and is promoting several initiatives in this area. But if the number of employees has to be reduced in the current crisis, many qualified workers will leave the machine-tool sector, thus endangering the future human capital base of the German machine-tool industry.

Annex
Case Studies and Technological Trends

This annex summarizes several interviews with experts in machine tools concerning possible future technological trends. The visited firms produced machine-tool machines and metal-remodeling machines. They were medium-sized enterprises, and each was affected in a different way by the current crisis.

CNC Controllers

There is a danger that, in about ten years, the Japanese will dominate the controller market, if German machine-tool producers are not able to develop and use a common controller. There was also skepticism about the realization of a single standard for a European control. There are too many different parties involved. Thus, essentially everything could remain as it is today, i.e., there will still be competing firms with different development of controllers with whom the machine-tool producers will work on a firm-by-firm basis.

Machining Centers

For approximately ten years, clients have used more and more flexible manufacturing systems. Flexible production is becoming increasingly important because of the added variety of parts and the decrease in parts produced per type, thus making mass production less profitable. The trend will carry over into CNC-controlled machines and machining centers. The aim is to make flexible production as cheap as mass production.

Another expert said that, today, clients prefer smaller machine units that can be run either alone or linked together. Total flexible manufacturing cells and systems have been too expensive and too susceptible to failure. The idea of automatically changing worn-out tools failed because of high costs and because the immature sensor technology that recognizes the wear was not accurate enough.

Station-Type Machines

Experts said that further development and employment of station-type machines depends on the parts that have to be produced. Parts that users cannot see in the final products, e.g., water or oil pumps in cars, will still be produced in big numbers. Station-type machines, such as dial-index rotary transfers and transfer lines, will still be used in production.

For parts that can be seen, e.g., bodies of cars, makers must take competitors and client taste into account to determine how long the parts can be sold unchanged. In this case, more flexibility will be necessary in the future. Thus, it is probable that flexible universal machines will more and more be substituted for station-type machines.

Bibliography

Arbeitsgemeinschaft für berufliche Fortbildung Stuttgart, *Fit durch Fortbildung*, 1992.

"Auch Strukturprobleme im Maschinenbau," *Stuttgarter Zeitung*, No. 142, June 24, 1992, p. 9.

"Auch Verbände Können in Strukturkrisen kommen," *Handelsblatt*, No. 63, March 31, 1993, p. 5.

Automobil-Industrie, Vol. 38, No. 1, February 1993, pp. 50–51.

Bayerische Hypotheken und Wechsel, *Industrial Survey: Crisis in the German Machine Tool Industry*, Munich, 1993.

Becher, G., et al., "FuE-Personalkostenzuschub-Programm," *DIW-Wochenbericht*, Vol. 57, No. 10, 1990, pp. 119–122.

Brödner, P., and W. Schultetus, "Rationalisierungs-Kuratorium der Deutschen Wirtschaft (RKW)," in *Erfolgsfaktoren des japanischen Werkzeug-maschinenbaus*, 5th ed., Eschborn, Germany, 1992, pp. 15–22.

Brusco, S., "The Emilian Model: Production Decentralisation and Social Integration," *Cambridge Journal of Economics*, 1982, pp. 167–184.

Bundesministerium für Bildung und Wissenschaft, *Berufsbildungsbericht*, Bad Honnef, Germany, 1993.

Bundesministerium für Forschung und Technologie (BMFT), *Bundesbericht Forschung VI*, Bonn, 1979.

Bundesministerium für Forschung und Technologie (BMFT), *Program Fertigungstechnik der Bundesregierung*, Bonn, 1980.

Bundesministerium für Forschung und Technologie (BMFT), *Program Fertigungstechnik 1984–1987 der Bundesregierung*, Bonn, 1983.

Bundesministerium für Forschung und Technologie (BMFT), *Fertigungstechnik Program 1988–1992*, Bonn, 1988a.

Bundesministerium für Forschung und Technologie (BMFT), *Bundesbericht Forschung*, Bonn, 1988b.

Bundesministerium für Forschung und Technologie (BMFT), *BMFT-Förderungskatalog*, Bonn, 1991.

Bundesministerium für Forschung und Technologie (BMFT), *Programm Qualitätssicherung 1992–1996*, Bonn, 1992.

Bundesministerium für Wirtschaft, *Unternehmensgrößenstatistik 1989/1990: Daten und Fakten*, prepared for Institut für Mittelstandsforschung im Auftrag des BMWi, Studienreihe 68, Bonn, 1990.

Buresch, K. D., "Erfahrungen und Bewertung der neugeordneten industriellen Metallberufe—ein Beispiel der Automobilindustrie," in *Berufsbildung in Wissenschaft und Praxis*, Vol. 21, No. 6, 1992, pp. 25–30.

"Deckel Maho schreibt weiter rot," *Stuttgarter Zeitung*, No. 159, July 14, 1993, p. 11.

"Deckel und Maho endgültingvereint," *Stuttgarter Zeitung*, No. 150, July 3, 1993, p. 16.

"Deckel und Maho gehen zusammen," *Stuttgarter Zeitung*, No. 150, July 11, 1993.

"Die Lage ist schlicht katastrophal," *Stuttgarter Zeitung*, No. 119, May 26, 1993, p. 11.

Edler, D., and K. Hornschild, Erfolgskontrolle am Beispiel der FuE–Personalzuwachsförderung, in *Erfolgskontrollen in der Technologiepolitik*, ed. Niedersächsisches Institut für Wirtschaftsforschung, Hannover, 1992, pp. 49–57.

Fritsch, M., "The Role of Small Firms in West Germany," Wirtschaftswissenschaftliche Dokumentation der Technische Universität, Berlin, Diskussionspapier 147, 1990.

Gawlik, E., "Aufwand für betriebliche Aus- und Weiterbildung in Groß- und Mittelbetrieben—Auswertung von Geschäfts- und Sozialberichten," in *Berufsbildung in Wissenschaft und Praxis*, Vol. 22, No. 1, 1993, pp. 32–36.

Hornschild, K., "Forschungspersonal–Zuwachsförderung," *DIW–Wochenbericht*, Vol. 56, No. 10, 1989, pp. 603–608.

Hornschild, K., and F. Meyer-Krahmer, "Technical Changes and the Network Between Enterprises as well as Science and Economy," paper presented at the Technical Development, Society and Government, symposium, Technische Universität, Berlin, December 1990.

IFO—Institut für Wirtschaftsforschung, *Berichtskreisergebnisse aus den Investitionserhebungen von 1977 bis 1992*, Munich, various years.

IFO—Institut für Wirtschaftsforschung, *Innovationsberichte 1985/86 bis 1990/91*, Munich, various years.

Institut der deutschen Wirtschaft, "Datenbank KURS DIREKT–Run auf Weiterbildung hält an," *IWD*, Vol. 19, No. 5, 1993.

Institut der deutschen Wirtschaft, *Zahlen zur wirtschaftlichen Entwicklung in der Bundesrepublik Deutschland*, Cologne, Germany, 1992.

Interview in *Wirtschaftswoche*, January 1993.

Kernforschungszentrum Karlsruhe, Projektträgerschaft Fertigungstechnik, *Forschungsbericht KfK–PFT 100, Programm Fertigungstechnik 1980–1983, Teil: Übersicht*, Karlsruhe, Germany, 1984.

Kernforschungszentrum Karlsruhe, Projektträgerschaft Fertigungstechnik, *Forschungsbericht KfK–PFT 146, Wirkungsanalyse der indirekt-spezifischen Förderung zur betrieblichen Anwendung von CAD/CAM-Systemen im Rahmen des Programms Fertigungstechnik 1984–1988*, Karlsruhe, Germany, 1989a.

Kernforschungszentrum Karlsruhe, Projektträgerschaft Fertigungstechnik, *Forschungsbericht KfK–PFT 146, Wirkungsanalyse der indirekt-spezifischen Förderung zur Entwicklung von Industrierobotern, Handhabungssystemen sowie zugehöriger intelligenter Peripherie*, Karlsruhe, Germany, 1989b.

Kernforschungszentrum Karlsruhe, Projektträgerschaft Fertigungstechnik, *Forschungsbericht KfK–PFT 150, Ergebnisse des Programms Fertigungstechnik 1984–1988*, Karlsruhe, Germany, 1989c.

Kernforsuchungszentrum Karlsruhe, Projektträgerschaft Fertigungstechnik, "Erste Ergebnisse der Evaluierung der indirekt-spezifischen CIM–Förderung," Dokumentation zur Zwischenpräsentation, Karlsruhe, Germany, 1990.

Kernforschungszentrum Karlsruhe, Projektträgerschaft Fertigungstechnik, "CIM im Programm Fertigungstechnik 1988–1992 des BMFT—Entwicklungstendenzen von Technik und Arbeitsorganisation," Dokumentation zur Ergebnispräsentation, Karlsruhe, Germany, 1993.

Krugman, P., *Geography and Trade*, Cambridge, Mass.: MIT Press, 1991.

Kuntze, U., "FuE–Kooperationen von kleinen und mittleren Unternehmen—Evaluation der BMFT–Maßnahmen auf diesem Gebiet," in *Erfolgskontrollen in der Technologiepolitik*, ed. Niedersaechsisches Institut für Wirtschaftsforschung, Hannover, Germany, 1992, pp. 59–88.

Lundvall, B. A., *National Systems of Innovation—Towards a Theory of Innovation and Interactive Learning*, London, ed., 1992.

"Maschinenbau-Holding gegründet," *Stuttgarter Zeitung*, September 22, 1992.

Ministry of Economic Affairs, press release, September 7, 1992.

Ministry of Economic Affairs, press release, September 17, 1992.

Ministry of Economic Affairs, press release, February 5, 1993.

Nerb, G., "Der Standort Westdeutschland im Urteil der Unternehmen," in *IFO SCHNELLDIENST*, Vol. 45, No. 8, 1992, pp. 6–9.

Piore, M. J., and C. F. Sabel, *Das Ende der Massenproduktion*; Jürgen Behrens, tr., Frankfurt am Main, Germany, 1989.

Puvogel, H. H., *Über den Zusammenhang von Humankapitaltrukur und Wettbewerbsfähigkeit im westdeutschen Maschinenbau*, Tübingen, Germany, 1992.

Rendeiro, J., "How the Japanese Came to Dominate the Machine Tool Business," in *Long Range Planning*, Vol. 18, No. 3, 1985, pp. 62–67.

Richter, Andreas, "Wir haben keine Patentlösungen," *Stuttgarter Zeitung*, No. 61, April 22, 1993, p. 17.

Rominski, Dietrich, "Maschinenbau in Krisenzeiten: Den Kunden produktiver machen," *Absatzwirtschaft*, Vol. 36, No. 3, 1993, pp. 20–22.

Sabel, C. F., "Flexible Specialisation and the Reemergence of Regional Economies," in P. Hirst and J. Zeitlin, eds., *Reversing the Industrial Decline?* New York: St. Martins Press, 1989, pp. 17–70.

Statistisches Bundesamt, *Verschiedene Fachserien*, Wiesbaden, 1992.

Verband Deutscher Maschinen- und Anlagenbau (VDMA), ed., *German Machinery and Plant Manufacturers; Company and Industry Information*; Frankfurt am Main, Germany: The Member Firms of the VDMA, 1991.

Verband Deutscher Maschinen- und Anlagenbau (VDMA), *Statistiken aus dem deutschen Werkzeugmaschinenbau 1991*, Frankfurt am Main, Germany, 1992.

Verband Deutscher Maschinen- und Anlagenbau (VDMA), *Statistisches Handbuch für den Maschinenbau*, Frankfurt am Main, Germany, 1992.

Verband Deutscher Maschinen- und Anlagenbau (VDMA), *Westdeutscher Maschinen- und Anlagenbau 1950–1991. Langfristige Entwicklung in Zahlen*, Frankfurt am Main, Germany, 1992.

Verein Deutscher Werkzeugmaschinenfabriken (VDW), *Internationale Werkzeugmaschinenstatistik 1991*, Frankfurt am Main, Germany, 1992.

Vieweg, H. G., and H. G. Hilpert, *Analyse der Wettbewerbsposition des deutschen Maschinenbaus—Werkzeugmaschinen, Gutachten im Auftrag des Bundesministeriums für Wirtschaft*, Munich, Germany: IFO—Institut für Wirtschaftsforschung, 1992.

Weber, Joachim, "Wir verstehen unsere Mitglieder als Kunden und Anteilseigner," No. 199, *Handelsblatt*, No. 199, October 14, 1992, p. 25.

Werner, R., "Neue und alte industrielle Metallberufe: statistische Analyse der Entwicklungen," *Berufsbildung in Wissenschaft und Praxis*, Vol. 21, No. 6, 1992, pp. 2–10.

Zechlin, H. J., VDMA manager, quoted in *Stuttgarter Zeitung*, No. 61, April 22, 1993.

Zedler, R., "Technologieentwicklung und berufliche Qualifizierung in den industriellen Metallberufen," *Berufsbildung in Wissenschaft und Praxis*, Vol. 21, No. 6, 1992, pp. 10–15.

Appendix C
The Italian Machine-Tool Industry

Antonello Zanfei, with the assistance of Alfonso Gambardella, University of Urbino

The Four Phases of the Italian Machine-Tool Industry's Evolution

Today, Italy's machine-tool industry plays a major role in the internationally competitive arena, in terms of both shares of world production and export performance.[1] Italy is particularly strong in the production of tools for the auto industry and small metalworking firms. This was not always the case. Unlike Germany, the United States, and the United Kingdom, which have been characterized historically by a clear dominance of world machine-tool markets, and like Japan, Italy is a relative newcomer. Although it has a rather long tradition in the manufacturing of machine tools, Italy held only a marginal position in the international arena until the early 1970s. Its share of world machine-tool production was just 1.6 percent in 1965, as opposed to Germany's 28 percent, the United States' 17 percent, and Great Britain's 13 percent.

Figure C.1 highlights four different phases in the Italian machine-tool industry's evolution, each of which is discussed in turn in the following sections:

1. The fast growth of the 1960s, which significantly increased Italy's share of world production to a high of 4.3 percent in 1970
2. The 1971–1980 period, which was marked by a slower but steady growth of Italy's share of world production (to 6.5 percent at the end of the decade) and by a fast increase in exports
3. The 1980–1985 period, when there was a sharp drop in global machine-tool demand and Japan became the world leader in machine-tool production
4. The recovery and high growth of the postrecession period, which had taken Italy's share of world production to 8.8 percent in 1992, although a slowdown has since taken place.

---

[1]This appendix was written by Antonello Zanfei, ISE–Università di Urbino and IEFE–Università Bocconi, in collaboration with Alfonso Gambardella, Università di Urbino and IEFE–Università Bocconi, on behalf of Centro Studi Impresa e Territorio (CESIT), Università di Urbino, Italy.

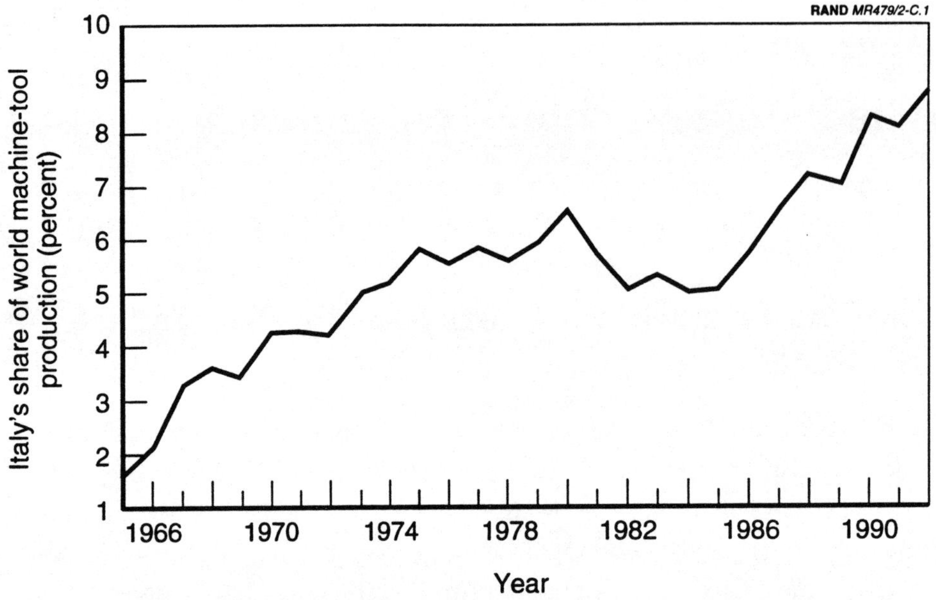

SOURCES: UCIMU and *American Machinist.*
NOTE: Number for 1992 is provisional.

Figure C.1—Evolution of Italy's Share of World Machine-Tool Production from 1965 Through 1992 (data based on U.S. $)

The Early Stages of Growth Led by Domestic Demand (1960–1970)

During the 1960s, a set of separate exogenous factors converged to sustain a high growth rate for the Italian machine-tool industry. The first half of the decade was characterized by a significant expansion of domestic demand for capital goods, reflecting exceptionally fast increases in gross national product (GNP) and private consumption.[2] In particular, machine tools played a fundamental role in sustaining the development and competitiveness of both traditional sectors and the more dynamic industries (metallurgical and transportation equipment) that spurred the country's industrialization in this period. While this fast increase in demand was partially satisfied by imports, it also opened up increasing opportunities for domestic manufacturers. In fact, geographic proximity put domestic manufacturers of machine tools in a better position to meet specific needs of the small- and medium-sized firms that played a crucial role in Italy's

[2]Between 1958 and 1964, real GNP, private consumption, and gross investments grew at rates of 5.7 percent, 6.8 percent, and 5.8 percent, respectively. These rates are higher than the corresponding average rates of European Community (EC) countries and the United States in the same period.

industrialization process. Large producers of durable consumer goods—for example, car manufacturers FIAT, Alfa Romeo, and Lancia in the northwest and the electrical household appliance firm Zanussi in the northeast—created extensive networks of suppliers of parts and components, which in turn were strong demanders of specialized machine tools (see Firm Size and Vertical Disintegration, below, for further details on regionalism).

Machine-tool demand continued to expand after 1965, although at a slower pace, in spite of severe monetary controls that considerably slowed the economy's expansion. The growth of the machine-tool industry was promoted from two directions. Machine-tool purchases and, more generally speaking, adoption and substitution of process technology reflected an important effort carried out by large firms to increase capital intensity and reduce the effect of growing labor costs. At the same time, a law (No. 1329 of 1965, known as the Sabatini Law) was introduced that favored the adoption of innovative machinery in the Italian industry by granting subsidies and financial aid to users, helping sustain machine-tool demand among small- and medium-sized firms (see Policy Measures and Related Issues, below).

Although the overall result was that demand growth continued to favor foreign machine-tool suppliers, Italian manufacturers also expanded production, increased the scale and efficiency of their processes, and gradually improved competitiveness in domestic and international markets. The improved competitiveness between 1965 and 1970 is reflected in the growth of imports by a factor of 2.3, of exports by a factor of 1.8, and of Italian manufacturers' domestic sales by a factor of 2.4.

The Industry's Internationalization (1970–1980)

Generally, the early growth phase of the 1960s was conditioned largely by positive trends in domestic demand for capital goods. By contrast, during the 1970s, the second phase outlined above, Italian machine-tool manufacturers were facing both lower GNP and slower domestic consumption growth rates. Figure C.2 shows that fixed investments in small user firms (less than 200 employees) and, even more so, of large firms (more than 500 employees) declined after 1972, with no significant improvement until the end of that decade. For machine tools specifically, the 1972–1978 period reflects an overall dynamic of negative "apparent consumption"[3] in real terms. However, Italian manufacturers were favored in their effort to increase exports by a remarkable increase in worldwide

---

[3]Apparent consumption = production – exports + imports.

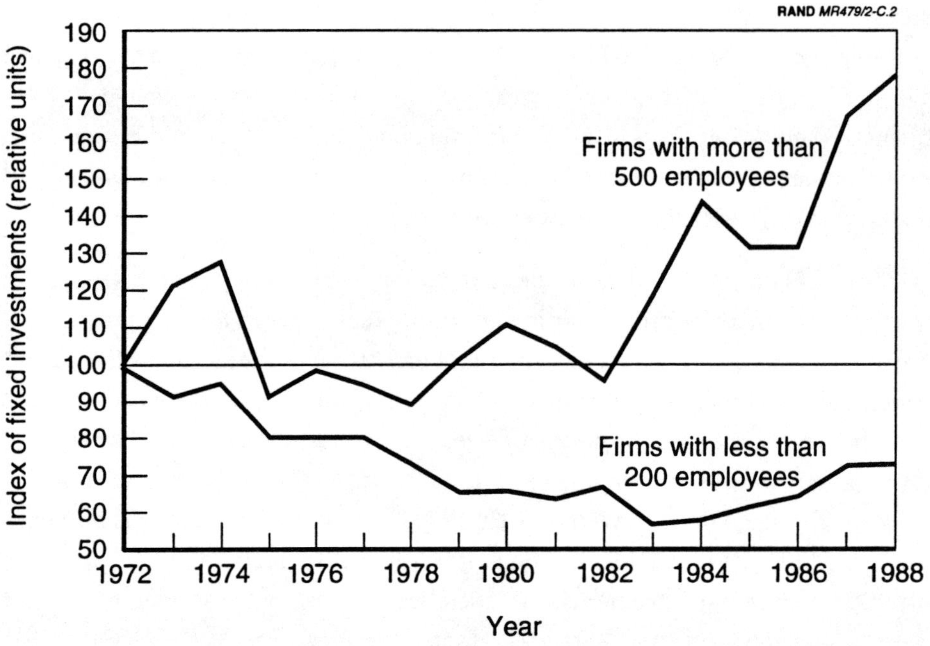

SOURCES: ISTAT and ISCO data.

Figure C.2—Index of Fixed Investments of Large (>200 employees) and Small (<200 employees) Firms, with Constant 1972 Prices

machine-tool demand in the most advanced countries. The combined total consumption in the 20 largest machine-tool–producing countries doubled between 1975 and 1980; in fact, most industrialized countries (with Italy lagging behind) were then making efforts to compensate for the first oil shock by building more productive plants, which required, among other factors, high-performance machinery and new production processes.[4]

On the supply side, two major factors help explain Italy's international machine-tool competitiveness during the 1970s. First, machine-tool manufacturers significantly increased their use of subcontracting, thus enhancing flexibility in their manufacturing activities. Parts and components were outsourced to specialized manufacturing units. Such decentralization is confirmed by data in Figure C.3, which shows a significant increase in the share of costs sustained by

[4]In the 1960s, Italy was still experiencing a stronger expansion than most industrialized countries. While fixed investments were growing slower than in the previous decade, because of the effects of the monetary restrictions of the mid-1960s, most of these investments were labor-saving, because Italian entrepreneurs aimed to reduce the strength of worker unions. When the oil crisis severely hit the most advanced part of Italian industry (which could be identified essentially with the automobile industry), smaller enterprises did not have the means to invest in new capital formation. Thus, big industry reduced investments while small- and medium-sized enterprises (SMEs) were not able to compensate.

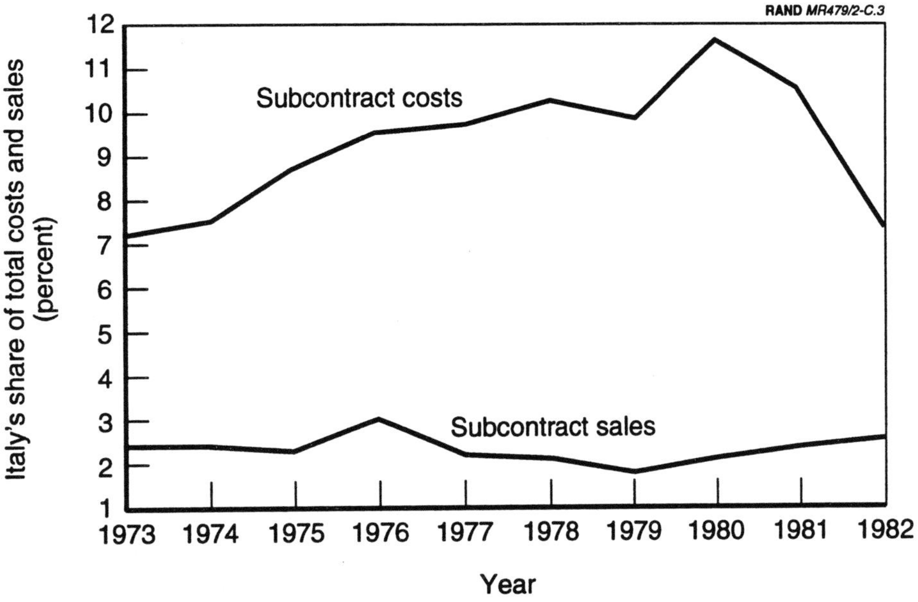

SOURCE: ISTAT, *Bollettino mensile di statistica.*

Figure C.3—Subcontracting Costs and Sales, 1973–1982

firms for subcontracting activities to external manufacturing units between 1973 and 1980. Note that the data refer to firms with more than 20 employees. Analysis of these data suggests that firms with more than 20 employees tended to decentralize activities either to firms external to the industry (e.g., computer numerical control (CNC) software) or to smaller machine-tool firms (less than 20 employees) involved in the manufacture of special parts or tools.

Second, a specialization process eventually gave Italian machine-tool firms a lead in the production of nonstandard products tailored for specific purposes. We shall see (in Surviving the Crisis, below) that this process guaranteed Italian firms some protection from direct competition from Japanese manufacturers, which concentrated on higher-volume, standard CNC tools.

Surviving the Crisis (1980–1985)

The early 1980s brought a far-reaching crisis that affected Italy's machine-tool production and exports, as it did those of most industrialized countries. As Figure C.4 illustrates, Italy was not hit by the crisis as hard as its main

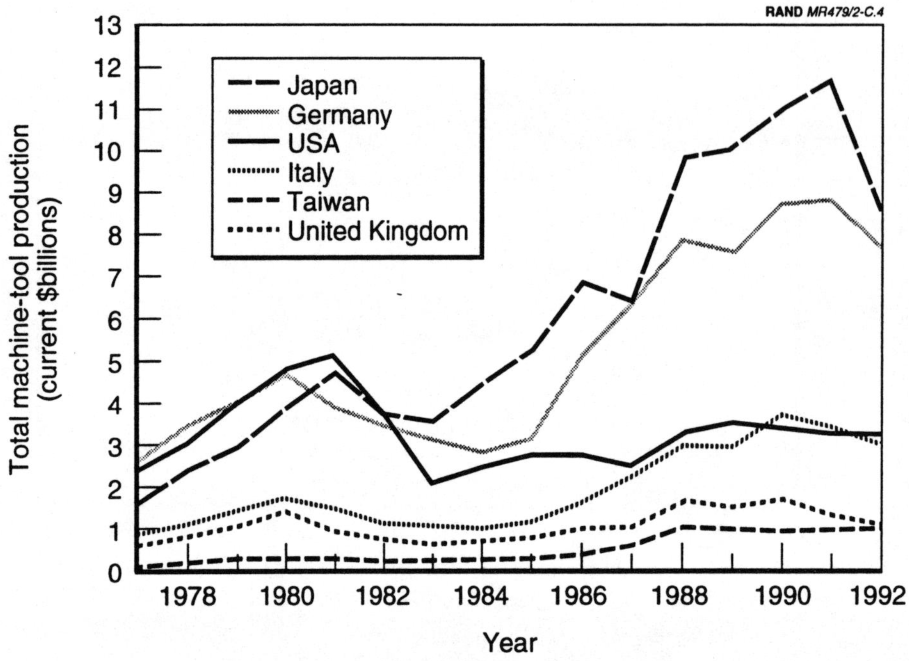

SOURCE: Elaborations of CECIMO data reported by UCIMU.

Figure C.4—Trends in World Machine-Tool Production

competitors. Moreover, if the production trend is considered in absolute terms, Italy also shows a slower reaction to the shakeout of the early 1980s.[5]

To explain the relatively low intensity of the 1980–1985 crisis, we must consider at least three factors:

1. Italian manufacturers were able to increase exports to those markets that grew more rapidly (or at least were characterized by a lower contraction).
2. Italy was less affected than other countries by aggressive Japanese and Asian competition.
3. Italian suppliers were relatively quick to introduce the "new" CNC technology that eventually became a fundamental competitive asset.

Let us consider these factors more closely. After the swift growth in demand during the second half of the 1970s, all industrialized countries experienced a slowdown in machine-tool consumption. The combined total consumption of the top 20 machine-tool manufacturing countries increased only 10 percent

[5]This view is also confirmed if values are translated into constant dollars and then deflated using the U.S. consumer price index (CPI).

between 1980 and 1985 (whereas it had doubled between 1975 and 1980). In the same period, Italy's machine-tool apparent consumption fell 4.7 percent per year, a larger decrease than that in most industrialized countries (France and Germany had an average consumption decline of 1.2 percent and 1.0 percent, respectively). In some countries, the contraction of demand was less severe; so, those countries managed to have a positive, albeit small, increase of apparent consumption over the whole 1980–1985 period (+1.5 percent in the United States, +3.6 percent in the United Kingdom). In Japan, apparent consumption fell only in 1982 and 1983, i.e., the briefest recession among the highly industrialized countries. The overall dynamics of the Japanese market, then, were largely positive during the examined period (+13 percent in 1980 through 1985).

Italian machine-tool manufacturers were able to compensate for the contraction in domestic demand by increasing foreign outlets. They expanded their export/production ratio from 49.1 percent in 1980 to 63.4 percent in 1985—by far the highest increase experienced by large industrialized countries in that period (see Figure C.5). They also augmented their penetration into faster-growing

RAND MR479/2-C.5

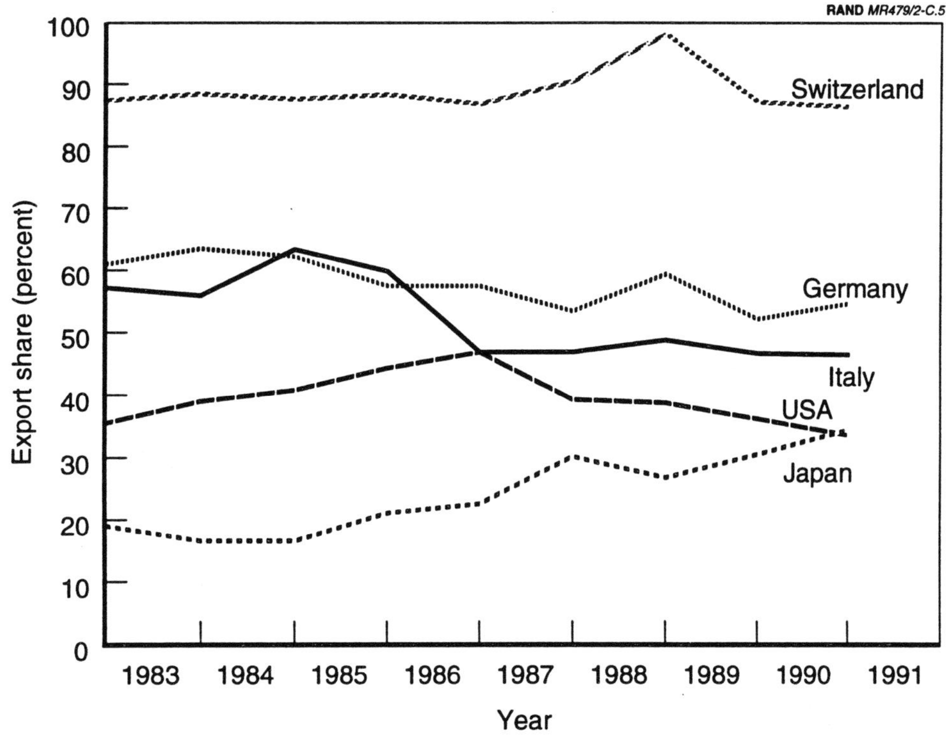

SOURCE: UCIMU's elaborations on national associations' data.

Figure C.5—Export Shares of Total Italian Machine-Tool Production in Comparison with Main Competitors' Shares

markets. For instance, Italy expanded its share of total exports directed to Germany (from 12.1 percent in 1980 to 14.6 percent in 1985) and to the United States (from 6.8 to 13.3 percent).

To achieve this result, Italian machine-tool firms had to increase their efforts to enhance productivity and lower their export prices to improve competitiveness. In fact, the first half of the decade was characterized by a substantial reduction in the number of employees—by one-third in five years (from 37,200 in 1980 to 28,200 in 1985)—and reintegration of decentralized activities, as illustrated by Figure C.3. Despite falling sales, new fixed investments continued to increase (except in 1982), thus revealing a strong effort to improve both manufacturing processes and product quality. Available data suggest that Italy actually was able to improve its price competitiveness substantially. Table C.1 shows that the ratio between wholesale prices of Italian machine tools and those of foreign manufacturers diminished markedly during the first half of the 1980s, especially when the comparison is made with Japan, the United States, and Germany.[6]

As far as the second factor (low impact of Asian competitive challenge) is concerned, the evidence is clear that, by 1985, Japan directed to Italy only 0.5

Table C.1

Competitiveness Indicator of the Italian Machine-Tool Industry (1980 = 100 Italian lire)[a]

	USA	Japan	Germany	United Kingdom	France	Average	Change (%)
1980	100.0	100.0	100.0	100.0	100.0	100.0	
1981	78.9	81.8	101.9	93.4	100.1	87.7	−12.3
1982	70.7	86.9	98.6	95.5	102.1	87.6	−0.1
1983	64.8	77.2	93.7	97.0	100.7	80.9	−7.6
1984	56.8	68.5	90.5	91.3	98.3	74.2	−8.3
1985	57.0	69.6	92.4	87.4	99.4	75.0	1.1
1986	76.9	73.7	89.8	101.5	99.7	81.6	8.8
1987	89.9	80.1	85.2	105.0	100.4	85.1	4.3
1988	89.2	72.1	83.6	94.9	99.6	81.2	−4.6
1989	84.4	68.8	86.2	94.2	101.0	86.9	7.0
1990	96.1	84.4	85.3	98.5	99.2	92.7	6.7
1991	91.5	76.2	83.0	95.1	99.0	89.0	−4.0

SOURCE: UCIMU's elaborations on CECIMO and UIC (Italian Exchange Rate Bureau) data.

[a]The indicator is the index of the ratio between wholesale prices of Italian machine tools and the wholesale prices in the indicated countries, corrected for changes in exchange rates. The decrease of the indicator means a gain of competitiveness of the Italian industry, and vice versa.

[6]This price information does not control for changes in product type or quality, and thus may miss the fact that Japanese machine-tool makers shifted to higher-value machines (see Volume 1 of this report, Chapter Four).

percent of its total exports (519.8 billion yen), as opposed to 52.5 percent to the United States, 6.3 percent to Germany, and 3.2 percent to the United Kingdom. The share of Japanese exports to Italy had grown to 1.2 percent by 1988, but that is still a minimal part of Japan's foreign activity. However, Italy's imports from Japan are higher than average for machining centers (2.4 percent of Japan's total exports in this category were directed to Italy in 1988), punching machines (4.7 percent), and CNC lathes (3 percent). Italy does not represent a major market for Japanese exports in these categories, however.

Two important reasons for this low penetration of Japanese machine tools into the Italian market in the early 1980s can be inferred. First, Italy has received almost no Japanese foreign direct investment in cars and other transportation equipment industries.[7] Therefore, Japan's machine-tool manufacturers could not take advantage of a presence in Italy of Japanese-owned automobile plants and their suppliers, a presence that in other countries (such as the United States) was used as a "bridgehead" for the penetration of related manufacturing and service activities (such as machine tools).

Second, the already-mentioned specialization of Italian machine-tool manufacturers in nonstandardized, tailor-made market segments has partially protected them from the aggressive competition of the Japanese. Japanese specialization has hinged on high-volume production of relatively standardized machines scaled to intensive user industries.

A further, and final, factor that helps explain Italy's success in coping with the international crisis of the first half of the 1980s was Italian firms' rapid introduction of computer numerical control technology. Several authors (Carlsson and Jacobsson, among others) point out that the adoption of CNC technology caused significant structural-adjustment problems for traditional machine-tool manufacturers, i.e., coping with shrinking markets for conventional machine tools, shortened product life cycles, and new commercialization needs.[8]

---

[7]There appears to have been a private agreement between FIAT and Japanese automakers, dating back to the 1950s, to avoid each other's markets. Competition from the Japanese is expected to increase in the near future.

[8]According to data reported by Edquist and Jacobsson (1988), between 1978 and 1984 the share of NC machine tools in total machine-tool investments grew from 15.6 to 54.3 percent in Japan, from 19 to 62.4 percent in the United Kingdom, from little more than 20 to 40.1 percent in the United States, and from 26 to 59.4 percent in Sweden. With reference to product life cycles, it is acknowledged that, in the case of CNC lathes, a design introduced in the mid-1970s would be phased out within eight years, whereas a design put on the market in the mid-1980s would have an expected lifetime of about three years (Schor, 1986). Generally speaking, the introduction of CNC technology radically changes the overall organization of machine-tool manufacturing processes, leading to a different approach to commercialization and post-commercialization services.

The timing of CNC technology adoption and commercialization is thus a fundamental aspect of the changing competitive scenario. Italian manufacturers were relatively early adopters of this technology. The share of CNC machine tools in total Italian machine-tool production was already high in the mid-1970s (15.2 percent in 1976), when the "electronic revolution" applied to CNC had just started. Note that this share was just as high as Japan's, almost twice as high as the United Kingdom's, 50 percent higher than Germany's, and 25 percent higher than France's. From then on, Italian machine-tool manufacturers continued investing in the new technology at a faster pace than did most industrialized countries, except Japan and Germany, which took the lead in this field.

This ability to enter the CNC market faster than most competitors has favored Italian suppliers in both domestic and international markets and has helped them survive the international crisis with less damage than most competitors. The domestic market was particularly receptive to the new technology in the early 1980s. In that period, Italian small- and medium-sized firms active in a number of traditional sectors were undergoing a restructuring that opened up new opportunities in domestic machine-tool markets. Such restructuring is consistent with the evolution of small firms' fixed investment patterns illustrated in Figure C.2. As this reorganization and capitalization process was taking place in the early 1980s, with some delay in comparison with the most advanced industrial countries, small- and medium-sized machine-tool users were able to leapfrog to the new technology, with lower installed-base effects.

The Recovery and Problems Ahead (1985–Present)

The previous discussion helps explain why Italy was hit less hard by the international crisis of the first half of the 1980s. But what about the recovery? We have already noted that the 1985–1991 upswing was not as strong for Italy as it was for some of Italy's direct competitors. Figure C.6 further illustrates that, while exports kept growing fast in real terms, the gap between export and import growth has been narrowing significantly since 1985.

This general trend is the result of a gradual but significant erosion of both price and nonprice advantages that Italian manufacturers had enjoyed until the early 1980s. Table C.1 provides some evidence of the increasing difficulties Italian manufacturers encountered in keeping up with the prices of their direct competitors, Japan and the United States in particular (it may also help explain the swift decline of Italian exports to the U.S. market). Taiwan has also emerged as an aggressive competitor in both domestic and international markets. Italy's

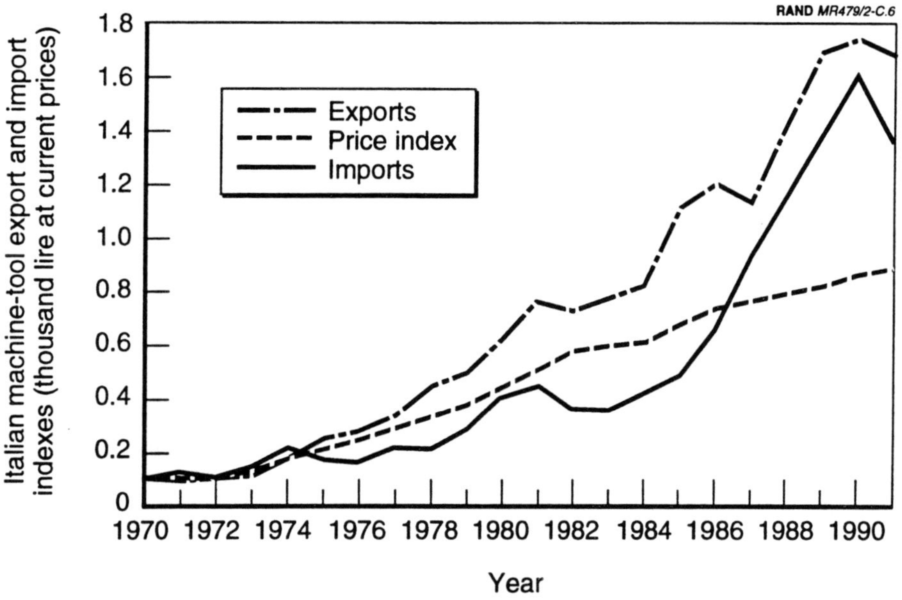

SOURCE: UCIMA on ISTAT data.

Figure C.6—Evolution of Italian Machine-Tool Imports and Exports, 1970–1991

machine-tool imports from Taiwan increased from 0.4 percent of total Italian imports in 1980 to 3.4 percent in 1991 (and 3.8 percent in 1992). Although Italy does not represent a key market outlet for Taiwanese manufacturers (exports to Italy were 0.9 percent of total Taiwanese exports in 1980 and 4.6 percent in 1991), their machine tools are sold on the Italian market at an extremely competitive price: In 1991, the unit value (per kilogram) of Italy's imports from Taiwan (9,546 lire [L]) was less than half the average price of Italian exports (20,965 L). Of course, this disparity also reveals the lower quality of the machine tools produced by Taiwan. However, it is hard to deny that, given these prices, Taiwanese machine tools became highly attractive for standard uses.

As far as nonprice factors are concerned, and thanks to the flexibility of new technology embodied in CNC machine tools, a number of foreign manufacturers are markedly and rapidly improving the extent of their products' capabilities through new software and modular add-ons. These manufacturers are often able to work out tailor-made solutions that are highly competitive with Italian firms' custom machines, which is probably a fundamental reason for the substantial increase in imports from Japan: Italy received more than 10 percent of its total imports from Japan in 1991 (15.7 percent in 1992; 5.2 percent of total Italian consumption), as opposed to 4.3 percent in 1985. Note that nonconventional machinery and machining centers make up the bulk of Japanese imports (47.6

billion L in 1991, i.e., 42.3 percent of Italy's total imports from Japan). The trade balance with this country worsened in the second half of the 1980s, from a deficit of 9.3 billion L in 1985 to 156.3 billion L in 1990 (the negative trend was partially curbed in 1991 and 1992, when the trade deficit fell to 88.6 and 124.5 billion L, respectively).

Germany is the single-largest exporter to Italy. Its machine-tool trade balance has improved dramatically in recent years (from –130.6 billion L in 1988 to +1.8 billion L in 1991 and 22.6 billion L in 1992). Italy imports mostly standardized lathes (90.4 billion L, i.e., 22.2 percent of total imports from Germany in 1991, with a trade deficit of 10.1 billion L in this category) and is also largely dependent on German suppliers for a number of metal-cutting machines (grinding, surfacing, and gear-cutting machines). In spite of their propensity to manufacture and export high-end standardized machinery, several German manufacturers are also increasing their competitive strength in the field of customized machines and are often able to erode market shares of Italian manufacturers in this field. This is the case of Gildemeister of Bielefeld, which has a manufacturing unit in Italy (Lombardia) and is producing a wide array of lathes, CN controllers, and factory-automation processes. According to officers of the Italian machine-tool industry association (UCIMU), once this plant was acquired, it was specifically organized to develop tailor-made solutions from standardized machine tools that continue to be manufactured in Germany. These products are sold through Gildemeister's distribution channels, and some personnel are specifically dedicated to sales and promotion of these products.

As foreign firms have become more aggressive in producing and marketing their nonconventional, customized machinery, Italian manufacturers have failed to respond. In fact, they appear to have slowed their fixed capital investment activity and to have overlooked the importance of building adequate marketing and distribution structures (see later in this section).

As regards new capital formation, after the peak of 1985, per capita investment increased at a slower, although still rapid, pace (Figure C.7). Instead, machine-tool firms returned to the strategy, adopted in the early 1970s, of increasingly resorting to subcontracting (Figure C.8). In other words, they chose to defend their competitiveness by flexibly organizing their manufacturing processes (through subcontracting) rather than investing in new technology or in new marketing and distribution networks.

Based on the few data that are available, an overall increase in the skills of the labor force also has occurred in the industry. First, the ratio of technicians and white-collar workers to total employees increased from 31 to 39 percent from

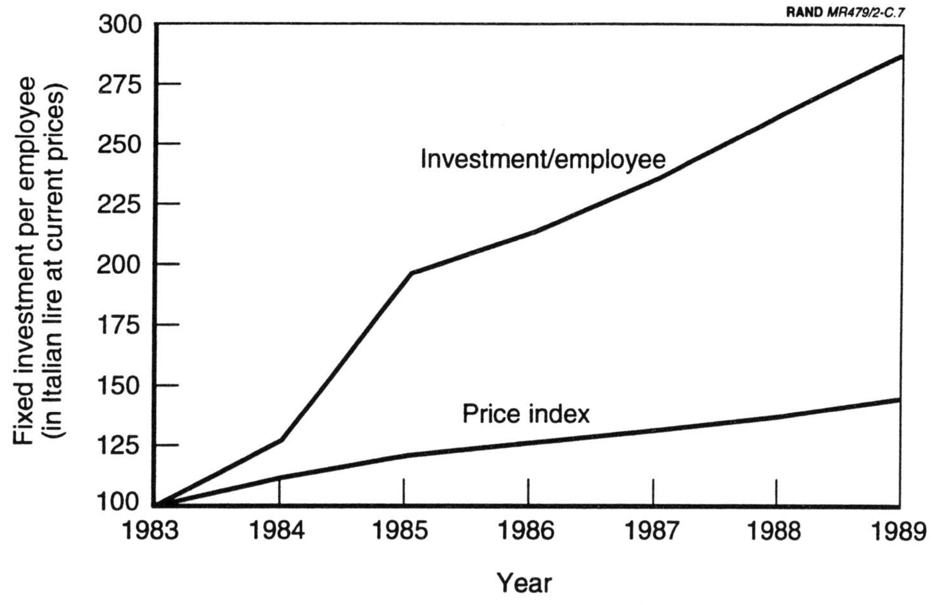

SOURCE: ISTAT, *collana d'informazione.*

Figure C.7—Evolution of Per Capita Investments

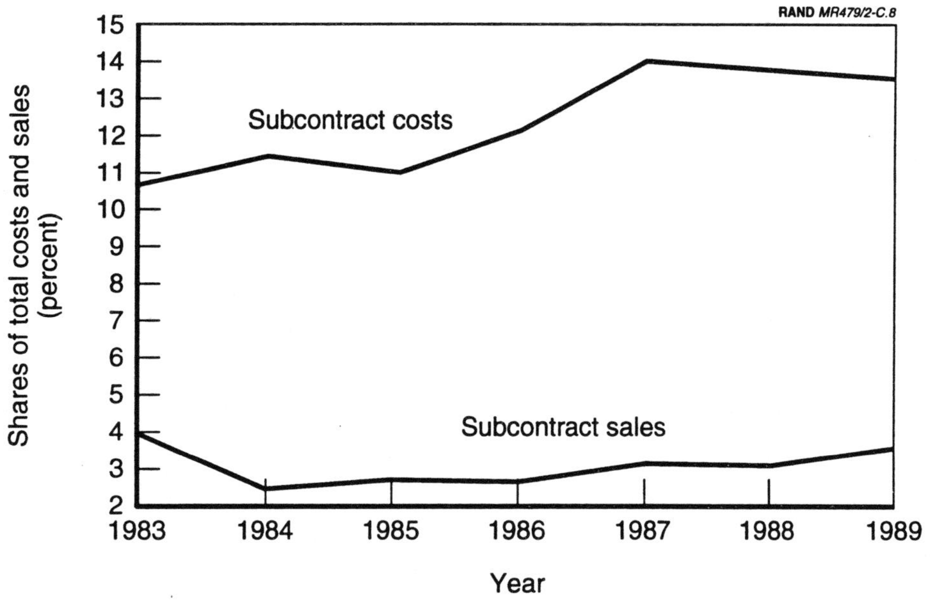

SOURCE: ISTAT, *collana d'informazione.*

Figure C.8—Subcontracting Costs and Sales, 1983–1989

1984 to 1990 (UCIMU, 1991). To the extent that this evolution reflects an attempt to increase management and coordination skills, it is certainly an asset for future competitiveness.

Second, the ratios of R&D expenses to total sales and personnel to total employees increased in the same period, from 0.62 to 1.43 percent and from 0.8 to 2.3 percent, respectively. This observation needs to be qualified, however. On the one hand, both ratios appear to be much lower than those for other Italian capital goods and high-technology industries. On the other hand, institutionalized R&D data most probably underestimate the actual innovative (development) activities carried out by small- and medium-sized firms in the machine-tool industry. In fact, to meet highly specific user needs, machine-tool manufacturers of the type prevailing in Italy—i.e., highly specialized in the design and production of personalized machine tools—are compelled to improve and adapt the original design continuously. Moreover, given the importance of CNC machinery in overall Italian machine-tool production, manufacturers have to interact with, and learn from, both suppliers of high-technology components and machine-tool users.

If we now turn to provision of marketing structures and after-sale services, a number of sector studies (Onida, 1991; Vitali, 1990) have pointed out that Italian manufacturers are largely underdeveloped in this role. Among the 235 UCIMU members in 1992, only 114 had some kind of permanent sales and distribution structure abroad, either in the form of sales agents or of subsidiaries and branch offices. Only 39 of these were active in the U.S. market. Twenty-nine firms had a trading or manufacturing subsidiary abroad, i.e., a more structured presence in a foreign market than simply a network of agents.

This weakness is increasingly penalizing Italian manufacturers' efforts to compete in distant foreign markets, especially compared with German and Japanese firms, which are endowed with greater export supports. For instance, it is apparent that the inadequacy of Italian distribution services is a fundamental obstacle to exports of complex machinery, as in the case of robots, which is clearly shown in Table C.2. One should also note that, in 1991, Italy had a trade deficit of 15.6 billion L in this field and that 49.4 percent of total exports was directed to France, whereas a much smaller share was directed to more distant markets (6.4 percent to the United States).

Italy is far more competitive in the production of customized machinery, flexible manufacturing systems (FMS), and cells. However, Italian machine-tool makers are moving away from customized CNC machinery in favor of more commodity-

Table C.2

Export/Production Ratios by Type of Products (percent)

	Year				
	1987	1988	1989	1990	1991
Nonconventional stand-alone machine tools	37.2	35.9	38.5	45.3	46.8
Robots	31.8	30.4	31.5	29.2	29.3
Cells and FMS	60.8	61.9	65.9	56.4	52.4

SOURCE: UCIMU, *Lettera economica*, No. 15, 1992.

type machine tools. This might be a negative sign for Italy's competitiveness in the long run.

Firm Size and Vertical Disintegration

Firm size and the coordination of the machine-tool manufacturing process have frequently emerged in the previous sections as crucial factors in the evolution and future prospects of the Italian industry. Are issues related to these factors of greater magnitude than in other countries? How can these issues be better qualified and quantified?

A very superficial observation reveals that some fundamental structural differences in coordination do exist across countries. For instance, the United Kingdom today produces a little more than one-third of what Italy produces but has over 70 percent more employees; Germany has slightly more than double Italy's production but three times as many machine-tool employees. This observation reflects differences in productivity, as well as in degree of vertical integration, with a higher specialization and a more extensive outsourcing of components by Italian firms.

The available data permit us to better quantify and qualify this view as follows:

1. The average size of Italian machine-tool firms is actually low, however measured. When using Italian Central Bureau of the Census (ISTAT) data based on a large sample of firms with more than 20 employees and an extensive definition of machine tools, the average size was computed to be 61.7 employees per unit in 1989 (it was 63.6 in 1983). Using UCIMU data, which refer to a smaller sample of firms covering a more restrictive definition of machine tools, the average size was 52.5 employees. More specifically, 68.1 percent of all firms had less than 50 employees in 1991 (72.2 percent in

1986). This class of firms (with less than 50 employees) employs 24.0 percent of the total labor force of the sample. If one splits these data by product category, it appears that the share of total labor force employed in this class of firms is higher for stand-alone machine tools (25.8 percent). In the case of cells and FMS, only a few firms (about 30) are active in Italy, and they tend to be larger than average. The exceptions to the norm of small machine-tool companies are Mandelli and Comau. Comau is a subsidiary of FIAT and is the only Italian firm that ranks among the top global machine-tool makers. Its diversified product line includes strengths in FMS and robotics.

2. Such a highly fragmented industry is geographically concentrated in a very limited area (see Figures C.9 and C.10). This concentration was favored

RAND MR479/2-C.9

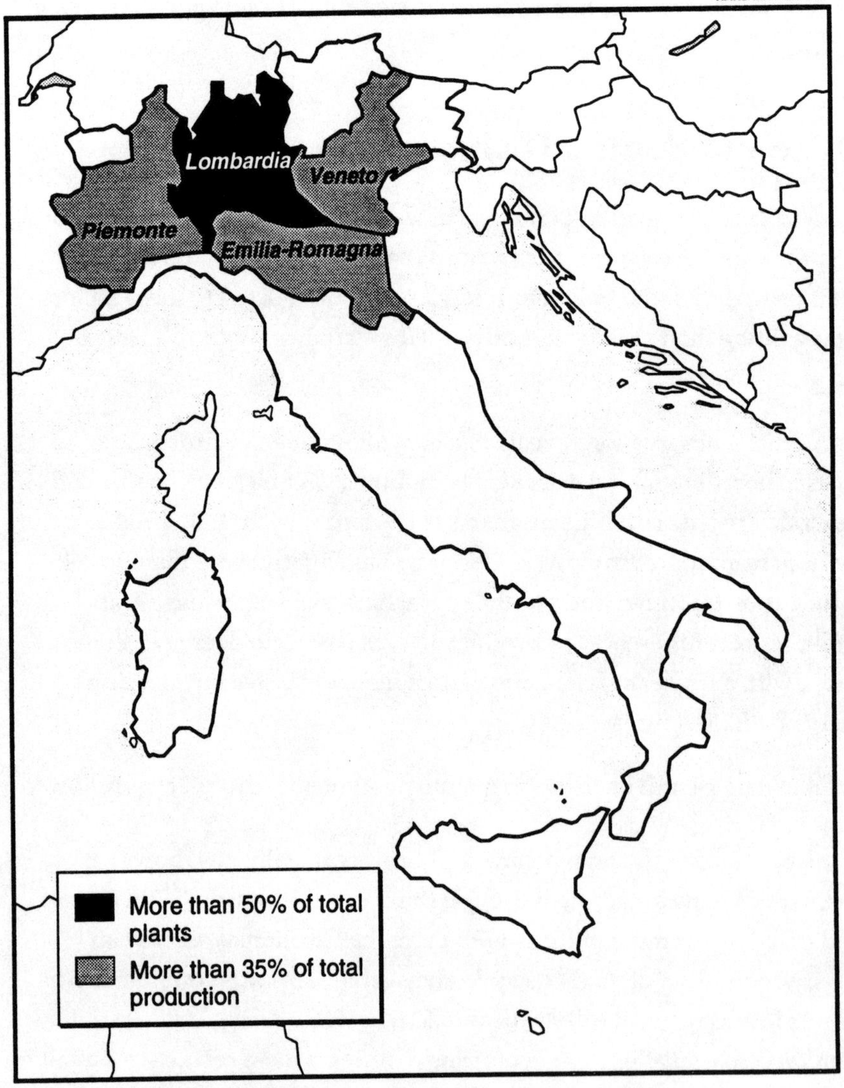

SOURCE: Elaborations of UCIMU data.

Figure C.9—Geographic Distribution of Italian Machine-Tool Manufacturers

RAND MR479/2-C.10

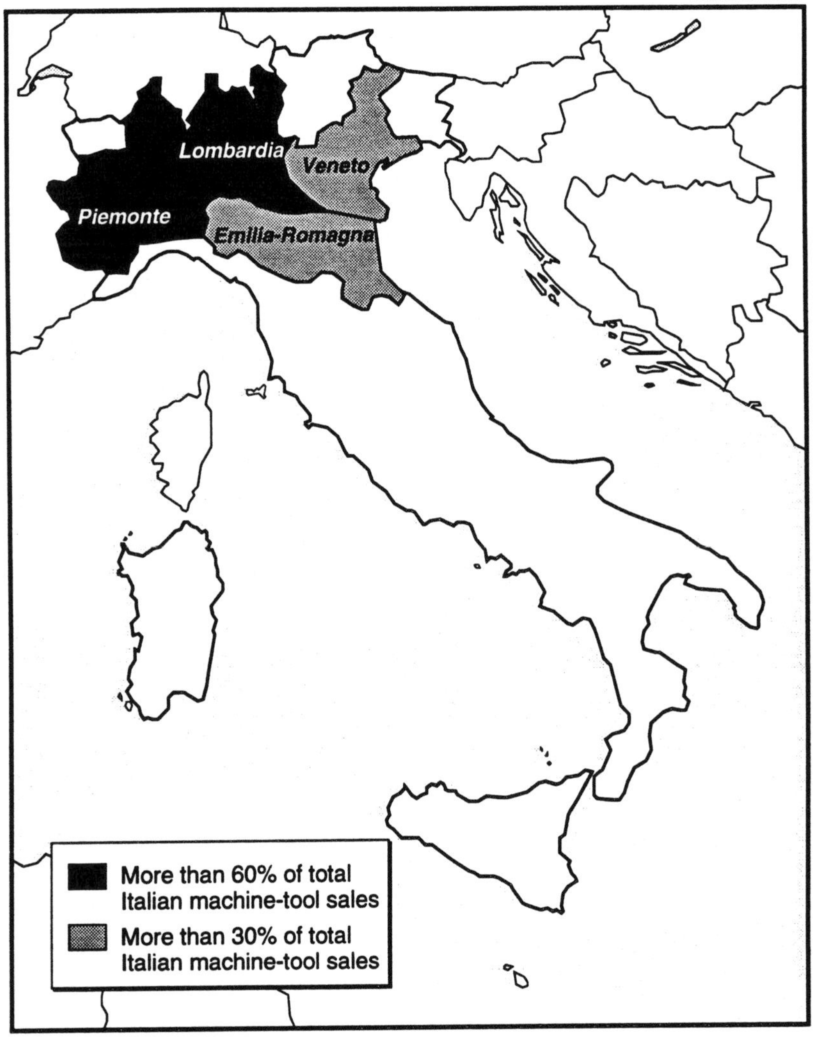

SOURCE: Elaborations of UCIMU data.

Figure C.10—Geographic Distribution of Italian Machine-Tool Sales

historically by the closeness to either large users (automakers, e.g., FIAT, Alfa Romeo, and Lancia; electronic and electromechanic equipment manufacturers, e.g., Olivetti, Italtel, Siemens, F. Tosi, and Aermacchi in the northwest; electrical household appliance producers, e.g., Zanussi, now Electrolux, in the northeast) or small firms active in different metalworking and nonelectric machinery sectors (e.g., Emilia). In either case, demand from large users is only a small portion of the overall consumption. In fact, demand is led by specialized small firms active in these areas that need efficient, tailor-made machinery to supply both local and foreign manufacturers with parts and components. Examples of foreign companies that purchase components on the Italian market and indirectly feed demand for machine tools are Bosch, Volkswagen, Opel, and BMW. According to UCIMU's officers, BMW's purchases of automobile-engine components in Italy can be estimated to reach 230 billion L per year.

3. The diffusion of machine tools by large regions roughly corresponds to the degree of geographic concentration of suppliers. MIP-Politechnique of Milan (Mariotti and Mutinelli, 1991) reviewed 1989 data for over 3,019 adopters of manufacturing automation equipment active in different industrial sectors (steel; electric and nonelectric machinery, including metalworking machinery; electromechanic equipment; computers; transportation equipment; and precision instruments). This study allows some quantification of the regional diffusion of machine tools. It appears that 55.3 percent of adopters of NC machine tools are concentrated in the northwestern area, 21.6 percent in the northeast, 15.3 percent in the center, and 7.7 percent in the south. When the adoption rate is considered (calculated as number of adopters out of the total number of plants active in the industries considered in the survey), the central part of Italy shows the highest intensity of adoption, with 24.2 percent, as opposed to 20.7 percent in the northwest, 16.4 percent in the northeast, and 16.5 percent in the south. Note, however, that the adoption rate is different if CNC machine tools are considered (i.e., machine tools whose NC is governed by computers), with the northeast and the northwest taking the lead (22.7 percent and 22 percent, respectively), the center at 17.4 percent, and the south at 13.4 percent. The individual regions with the highest number of adopters are Lombardia, Piemonte, Veneto, and Emilia.

4. In spite of the high geographic concentration of both suppliers and users of machine tools, the local organization of the industry is different from the typical "industrial district" in Italy. Most of these districts (like Prato and Biella for textiles, Carpi for knitwear, and Sassuolo for tilemaking) are characterized by (1) a strong specialization of manufacturers in a single industrial *filiere* (literally, die or die plate, channel); (2) well-defined hierarchical relations between firms, which are shaped by history in a way that is specific to each geographic and social context; (3) a significant role played by recent public interventions aiming to enhance technical change, organizational innovation, and competitiveness of a specific industry on a regional basis with a related contribution of local manufacturers' associations (e.g., the SPRING program at Prato). The areas with a high concentration of machine-tool suppliers and a high machine-tool adoption rate, however, are characterized by (1) a low degree of sectoral specialization, with machine-tool suppliers coexisting with a large number of manufacturers from differential sectors and of all sizes, often playing a key role as machine-tool

users; (2) the presence of a few leading companies with high international visibility, such as Comau, Dea, and Prima in the Turin area, and Mandelli and Marposs in Emilia; (3) a large majority of smaller manufacturers of machine tools and accessories, acting either as subcontractors for larger manufacturers or as specialized suppliers of small and large users located within and outside the area; (4) no public intervention at a local level that is specific to the machine-tool industry, and a high geographic concentration (in Lombardia) of services provided by UCIMU.

5. As a general statement, one may venture to say that, *on a local level*, most relations between suppliers are subcontracting agreements, while a crucial role is played by user-producer linkages. Arms-length agreements with large manufacturers of final goods (i.e., automakers) are only part of the story. Such large manufacturers are not only responsible for high volumes of machine-tool purchases, but they also demand highly specific technical features and influence machine-tool suppliers' innovative activity. Moreover, large end-users also rely on a great number of suppliers of parts and components, which also demand specialized machine tools. To some extent, adopters of machine tools also interact with suppliers for the design of flexible manufacturing systems. According to the MIP-Politechnique research quoted above (Mariotti and Mutinelli, 1991), 45.6 percent of the 1,316 systems adopted by a sample of 521 firms with less than 500 employees in 1989 was completely developed by equipment suppliers. (It is even 57.4 percent for adopters with number of employees ranging from 200 to 499.) Furthermore, 27.2 percent of these systems was designed jointly with external parties (other adopters, system integrators, or equipment suppliers). Such collaboration appears to happen most frequently in very small firms, ranging from 20 to 49 employees (43.5 percent of total systems adopted is designed together with external parties). Considering the geographic distribution of this phenomenon, the whole design of flexible systems is more frequently decentralized entirely to equipment suppliers in the northeast (42.7 percent) than it is in the center (34.8 percent) and in the northwest (42.7 percent). Reliance on collaboration with external parties is most frequent in the center (39.1 percent) and much lower in the northwest (19.6 percent) and in the northeast (11.2 percent).

6. Differing from firms in other countries, Italy's firms active in these local regions have developed no strong ties with universities. (The only possible exception of a university playing an active role in the machine-tool industry is the Politechnique in Milan.) It appears that firms active in these concentrated areas enjoy network externalities of a different nature. First, large users are interested in the proliferation of machine-tool suppliers,

because this enables them to second-source if necessary. Second, specialized suppliers of larger users are interested in maintaining their role as "technological gate-keepers" between machine-tool manufacturers and users, because this role increases their bargaining power. Third, machine-tool suppliers take advantage of the existence of different categories of purchasers, because it increases the possibility of learning and may also reduce the cyclical instability of demand.

7. During the second half of the 1980s, a significant reduction of the ratio between value added and sales (in real terms) occurred, as illustrated in Figure C.11. This figure reveals both a requalification of inputs, as a result of restructuring processes and increasing reliance on high-technology components, and an outsourcing strategy that is consistent with the data on subcontracting we have already discussed. This interpretation is also confirmed by the dynamics of the ratio between the wholesale price index of machine tools and the price index of inputs (Figure C.12). Therefore, not only are manufacturer-supplier networks a common feature of this industry, but they also involve increasingly valuable resource flows.

In spite of the mutual advantages manufacturers and users derive from such high vertical disintegration, a number of Italian machine-tool manufacturers believe that there is an urgent need to better coordinate resources to face new

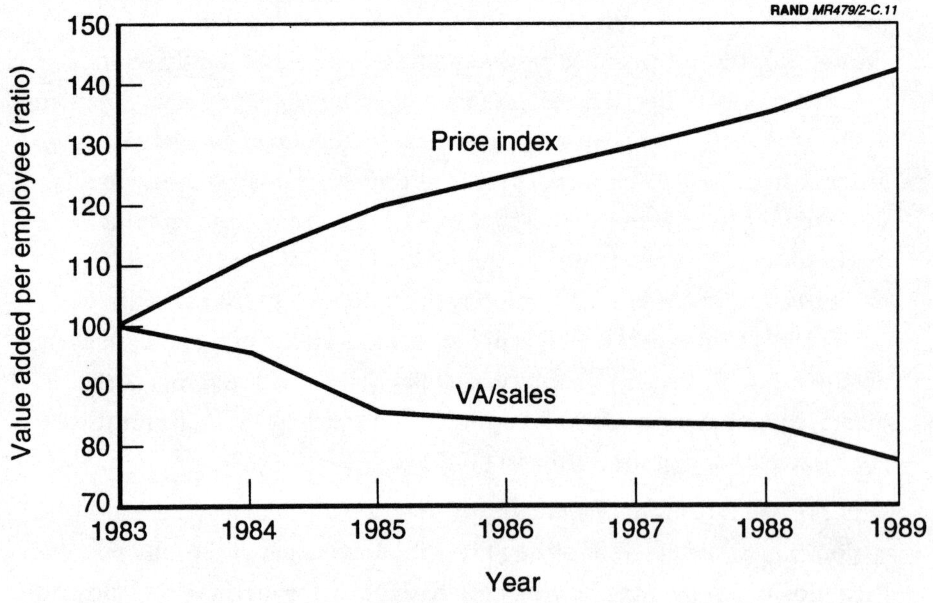

SOURCE: ISTAT, *collana d'informazione.*

Figure C.11—Evolution of Machine-Tool Value Added/Sales Ratio

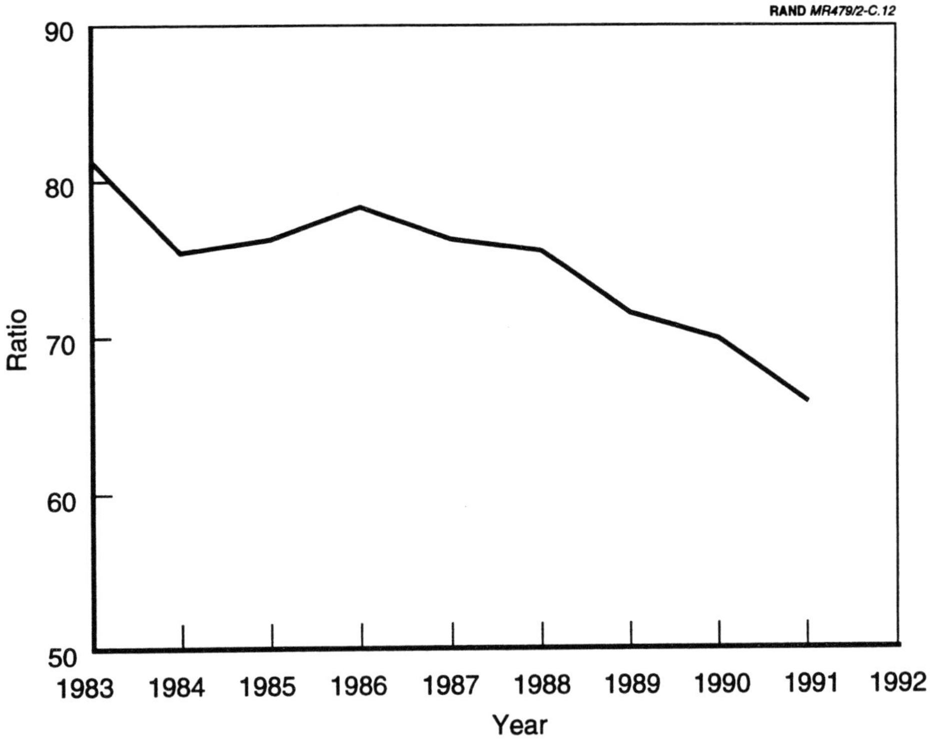

SOURCE: UCIMU, *Rapporto di settore.*

Figure C.12—Ratio Between the ISTAT Wholesale Price Index and the UCIMU Price Index of Inputs for the Italian Machine-Tool Industry

competitive challenges. This perception accounts for the increase in mergers, acquisitions, and strategic alliances. Mandelli and Comau are the most active movers in this direction. According to a recent survey, there were some 25 interfirm agreements in 1991 (Cilona and Trona, 1993). Many of the agreements aimed at the joint development and commercialization of new products (as in the case of the Comau-Daifuku alliance in the field of automatic motion systems for the automobile industry); others aimed at the formation of consortia for commercialization in distant markets (as the one between OCN-PPL and Rambaudi to enhance exports to extra-EU markets).

Also, the national association of machine-tool manufacturers has increased efforts to enhance interfirm coordination and is constantly organizing training initiatives to improve human capital. Among other organizations, UCIMU has created the so-called Subcontracting Interassociation Committee (CIS) to facilitate information interchange between component suppliers and machine-tool manufacturers; Italian M3T and Consorzio Enfapi were formed to provide training services for technology management and professional upgrading with support from the European Union. For instance, in a recent seminar organized at UCIMU, FIAT executives and technicians were invited to discuss their specific user needs with selected members of the association.

Policy Measures and Related Issues

Italy's machine-tool industry was directly and indirectly influenced by a rather limited set of public policies between 1965 and 1991. Two major policies favored technological innovation:

- Incentives for applied research. These have benefited machine-tool manufacturers insofar as manufacturers invested in the development of new processes and products.
- Incentives for adopting innovation and investing in new plants and machinery. These directly affect machine-tool users and indirectly affect machine-tool manufacturers.

Within the first policy category, an initial set of measures was provided by law No. 46 of 1982, which organized a "special fund for applied research." Originally meant to be a selective instrument to favor technological innovation at the industry level, the law was supposed to distinguish between three different levels of innovative programs to be financed (reduced to two levels in 1988) and to favor southern regions and small- and medium-sized firms in the allocation of funds. In practice, it is widely acknowledged that this law led to bureaucratic obstacles to highly innovative projects. Moreover, although some funds were reserved for southern regions and small enterprises, around 75 percent of total funding was concentrated in Piemonte and Lombardia, and 73 percent went to firms with more than 300 employees from 1984 to 1988.

Another policy to promote technological developments is a number of "finalized projects" promoted by the National Research Council. These efforts include one for the development of computer-aided design (CAD) technologies and related interfaces with manufacturing processes (13 billion L), one for the implementation and integration of flexible manufacturing systems (31 billion L for 1983 through 1988), and one for studies in the field of robotics.

A more recent provision to promote innovation was introduced in 1991 (law No. 317). The law will specifically fund R&D within small firms.

As far as the diffusion of innovation is concerned (the second public policy mentioned above), the key instrument has long been the so-called Sabatini Law

(No. 1329 of 1965). It provides financial support and credit incentives for the adoption of innovative machinery. Funds are managed by Medio Credito Centrale. From 1984 through 1988, this law provided investment in machinery for 10,690 billion L. It is estimated that, in 1987 and 1988, an average of 5.5 percent of total fixed investments was actually funded by this law.

Finally, law No. 696 of 1983, subsequently modified and re-funded with laws No. 399 of 1987 and No. 165 of 1989, introduced incentives and aids for purchasing and leasing CNC machine tools, as well as electronic equipment for manufacturing automation. After 1987, aid was extended to software purchases. Contributions can reach 25 percent of tax-free costs of machinery and are directed to small- and medium-sized firms. Further aid was introduced to favor southern firms. Until 1987, over 16,000 firms had had access to such funding.

Case Studies

To understand the major differences that exist within the machine-tool industry, let us now look more closely at four key product types and related technologies: machining centers, transfer lines, CNC controllers, and laser beam cutting.

Machining Centers

Machine tools combine different metal-cutting tasks and are optimized with low production volumes. Therefore, they are particularly suitable for small-scale metalworking enterprises, which are very common all over Italy, as confirmed by the very high share of machining centers in total machine-tool consumption: 13.2 percent in 1991 (it was even higher in 1988: 17.2 percent). Since the mid-1970s, machining centers have represented the single largest product aggregate of total CNC equipment production. Most of this production covers domestic demand, with exports amounting to a very small fraction of total sales until the late 1980s (only 4.7 percent in 1988). Import penetration has grown significantly, from 17.2 percent of total machining center consumption in 1988 to 29.4 percent in 1991. However, as exports have grown even faster (from 20 billion L in 1988 to 110.1 billion L in 1991, bringing export-to-production ratios from 4.7 percent to 13.1 percent between 1988 and 1991), Italy has improved its trade balance in this subsector in recent years.

About 40 out of the top 200 machine-tool firms classified by *Tecnologie meccaniche* have some involvement in machining center production. On average, machining center manufacturers in this sample had 215.2 employees with 48.5 billion L in sales in 1992. Two very large firms (by Italian standards) are included: FIAT's Comau, with 2,658 employees and 952.6 billion L in sales, and Mandelli, with 1,940 employees and 264.5 billion L in sales. If one excluded these companies from computation, the average size would drop to 102.5 employees and 18.3 billion L in sales.

Table C.3 shows that no firm covers the whole machining center product line. A large majority of listed companies commercialize "moving-column" machining centers. Fifteen suppliers of moving-column machining centers (out of 32) also provide, on request, fixed-column solutions, to cover the widest possible array of user needs. However, only a few suppliers of machining centers are able to cover a very large range of solutions (Vecchia of Foglizzo, Turin, in the field of moving-column machining centers, and Bragonzi of Lonate, Varese, for fixed-column machining centers). Generally, in both market segments, it seems to be more common to supply relatively small-capacity machines (equal to or less than 1,000 mm^3), which can be easily adapted to the manufacturing of tiny metal pieces.

Some firms supply machining center solutions tailored for highly specific user needs, thus covering a limited but protected market niche: This is the case of Carnaghi's machining center with a movable portal, Cortini's equipment for training purposes, Rambaudi's vertical machining center with a portal offering a work capacity of 850x500x360 mm, and Schiess-Pensotti's machining center with a vertical spindle for turning, milling, and boring with a movable table.

Transfer Lines

In their conventional, automatic version, transfer lines can be considered as manufacturing solutions, allowing several work-processing locations in a single machine, with low unit costs of products at the expense of a relatively high rigidity. While the introduction of CNC has allowed some degree of flexibility, the use of such machines (much like other station-type machines) still tends to be optimized for high-volume production. This characterization has three important implications for the Italian case. First, since there is a relatively low number of high-production-volume firms in Italy, there are also relatively few Italian transfer-line manufacturers. Only 19 of the top 200 machine-tool manufacturers are active in this market segment (see Table C.4). The average size of such firms is 111.5 employees, with 21 billion L in average sales. Altogether, Italian manufacturers covered 91.4 percent of apparent consumption (560.9 billion L) in 1991. In this area, Italy has a positive, although diminishing, trade balance: The surplus was 31.4 billion L in 1991 (+0.24 normalized) as opposed to 91.3 billion L in 1988 (+0.72 normalized).

Table C.3

Italian Suppliers of Machining Centers by Firm Size and Product Range

Company Name	1992 Sales (million L)	1992 Employees	UCIMU Product Categories[a]					
			3.2.1	3.2.2	3.2.3	3.2.4	3.2.5	3.2.6
Alesamonti	7,300	70			X	X		
Bolla	NA	NA			X			
Berardi	32,000	205			X			
Braganzi	4,900	46			X	X		
Castel	14,000	103				X	X	
Carnaghi	27,000	100	X		X		X	X
Castor[b]	4,000	30	X					
Ceruti	32,000	205				X	X	
Comau	952,600	2,658				X	X	
CNT	8,900	100	X					
Deber	8,100	50				X		
Duplo Standard[b]	20,000	72	X	X	X		X	
Fa.M.U.P.	18,000	100			X	X		
C.B. Ferrari	35,200	96			X	X	X	
FMS/PAMA	NA	NA			X	X		
Gildemeister Italy	63,600	383		X				
Int Internato	9,300	21				X	X	
INT[b]	7,500	12				X		
Innse	NA	NA			X	X		
Jobs	32,000	150				X	X	
Lazzati	7,000	32			X	X		
Mandelli	264,500	1,940				X		
MCN	24,300	74			X	X		
Meccanica Cortini	6,500	47			X		X	X
MECOF[b]	44,600	215				X		
Mival	12,000	70			X	X		
Norma	11,600	43				X		
Novar	23,000	54			X	X		
OCN-PPL	NA	NA				X		
Oerlikon	NA	NA				X		
Omba	NA	NA			X			
OMV	NA	NA				X	X	
OMZ	NA	NA			X			
Parpas[b]	57,000	390				X	X	
Pear	4,100	30			X			
Rambaudi	60,000	356			X	X	X	X
Riva Officine	6,900	75			X		X	
Sachman	16,500	90			X	X	X	
SAIC Casati	NA	NA			X			
SAIMP Sistemi	NA	NA				X		
San Rocco Macchine	NA	NA			X	X		
Schiess Pensotti	9,500	54					X	X
Sechu FAS	NA	NA			X	X		
Sigma	18,500	190				X		
Temco M.U.	3,200	16					X	
TMA FAS	NA	NA			X	X		
Vecchia	26,800	96				X		

SOURCE: Our elaborations on UCIMU and Technologie meccaniche data, June 1993.

[a]3.2.1 = machining center turning with rotating tools (single spindle).
3.2.2 = machining center turning with rotating tools (two spindle).
3.3.3 = fixed column.
3.2.4 = machining center moving column.
3.2.5 = machining center vertical.
3.2.6 = other machining center.

[b]Data refer to 1991.

Table C.4

Italian Suppliers of Transfer-Line Machines by Firm Size and Product Range

Company Name	1992 Sales (million L)	1992 Employees	UCIMU Product Categories[a]								
			2.1.1	2.1.2	2.1.3	2.1.4	3.1.1	3.1.2	3.1.3	3.1.4	Other
AMCA	NA	NA	X	X	X	X					
Berardi	32,000	205	X	X	X	X					
Cattaneo	5,000	25	X	X	X	X					
Cimat[b]	28,200	144		X	X	X					X
Dell'orto	19,000	137		X		X					
Duplo Standard[b]	20,000	72	X	X		X					
Fa.M.U.P.	18,000	100		X							
Fimat	NA	NA	X	X							
T. Giuliani	16,800	125	X								
Gnutti[b]	25,000	168	X	X	X	X					
Gozio	7,500	51									X
Pedrazzoli[b]	30,000	200	X								
Porta	6,000										X
Riello	24,400	172		X	X	X		X	X	X	
Rovetta Presse	49,000	164	X								
Streparava	2,000	10					X	X			
Temco Mu	3,200	16	X	X		X					
Vecchia	26,800	96	X	X	X	X					
Vigel	44,000	170	X	X	X	X					

SOURCE: Our elaborations on UCIMU and *Technologie mecchaniche* data, June 1993.

[a]2.1.1 = Linear automatic transfer.
2.1.2 = Automatic transfer with rotary indexing table.
2.1.3 = Automatic transfer with rotary indexing drum.
2.1.4 = Automatic transfer single station.
3.1.1 = Linear CNC transfer.
3.1.2 = CNC transfer with rotary indexing table.
3.1.3 = CNC transfer with rotary indexing drum.
3.1.4 = CNC transfer single station.

[b]Data refer to 1991.

Second, large, high-volume producers are typically located in the northwest; therefore, Italian transfer-line manufacturers tend to be more geographically concentrated than average. Twelve out of the 19 transfer-line suppliers recorded in the *Technologie* classification in 1991–1992 were localized in Lombardia or Piemonte. Three rather large manufacturers (Vecchia, Vigel, and Cimat) and a highly specialized, small supplier are located in the Turin area, where they take advantage of demand fueled by FIAT, both directly and indirectly (through component suppliers).

Third, as demand for flexibility expands and as technical possibilities to satisfy such requests also increase, transfer-line suppliers have entered into fierce competition with both FMS and machining-center manufacturers. On both sides, some of the most challenging competitors are already active on the domestic market: Comau of Turin, Mandelli of Piacenza, Elsag of Genova, and Sigma of Vigevano. However, it appears that only a few firms are active in the field of CNC transfer-line machines (see Table C.5 for the following subsection), with Riello being the only manufacturer covering the whole product range. The two major CNC transfer-line manufacturers, Riello (from Verona) and Streparava (from Brescia) both supply solutions with no more than 12 workstations. Porta (from Turin) can be distinguished in this scenario for its specialized production of flexible transfer lines ranging from 4 to 20 units, with electro-hydraulic operation, integrated with robots and automated loading and unloading stations.

Computer Numerical Controls

CNC technology allows control, test, and measurement of production through prerecorded, symbolic instructions that are processed by one or more computer units. Available data do not allow a precise evaluation of the Italian market for this electronic device.[9] However, as CNC machine-tool manufacturing has increased in importance in Italy, one can easily maintain that domestic consumption in this field must have grown significantly over the past decade. In spite of such growth, no international-level CNC manufacturer has emerged in Italy. It is acknowledged that most Italian machine-tool manufacturers purchase CNC technology on the market, mostly favoring internationally manufactured

---

[9]According to the National Association of Electronic Industries (ANIE) estimates, the market for electronic measurement and control equipment amounted to 4,078.2 billion L in 1991, i.e., 8.24 percent of the total (consumer and business) electronics commercialized in Italy, making this market approximately 10 percent larger than the total machine-tool market, as estimated by UCIMU. Unfortunately, no precise product-line definition is provided for this estimate, and it is explicitly reported that parts of factory automation (robotics and FMS) and other heterogeneous equipment (such as electronic security systems) are included.

Table C.5

Italian Suppliers of Control Units by Firm Size and Product Range

Company Name	1992 Sales (million L)	1992 Employees	UCIMU Product Categories[a]						
			8.2.2	8.2.3	8.2.4	8.2.5	9.3.1	9.3.2	9.3.3
ABB-Robotica	18	42							X
BLM	24	114					X	X	X
DEA	148,000	850			X				
Dec Italia	NA	NA					X	X	
ECS	NA	NA	X						
Elsag	NA	NA	X			X			
Emmegi	18,300	80	X				X	X	
FAS	NA	NA	X						
Ficep	NA	NA		X					
Fidia	26,000	110	X		X		X		
Hitec Campania	NA	NA					X		
Jobs	32,000	150			X				
Mandelli	264,500	1,940	X				X	X	
Microcontrol	NA	NA						X	
Oerlikon	NA	NA				X			
OSAI A-B	NA	NA	X	X		X			
Program NC	NA	NA					X		X
Rexroth	NA	NA							X
Seiaf	NA	NA					X		X
Siemens Italia	NA	NA					X	X	
Spring	NA	NA					X		X
Telemecanique	192,000	300							X

SOURCE: Our elaborations on UCIMU and *Technologie meccaniche* data, June 1993.

[a]8.2.2 = CNC for metal cutting.
8.2.3 = CNC for metal forming.
8.2.4 = CNC for measuring and testing.
8.2.5 = other CNC.
9.3.1 = software for production planning and control.
9.3.2 = software for quality control.
9.3.3 = other software for production management and control.

devices (Siemens or FANUC, as a rule). Italian CNC manufacturers do exist, but they either cover limited and specialized niches or they design ad hoc solutions for their own machine-tool manufacturing needs. Fidia (from Turin) and ECS (from Florence) belong to the former group (niche of CNC suppliers). ECS has specialized in CNC controls for metal cutting machine tools, particularly conceived for machining centers, four-axis lathes, milling machines, and copying machines. It also services machining centers, boring machines, and cells, and up to 16 axes can be controlled simultaneously. Fidia supplies CNCs for metalcutting and for measuring and testing machine tools. In both market segments, its products can be distinguished by their capacity to carry out such functions as copying, digitizing, measuring, and graphic programming.

Examples of machine-tool firms manufacturing their own CNC that can subsequently be sold to third parties are Mandelli, Jobs, and DEA. Mandelli has designed a control called "Plasma," with a specific interface for complex FMS production. Jobs (from Piacenza) needed more powerful routines for its robot line and has developed them from existing CNCs. DEA (from Turin) has commercialized electronic control and diagnostic systems it had designed for its own robot production, as well as CNCs for the measuring and testing machines it also had manufactured.

A few CNC (hardware) manufacturers also design the related software (see Table C.5). This is the case of Fidia, Elsag, and Mandelli. However, there appears to be ample room for specialization in this field. Computer firms enjoy some competitive advantage, especially if they are located in high-demand areas (DEC and Siemens have plants in Lombardia). Furthermore, specialized software branches of larger machine-tool and factory automation manufacturers can easily commercialize software that was designed for internal uses (e.g., Seiaf, created by Elsag and IBM). Finally, some small software houses, e.g., Hitec Campania (from Avellino) and Program NC (from Milano), are able to adapt their packages and provide tailor-made solutions.

Laser-Beam Cutting

The laser-beam cutting process uses laser light to melt metal and obtain high-precision cuts. According to UCIMU officers, this technology is not highly diffused in Italy. No estimate of market size is available. Metal-cutting machine tools (especially punching machines) can be supplied with laser-cutting devices, upon request.

Although both light sources and cutting devices are predominantly purchased as a commodity, mostly from other European and U.S. manufacturers, a few suppliers are also active in Italy (see Table C.6). The top 200 classification records seven firms active in this field, with an average size of 95 employees and 19.9 billion L in sales. None of these firms is specializing exclusively in this product segment.

Some Italian manufacturers appear to be covering very limited niches, with high value-added products. For instance, Prima (from Turin) has developed a five-axis laser-cutting system that is used for tube cutting and refining. This is supposed to be a significant departure from standard technology, which has mainly applied laser cutting to flat surfaces.

Table C.6

Italian Suppliers of Laser-Beam Cutting Equipment by Firm Size

Company Name	Location	1992 Sales (million L)	1992 Employees
Automator Italia	Corsico, Lombardia	5,000	15
Jobs	Piacenza, Emilia	32,000	150
Omes	Santorso, Veneto	8,300	18
Prima	Turin, Piemonte	53,000	230
Sala	Levico, Trentino	25,000	152
Soitaab	Ronco, Lombardia	10,000	60
WA Witney Italia	Turin, Piemonte	6,200	40

Conclusion

Italy's positive performance (at least until recently) can be explained essentially in terms of two structural characteristics and two historical coincidences. The first structural characteristic is a highly fragmented domestic demand. Italian manufacturers are smaller on average than their main competitors. Key users are not only large companies, such as FIAT, F. Tosi, Aermacchi, or Electrolux, but also a large set of suppliers of those firms and a variety of small- and medium-sized enterprises that are active in both traditional and high-technology industries. This characteristic seems to have played a fundamental role, especially in the early phases of the industry's evolution, in stabilizing domestic demand and favoring machine-tool suppliers' learning about user needs. Quite early in their history, machine-tool manufacturers had to become flexible to adapt products and technologies to highly specific and differentiated demands.

The second structural feature is a high degree of outsourcing that enhances flexibility and competitiveness on the supply side. This is not so much a matter of reducing total costs as gaining access to external parties to increase the variety and quality of inputs in accordance with the evolution of technology and of demand. More than in other countries, it appears that the sources of innovation have been largely outside the single manufacturers, and, most often, outside the industry itself. This is one important reason why Italian machine-tool manufacturers appear to invest so little in R&D. Most innovations in the market segments covered by Italian manufacturers stem from the development and adaptation of products to specific user needs, activities not frequently accounted for as R&D in balance sheets.

The historical coincidences are (1) Italian machine-tool manufacturers could become early adopters of CNC technology because they have sustained lower fixed costs for the production of conventional machines than have most competitors; and (2) during the international crisis of the early 1980s, export expansion toward countries with higher-demand growth rates was favored by a strong devaluation of the Italian lira against the U.S. dollar and the German mark. The former coincidence helps explain why the Japanese challenge did not hit so hard. Italy seems to have taken advantage of being an early adopter, rather than being a producer, of CNC technology, which is consistent with the hypothesis on outsourcing. During the 1970s, Italian machine-tool manufacturers increased their reliance on external suppliers of technology as a means to increase the competitiveness of their final products. According to interviews with UCIMU officers, the domestic market for such components is competitive enough to ensure their availability at a reasonable cost.

The latter coincidence (exchange rate factor) has probably played a relevant role, especially in a phase when domestic consumption was falling at a faster rate than in other countries. However, devaluation of Italian currency between 1980 and 1985 does not *per se* explain increasing exports in that period.[10] This result was attained also by means of strong capital expenditures aiming to increase productivity and product quality.

As exchange rates have become less favorable and early adopter advantages have eroded, the relative importance of the structural weaknesses that the Italian machine-tool industry faces has increased. These factors include, among others, a low emphasis on skill development, lack of linkages with universities, and poor marketing and distribution methods. These problems will most probably damage Italian manufacturers in the years ahead, unless countervailing measures are taken by both companies and policymakers.

---

[10]Exports also grew following the devaluation of the lira against other European currencies in 1993.

Annex

List of Interviewed Experts

Broglio, A., National Association of Electronic Industries (ANIE), Milan.

Cavazzana, M., National Association of Machine Tool Manufacturers (UCIMU), Milan.

Ciocca, A., UCIMU, Milan.

Costa, A., ANIE, Milan.

Falzoni, A., Center for Studies of Internationalization Processes (CESPRI), Milan.

Lunghi, D., UCIMU, Milan.

Mandelli, M., UCIMU, Milan.

Morandini, C., Nomos–Market Analysis, Milan.

Mutinelli, M., MIP-RP, Politechnique of Milan.

Pattarozzi, M., Research on Electronics and Automation (RESEAU), Milan.

Pellegatta, F., UCIMU, Milan.

Rolfo, S., Center for Social Research (CERIS), Turin.

Taccini, P., Central Bureau of Statistics (ISTAT), Rome.

Vitali, G., CERIS, Turin.

Bibliography

ANIE [National Association of Electronics Industries], *Rapporto 1991*, Milan, June 1992.

ANIE [National Association of Electronics Industries], *Il punto trimestrale*, Milan, March 1993.

Balloni, V., E. Santarelli, and A. Sterlacchini, *Ristrutturazione dell'industria e innovazione nelle piccole imprese*, Ancona, Italy: Clua, 1992.

Baumgartner, P., "La macchina utensile europea," *Technologie meccaniche*, August 1992, pp. 38–44.

Bucci, G., A. Del Bimbo, and P. Nesi, "Sistema flessibile e multiprocessore per la gestione di aree industriali robotizzate," *Automazione e strumentazione*, Nos. 7–8, 1991, pp. 117–122.

Cainarca, G. C., and M. Colombo, eds., *Tecnologia e organizzazione nell'automazione integrata della fabbrica*, Milan: MIP, 1991.

Carlsson, B., "Small Scale Industry at a Crossroad: U.S. Machine Tools in Global Perspective," *Small Business Economics*, Vol. 1, 1989, pp. 245–261.

Centro Studi Economici Stammer, "La classifica dei costruttori di macchine utensili: le prime 200," *Technologie meccaniche*, various issues, June 1992–1993.

Cilona, O., and M. Trona, "L'industria delle macchine utensili negli anni 90: mercati, innovazione e sistema delle impresse," *Economia e politica industriale*, No. 77, 1993, pp. 207–220.

Cominotti, R., and S. Mariotti, eds., *Italia multinazionale 1992*, CNEL-R&P, Milan: Etas Libri, 1992.

Edquist, C., and S. Jacobsson, *Flexible Automation: The Global Diffusion of New Technology in the Engineering Industry*, Oxford: Basil Blackwell, Ltd., 1988.

ISTAT, *Supplemento al bollettino mensile di statistica*, Rome, various issues, 1975–1983.

ISTAT, *Collana d' informazione*, Rome, various issues, 1984–1993.

Jacobsson, S., *Electronics and Industrial Policy: The Case of Computer Controlled Lathes*, London: Allen & Unwin, 1986.

Marchesini, F., ed., "L'industria italiana delle macchine utensili per la lavorazione dei metalli," *Problemi e analisi*, No. 5, 1990.

Mariotti, S., and E. Mutinelli, eds., *Rapporto sull'automazione nell' industria Italiana*, Milan: MIP, 1991.

Onida, F., ed., *Gli scambi internazionali di macchine utensili: analisi per mercati e concorrenti e prospettive per l'Italia*, Milan: Cespri, 1991.

Rolfo, S., "L'industria europea delle macchine utensili: una struttura in evoluzione," *Quaderni Ceris*, No. 2, pp. 7–39, 1990.

Rullani, E., and A. Zanfei, "Area Networks: Telematic Connections in a Traditional District" in C. Antonelli, ed., *New Information Technology and Industrial Change*, Boston: Kluwer Publ. Co., 1988.

Schor, Adam, "Some Small Companies Sidestep the Falling Machine Tool Industry," *Cincinnati Business Courier*, November 10, 1986.

UCIMU, *Relazione del presidente per l'anno 1977*, Milan, 1978.

UCIMU , *L'industria italiana della macchina utensile*, Milan, 1979–1980.

UCIMU, *Rapporto di settore*, Milan, 1981–1993.

UCIMU, *L'industria italiana della macchina utensile, automazione e robotica: analisi dell'evoluzione recente*, Milan, 1988.

UCIMU, *Lettera economica*, various issues, 1990–1993.

Vitali, G., "Determinants of International Trade of Machine Tools During the Eighties: A Shift-Share Analysis, *Technovation*, Vol. 10, No. 8, 1990, pp. 507–519.

Appendix D
Case Study: Computer Numerical Controllers

Stan Przybylinski, Industrial Technologies Institute

Introduction

This case study describes the technological and market evolution of numerical control (NC) and computer numerical control (CNC) technology. While NC development began in the 1950s, the case study focuses on the period from 1977 to the present. We derived the material for this case study from books, literature on the industry and the technology, interviews with industry representatives, and the first detailed analysis of trade figures on stand-alone and integrated controllers for machine tools.

The information in this study is not meant to be comprehensive. Our goal in preparing this case study was to use a multidisciplinary approach to illustrate possible reasons why the United States lost its market position in the global CNC market. As such, it can form a basis for discussion about the issues facing this industry and the development of policies to address these issues.

Definition

NC technology controls a machine tool with prerecorded, symbolic instructions (Graham, 1988, p. 412). These instructions command the machine to move its axes at certain speeds and directions; start and stop the spindle at a specified speed; and control external devices, such as coolant pumps and clamping systems. Initially, NC programs were recorded and input to the machine using punch cards, and later punch tape. With the advent of microprocessors and better memory, instructions were electronically recorded, input, and modified with the use of a personal computer or workstation. Thus, the "C" for computer was added to the acronym. Most machine control technology sold today is CNC. The benefits of CNC include versatility, speed, accuracy, increased uniformity, lower tooling costs, and increased ease in integrating the design and manufacturing process through such technologies as computer-aided design and computer-aided manufacturing (CAD/CAM). The major elements of today's

CNC technology are microprocessors, input-output devices, memory devices, and software.

CNC Market Structure

Controllers for CNC equipment can be acquired through two channels, as illustrated in Figure D.1. In the early stages of CNC evolution, controllers were purchased from industrial control firms and were integrated with different kinds of machine tools, either by machine-tool firms or by users themselves. CNC machine tools could also be purchased from machine-tool firms with in-house controller groups, such as Cincinnati Milacron or Ingersoll Milling Machines. This combination of acquisition paths makes it difficult to obtain hard data on market size. Data on CNCs sold integrated with machine tools are "buried" within the larger 3541/3542 machine-tool Standard Industrial Classification (SIC) codes, although the data are available. Stand-alone controllers are classified in an entirely different category under the electronic equipment code (SIC 36), although their seven-digit code has shifted significantly over time. Thus, many of the market share estimates contained within this case study are based on the opinions of industry experts.

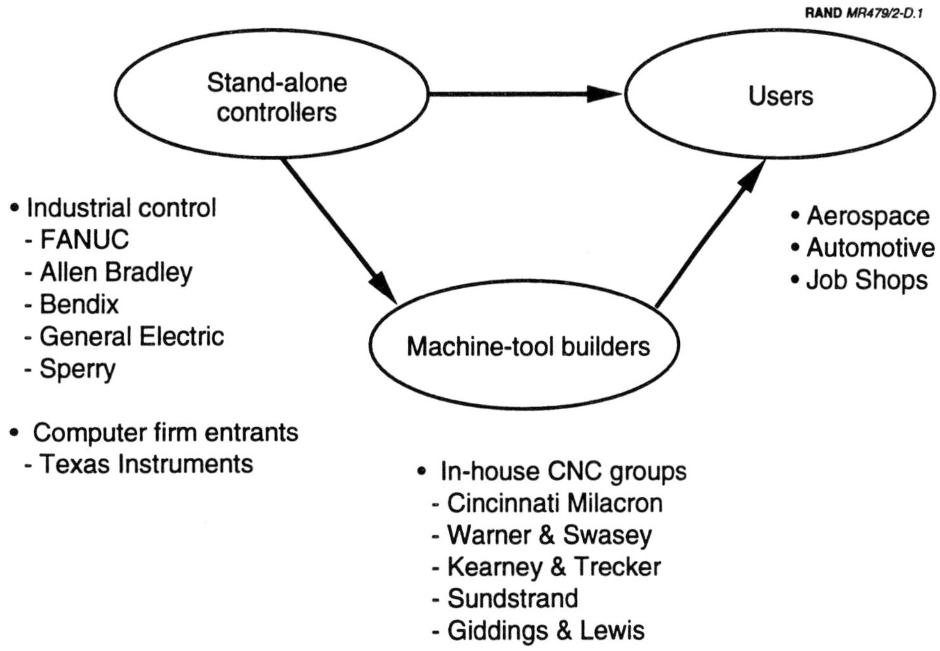

Figure D.1—Ways Users Can Acquire Controls

Since 1977, market demand for all machine tools has shifted (as shown in Chapter Three of Volume 1). At the start of the period, the United States was the single largest market for machine tools. Now, the Japanese market has assumed the leadership position, with the European Union providing the largest regional market. In addition, the U.S. market for machine tools is growing slower than these other regions. Other countries have experienced incremental increases in their consumption of machine tools, while the United States had a peak in 1980, with a decline thereafter. However, although the overall machine-tool industry has remained stagnant since 1980, the NC industry has experienced large gains since it bottomed out in 1983. In fact, U.S. consumption of stand-alone and integrated NCs nearly doubled from the $1.25 billion low of 1983 to nearly $2.2 billion by 1991. However, the demand has shifted from being traditionally supplied by U.S. manufacturers through 1978 to being predominantly supplied by foreign manufacturers. In fact, at the 1988 peak of this growing "import gap" between U.S. consumption and U.S. shipments, almost 54 percent of the entire U.S. market for NCs was supplied by imports (see Figure D.2). Regional shifts in consumption for all machine tools between 1980 and 1990 have also occurred, with Western Europe increasing 55 percent, and the Pacific Rim increasing 104 percent, while the United States declined 37 percent (AMT, 1992). As a result of these shifts, firms in the machine-tool and NC industries have had to restructure their marketing and production strategies.

Market supply for all machine tools has also shifted from U.S. to Japanese leadership, as illustrated in Table D.1. In 1975, U.S. and German firms were even, with Japanese firms a distant third. In 1990, Japan had a large lead, with the United States now in that distant third spot. This represented a 58 percent decrease for the United States and a 200-percent increase for Japan. During this period, Germany was able to maintain its market share, while Japan successfully entered the industry, with the United States unable to maintain its hold on the market. The key question is why the various countries responded to the market and technological changes in different ways and with different levels of success.

Study Overview

This case study will review the history of CNC development, with a quick overview of the postwar period focusing on developments since 1977. It is organized into the following segments:

- 1948–1977
- 1977–1982

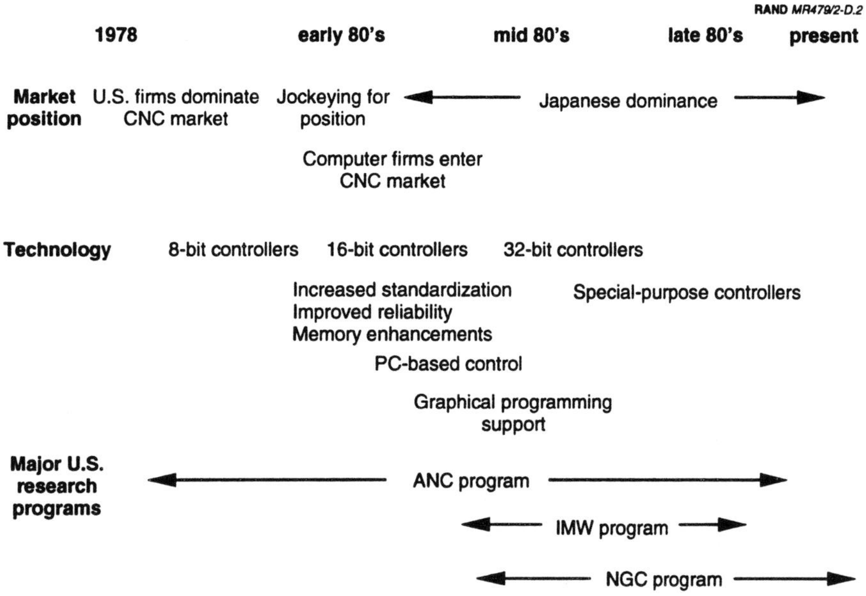

Figure D.2—The Evolution of CNC and Related Government Programs

Table D.1

Japanese Firms Are the Dominant Machine-Tool Suppliers

	Percentage of World Production	
	1975	1990
United States	17	7
Germany	18	19
Japan	8	24

SOURCE: *Bundesministerium für Wirtschaft* (1990).

- 1983–1986
- 1987–1989
- 1990–onward.

Within each period, the discussion will focus on changes in the CNC market. As will be seen, CNC technology and the relative market position between the United States and Japan have changed significantly. Furthermore, between 1976 and 1992, three large-scale U.S. research projects were initiated that concentrated on CNC, one with private sponsorship and two funded primarily by the federal government:

- The Advanced NC Program (ANC), sponsored by Computer-Aided Manufacturing International, Incorporated (CAM-I)
- The Intelligent Machining Workstation (IMW), sponsored by the U.S. Air Force Manufacturing Technology (MANTECH) Program
- The Next Generation Controller (NGC) Program, sponsored by the MANTECH Program and the National Center for Manufacturing Sciences (NCMS).

Overviews of the activities and results of each program are provided. These research and development (R&D) efforts in CNC are in one sense symbolic of the well-known strengths and weaknesses of U.S. R&D more generally. Efforts tended toward solving interesting technical challenges and focusing on basic research, while failing to address technology transfer, business, and market issues "early and often" in program planning and execution. Finally, the major issues relevant to each period will also be discussed. Figures D.2 and D.3 provide an overview of the entire study period and trends in the market for machine-tool controls.

1948 Through 1977: Early Development of NCs

The first period in the development of the NC industry began in 1949 when the U.S. Air Force granted a contract to John Parsons to develop NCs to enhance the output and flexibility of aircraft production. Working with the Massachusetts Institute of Technology (MIT), Parsons demonstrated NC technology in 1952. By 1955, NC technology was sufficiently developed to allow the Air Force to change its specifications for automated machine tools from tracer technology to NC technology and to allow the purchase of more than 100 NC machines at a cost equivalent to $154 million in 1987. This "core demand" provided a significant boost to the industry by reducing the uncertainty associated with the potential demand. Further Air Force development funding at MIT led to the development of a FORTRAN-based programming system known as Automatically Programmed Tools (APT), which offered significant flexibility and was applicable to nearly every type of machine tool. Given this versatility, the Air Force and the Aerospace Industries Association chose APT as the standard programming language for NC machine tools. By 1959, Air Force spending on NC development totaled $273 million (1987). This strong Air Force role in the early days of the NC industry led to a significant U.S. "first-mover" advantage over international competitors.

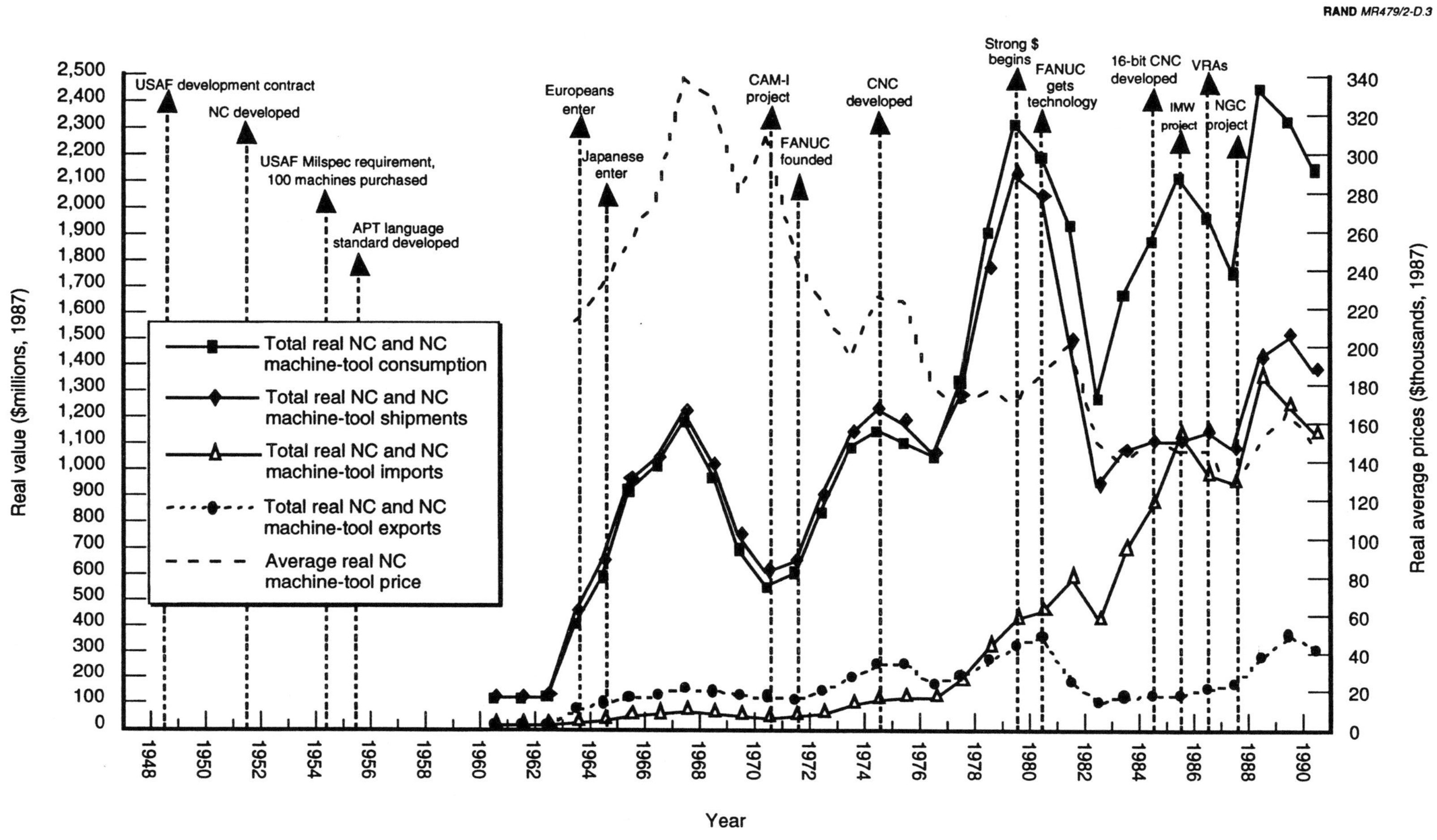

Figure D.3—Financial Evolution of CNC and Related Government Programs

From 1960 to 1964, those producers that were first to adopt NC technology began production, and the first customers began adopting and using NCs. Entry into the NC market was eased by Parsons' liberal licensing of the patented technology. The first customers were typically very large transportation-equipment firms (i.e., automobile and aerospace companies) with the extensive resources required to purchase expensive NC machines and train staff in their use.

Later in the decade, the technology was becoming more refined, experience with the technology led to an enhanced customer base, and imitators began entering the market. Consequently, production and consumption increased greatly, but more-advanced technology led to sharply increasing prices. Foreign entry into the industry began during this period, with European production beginning in 1964 and Japanese production beginning in 1965 (Schmidt, 1988).

By 1969, the value of U.S. consumption of NCs began dropping significantly. A shift in demand from purchasing NCs integrated with a machine tool toward greater demand for stand-alone NCs for retrofitting older NC machine tools occurred. This shift from integrated to stand-alone controls led to a substantial drop in the real average price for integrated tools—from a high of nearly $340,000 in 1968 to a low under $190,000 by 1977.

1977 Through 1982: CNC First Adopters—U.S. Firms Dominate

Technology and Market Issues

In the 1970s, the five major U.S. controller firms were General Electric, Bendix, Allen Bradley, Sperry UMAC, and Actron. Bendix owned all the basic NC patents, having bought out Parsons in the mid-1960s. These five firms, as well as FANUC and others, licensed the technology from Bendix, at a cost of $500,000 to $1,000,000 per license. The major U.S. controller firms produced controllers for integration with machine tools manufactured and sold by other companies. Some large machine-tool firms, such as Cincinnati Milacron, Warner & Swasey, Kearney & Trecker, Sundstrand, and Giddings & Lewis, had CNC divisions to support their machine tools. These CNC divisions sold their controls in the marketplace, but with limited success. Most CNC technology was proprietary, making equipment integration and substitution difficult and expensive. In this time frame, "CNC technology" included minicomputers as controllers that used punch cards or mylar tape to store programs, making any change in programming relatively complex. Even though CNC was a small percentage of the overall machine-tool market, U.S. firms played a dominant role in production and consumption.

In the late 1970s and early 1980s, FANUC was the dominant CNC firm in Japan, becoming the de facto standard, and began active global marketing, especially to the United States. Siemens remained strong in Europe. At this time, competition from foreign CNC or machine-tool builders in the United States was not yet overwhelming. The U.S. machine-tool industry, including machine builders and CNC suppliers, was busy serving the large automotive "Big Three" as they retooled their plants in response to market demand for front-wheel-drive cars and four-cylinder engines. According to one controller firm executive, domestic controller firms "dismissed the Japanese CNC firms as competitors" with "inferior" products.

However, that would soon change. Prior to this time, FANUC produced only open-loop controllers, severely limiting its ability to compete in some markets.[1] During this period, FANUC developed and introduced a closed-loop control system. They also purchased Gettys' closed-loop, servo-drive technology (Gettys, a Wisconsin-based, independent control manufacturer, was a relative leader in this market). This combination of closed-loop control and drives allowed FANUC to sell complete CNC packages, a development that was crucial to their evolution into the world leader in CNC. They also entered a cooperative agreement with Siemens that clarified their relative interests in the large U.S. market, increasing FANUC's ability to focus on its U.S. competitors.[2]

This evolution was also supported by the Ministry of International Trade and Industry (MITI). In 1938, the Japanese government passed the Machine-Tool Industry Law, one of several laws designed to protect industries for national defense purposes (Johnson, 1982, p. 133). Under these laws, the targeted industries received special government financing, taxes, and other protective measures. While these laws were not enforced during World War II, they resurfaced in the 1950s and 1960s and were important in the initial development of the protected industries. In the late 1960s and early 1970s, MITI's Machinery and Information Industries Bureau identified machine tools as a potential export leader. MITI worked to rationalize the Japanese machine-tool market, designating one firm as the leader in each machine-tool market segment (MIT

[1]Open-loop controllers send out signals to a motor to move the tool to a desired location. There is no feedback on whether the tool is indeed where desired. Closed-loop controllers have that feedback. They are constantly reading the error between the signal output and the actual position, providing more assurance of the desired outcome.

[2]According to a former machine-tool firm executive, the terms of this agreement stated that Siemens would focus on the high-end controls market and FANUC the low end.

Commission on Industrial Productivity, 1989, pp. 34–35). MITI also made direct efforts to link their burgeoning computer industry with machinery producers to advance the state of Japanese NC machine tools (Johnson, 1982, p. 302). FANUC, spun off from Fujitsu in 1972, already had this link and had ready access to Fujitsu's computer technology and expertise. According to an MIT study, MITI "encouraged" FANUC to become the single supplier of standardized controls in Japan (MIT Commission on Industrial Productivity, 1989, p. 36). According to a former Bendix executive, this MITI encouragement took the form of Oki being "pushed out" of the CNC business and "forced" to give up its Bendix licenses. With MITI's support, FANUC developed a simple NC control for each type of machine and then supplied the builders for each niche. MITI also regularly provided conditional loans, or *hojokin*, for R&D in important industries. Repayment of these loans was contingent on the success of the project (Okimoto, 1989, p. 78). It is not clear if FANUC qualified for or took advantage of this opportunity. However, MITI did support research in "flexible manufacturing" between 1977 and 1984 (Okimoto, 1989, p. 80).[3] This government assistance—combined with Gettys technology, a home market clearly preferring domestically produced products, and the needs of the growing Japanese automotive industry—provided a fertile environment for FANUC to grow and thrive.

Research: The Advanced NC Program

From 1976 to 1992, CAM-I sponsored the ANC Program. CAM-I is an international consortium of Fortune 500 manufacturing firms that performs precompetitive research. The goal of this research program was to automate the NC programming task, creating NC programs from CAD information. Achieving this goal required the development of several embedded technologies, including geometric modeling, interactive programming, process planning, and algorithms for volume reduction and decomposition. Many software issues were addressed. Member companies paid between $10,000 and $15,000 annually to support the contract research that CAM-I administered. Support for the ANC Program peaked in 1980, with 30 participating members. The CAM-I effort resulted in a 3,000-page specification to guide product development. Like most consortia, members had immediate access to the specifications, with public dissemination delayed for up to three years.

---

[3]This support was referred to as *itakuhi*, which is more akin to traditional contract research in the United States.

CAM-I member companies inserted the part and geometric modeling technology into their systems but really only took "parts of the technology for upgrade."[4] Automating the whole NC programming task would have made much of their existing equipment obsolete, an economically unfeasible option. Some feel that CAM-I's research was "ten years ahead of its time." If the CAM-I specifications could have been implemented in their entirety, the resulting systems would have provided a "technological leap."

Beginning around 1985, CAM-I results became publicly available and were accessible to the major CAD vendors who were not members of the consortium. In some instances, they created specifications for commercial products with "very little modification" of the CAM-I specifications, particularly for solid and three-dimensional modeling components. Thus, a "shoestring" private funding effort contributed to the development of usable commercial products. However, the bottom-line benefits of these products are difficult to measure. According to a CAM-I representative, while their work provided a solid foundation, no single product can be designated as resulting solely from the ANC Program. That is not to say there was no impact. For example, on a recent visit to a CAD firm, its technical staff were touting a new product. This product clearly could have been built on the ANC results, but the staff had no apparent knowledge of the ANC Program, even though they had ready access to the CAM-I final report.

Major Issues

Human Resources. The diffusion of CNC machine tools to the U.S. market required a substantial education and training effort in the machine-tool maker and user community. Engineers, technicians, operators, and managers all needed training in CNC during the entire period covered by this case study. The training focused on the concepts of NC and on equipment-specific procedures. The diffusion rate of this training varied by size of firm and industry.

These firms adopted CNC in the 1970s and early 1980s, when NC technology still required a mainframe or minicomputer. They had the resources and staff to train people in CNC and, in many cases, to establish specialized CNC programming and maintenance groups. According to one large CNC end user in the aerospace industry, they "established a three-year apprenticeship program in CNC" and "trained technicians while retrofitting their CNC during the 80s." He continued, "retrofitting the CNC of a machine tool is very good training for maintenance

---

[4]Interview with a CAM-I staff member who participated in the ANC Program. All quotes in the ANC section derive from that discussion.

people."[5] Many large firms also had on-site corporate computer services staff that could help solve CNC problems in production. Further, large firms were able to demand CNC service support from the CNC firms and machine-tool builders, because they were major, powerful customers.

In contrast, small- and medium-sized enterprises (SMEs) in the United States had great difficulties in adopting CNC technology. This was not the case in Japan, where SMEs could readily obtain assistance from their nationwide network of *kohsetsushi*, "technology upgrading centers" funded by prefectural and local governments. Dating from the Meiji restoration period, they became widespread in the 1920s and 1930s. These centers provide technological training, guidance, and development and are a major reason for the penetration of advanced manufacturing technology into Japan's SMEs. In fiscal year 1988, these centers provided technical guidance in 472,000 cases, including providing on-site assistance in 24,700 cases (Shapira, 1990). As a result of this assistance, and several other programs in Japan, there is a much higher penetration of advanced manufacturing technology in Japanese SMEs than in comparable U.S. firms, as illustrated in Table D.2 (Shapira, 1990).

While NC/CNC technology use is comparable in large U.S. and Japanese manufacturing firms, it has achieved a 40-percent–greater penetration rate in Japanese SMEs than in comparable U.S. firms. This higher adoption rate can also be attributed to the special tax incentives MITI provided until 1983 for investments in NC machines, robots, and other manufacturing technologies.

Table D.2

Japanese Firms Employ More Advanced Manufacturing Technology

	Japan-U.S. Ratio	
Type of New Manufacturing Technique	SME	Large
NC/CNC machine tools	1.4	1.1
Flexible manufacturing cells	4.3	1.9
CAD	1.1	0.9
Automatic inspection	2.9	1.5
Handling robots	4.1	1.4
Automatic warehouse equipment	5.8	1.8
Assembly robots	2.1	1.2

[5]This complex process varies between different machine types. For example, retrofitting a horizontal machining center would require removing the axis drive systems and work plates, dismantling the spindle, and removing all electrical controls. During the rebuild, a new electronic control system would be installed, including the CNC and new axis drives and ball screws; fitting of the work plates; rebuilding of the spindle, including new bearings; and realignment of the machine.

Companies received a 13-percent tax credit on the purchase price, over and above the normal depreciation allowance (Okimoto, 1989, p. 101).

Capital Investment. Capital investment by machine-tool users typically follows business cycles. In aerospace, these cycles are approximately 10 years long and significantly influence equipment purchases. These firms increase capital investment as the business cycle begins its upswing. Because of more frequent model changes and a greater dependence on the consumer market, the automotive sector is less predictable. Figure D.4 depicts the capital investment patterns of these two industries for the 1978 to 1987 period (Department of Commerce, 1990a and 1990b).

The availability of investment capital depends on many factors, including the competitive environment and firm goals. Respondents from CNC and machine-tool firms said "getting development dollars is always a problem." These experts estimate that it takes about $14 to 20 million to design, develop, and introduce a new CNC product. As already indicated, the highly competitive market environment and the low return on investment in the machine-tool market made resources for investment a rare commodity. In the early 1980s, controller firms invested to support their mainline markets, markets other than machine-tool control. However, control divisions of large machine-tool firms were profit centers, even though they faced some of the same problems as controller firms.

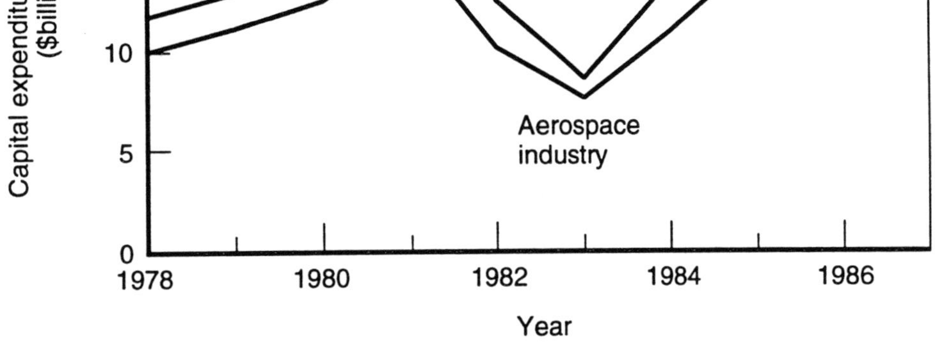

Figure D.4—Capital Expenditures in the Automotive and Aerospace Industries

Capital investment peaked in 1981, as automakers retooled their plants in response to the demand for more fuel-efficient cars. After a dip in 1983, investment grew rapidly through 1986 in both major machine-tool–using industries, providing a large market for machine-tool firms.

1983 Through 1986: CNC Commodity Tools—Jockeying for Position

Technology and Market Issues

In the early 1980s, several factors helped Japanese firms take the lead in CNC. From late 1979 until mid-1986, Japanese CNC firms introduced new products that were more technologically sophisticated and more reliable than existing products from U.S. firms. For example, in the early 1980s, FANUC introduced the Series 6000, a new controller incorporating bubble memory and CMOS random-access memory technology.[6] This "leap forward" in memory technology "really surprised us," said one U.S. CNC manufacturer. Customers wanted more memory, because the additional storage capacity made it much easier to store and use machine-control programs. Memory capacity at the machine is especially important to small- and medium-sized firms, because they cannot afford centralized minicomputers to store their program databases. It took U.S. firms two years to incorporate this technology in their product offerings. During this same 1979–1986 period, the high value of the dollar made all foreign products more attractive. In general, FANUC's products were also more reliable than rival U.S. products, a major selling point in the machine-tool market. Furthermore, economies of scale in production gave FANUC a better price-to-performance ratio and allowed it to become both the U.S. and world leader in CNC technology by 1985. At this zenith, FANUC's share of the global CNC market was up to 70 percent.[7]

Major Issues

Supplier-Customer Relations. U.S. controller firms provide industrial control products to a broad marketplace. Because machine-tool control is only a small

---

[6]Bubble memory is a nonvolatile, extremely rugged memory technology popular in the early 1980s. Its ruggedness made it popular for military and manufacturing applications. However, bubble memory is a sequential device, i.e., an item stored in memory must be accessed from the beginning and played through until completion or until it is stopped. This limits the application of bubble memory to sequential processes, such as storing CNC programs. The development of other rugged memory technologies and the need for random access for most applications reduced the usefulness of bubble memory technology.

[7]Interview with U.S. CNC executive.

market segment, controller firms chose, for economic reasons, to concentrate on more "mainline" domestic industries, such as general motion control for paper manufacturing, packaging, and web handling. Controller firms also "jumped on the robotics wagon" in the '80s, as did many other manufacturing firms. Since controller firms "don't have a lot of development funds, they put their dollars where the market is," said a machine-tool builder characterizing the strategy of controller firms. The largest market for these firms is more general industrial control. Without the investment dollars, the U.S. controller firms introduced fewer CNC products and were less able to respond to the needs of their CNC customers. This focus away from machine-tool control contributed to an arm's-length relationship between controller firms and machine-tool builders.

Human Resources. Most smaller firms began adopting CNC in the 1980s when microcomputer technology made CNC more accessible. It has been a gradual transition from manual to CNC equipment for most small firms, with penetration of CNC still low overall. There was a "lot of trial and error and mistakes," said a representative of a small die shop that uses CNC machine tools. They had to send employees to off-site apprenticeship programs to learn CNC concepts, typically at community colleges. For equipment-specific training, small firms relied on equipment suppliers, as did the large firms. As application problems arose, however, small firms had difficulty in obtaining the necessary support from their suppliers. Possible explanations include their relative insignificance as customers or their inability to pay for the support services rendered.[8]

CNC human-resource development varied by industry, as well as by firm size. The Air Force's early involvement in CNC development resulted in a highly educated and well-trained workforce in the aerospace industry. This familiarity was prevalent in defense and commercial aerospace applications. "We are fortunate that we had a well-experienced gang and that CNC knowledge was resident in the aerospace industry," said one manager for CNC specification projects. Generally, CNC skills in aerospace firms reside in the manufacturing engineering groups who create CNC programs for use on the floor. Thus, aerospace CNC operators need little or no in-depth knowledge of CNC technology. The recent slowdown in the aerospace industry is likely to cause the industry to "lose a lot of (well trained) people." It remains to be seen whether these trained people will end up applying their skills in aerospace firms or even firms in other sectors.

---

[8]Interview with a small CNC user.

Based on our interviews, we believe that the automotive and heavy-equipment industries had a more difficult time adopting CNC technology. Aerospace needs appeared to focus on CNC development for contouring applications. Furthermore, fewer people in the automotive sector were exposed to CNC concepts and equipment than in the aerospace sector during the 1950s, 1960s, and 1970s, while CNC was in its developmental stages.

Customer Base for Exports. Some firms began to realize the need to collaborate to develop and introduce new technology. For example, in 1983, Allen-Bradley entered into a joint venture with Olivetti of Italy. They subsequently introduced the 8600 controller, a product designed and built by Olivetti. This early deal was a harbinger of things to come, as more and more U.S. firms came to act as distributors for foreign-made CNC and machine tools. U.S. technology also flowed in the opposite direction. In the 1960s and 1970s, Bosch was one of the many firms that licensed the Bendix-owned NC patents. They mainly imported controls into Germany for use on Bendix designs. By the early 1980s, they had assimilated the U.S. technology and decided to dissolve their licensing and distribution agreement with Bendix. They subsequently designed and built their own controllers, focusing mainly on the German market, with limited distribution in the United States.

Other CNC firms were simply acquired by foreign interests. One such example is AEG's purchase of Modicon.

Thus, makers of early U.S. CNC machines focused on large, sophisticated users in the automobile and aerospace industries with the available resources and complex requirements to enable adoption of large, expensive, difficult-to-use mainframe and minicomputer-based CNC machines. By developing less sophisticated "commodity" CNC machine tools using microcomputers, the Japanese were able to expand into the less-sophisticated user community, as well as to gain a share of the more sophisticated users who were willing to trade capability for price. Consequently, U.S. consumption of NC realized enormous gains, but U.S. production remained quite stagnant. However, U.S. imports increased greatly, almost tripling during this period from a low of $400 million in 1983 to a high of nearly $1.2 billion by 1986. It is during this period that the huge "import gap" developed (see Figure D.2).

1986 Through 1989: CNC Commodity Tool Refinement and Specialty Tool Introduction

Technology and Market Issues

The mid-1980s saw rapid increases in NC processing power from U.S. computer firms. This meant that users could use microcomputers instead of the expensive and complicated mainframe and minicomputers for their NC. The 16-bit microprocessor, capable of processing 0.2–0.3 million instructions per second (MIPS), was incorporated into CNC products around 1985. A 32-bit processor with 1 MIPS capability was available soon afterward. One practical result of increased computing power was that users could program their machines to control more things simultaneously. However, U.S. controller firms were slow to pick up on this advantage. The large firms had proprietary CNC technology to protect, limiting their willingness to cannibalize their market position to outsource this vital component. This "not invented here" syndrome extended to hiring experts from the computer industry into the CNC firms. Their unwillingness to capitalize on home-grown computer talent was another factor leading to their decline.[9]

In addition, these microprocessor advances also facilitated the emergence of two-dimensional and three-dimensional graphics-based programming systems used to create CNC programs. Previously, there was no digital link between part design and part fabrication. In addition, programmers had to create CNC programs for geometric parts without the luxury of graphic support. This new processing power and the supporting graphics software allowed machinists or CNC programmers to use part-design information as a foundation for CNC programming. As a result, more-accurate CNC programs could be produced faster and by less experienced, less computer-literate personnel.

Many of these innovations were pioneered by U.S. researchers. However, U.S. controller firms did not take advantage of these technological advances. With the shrinking of the U.S. CNC market and limited CNC export opportunities, U.S. controller firms pursued other controls markets. The numbers simply did not justify the expenditures necessary to assimilate the new technology into CNC products. Thus, many controller firms fell further behind their competition. Even those firms that did offer new CNC products found they had lost their customers, and the costs necessary to switch made it difficult to get them back. In contrast, FANUC had a significant worldwide market position with no real

[9]Interview with CNC experts from the computer industry.

competition in its home market. As the de facto standard with dominant positions in each machine-tool market segment, the costs of any efforts to improve technology or increase standardization could be spread across all of its markets.

Research: The IMW Program

Somewhat concurrent with the ANC Program was the IMW Program funded by the Air Force MANTECH Program. Program documents provide a good overview of the IMW goals (U.S. Air Force, 1989, p. 1-1):

> The Intelligent Machining Workstation Initiative (IMW) is a research and development program to develop the requirements and specifications defining the machining workstation of the future. IMW is being designed to manufacture a variety of aerospace parts with the objective of creating a "good first part." IMW will accept a generic Product Definition Data (PDD) description of an incoming and expected outgoing discrete part, and perform the transformations necessary to correctly produce the part. The workstation will be used to demonstrate automated, unmanned operation of a machining workstation. The workstation will have the ability to plan, execute, and control all elements comprising its processing domain.

Cincinnati Milacron was the prime contractor for this 42-month program. The Carnegie Mellon University Robotics Institute added research expertise in manufacturing and artificial intelligence to the team. Finally, Pratt & Whitney was the target test site because of its reputation for "production of tough-to-machine, complex engine parts" (U.S. Air Force, 1989, p. 1-3).

This program developed some very innovative technology. Indeed, several respondents believed the technology significantly advanced the state of the art. Multiple, cooperating expert systems were developed to create process plans and CNC programs directly from part geometry data. Special grippers, tools, and fixtures were created to allow the machine tool itself to create the fixtures necessary to build a given part under software control.

Transferring radical, state-of-the-art technology like this from a research project to the marketplace may be best accomplished with aggressive, proactive measures. However, the technology transfer mechanisms selected were passive. As with most MANTECH programs, an industry–university review board was created to "serve as a forum for prioritizing industry needs and assessing industry response to the program." These review boards provide a peer review function and can act as passive technology transfer mechanisms as board members interest their firms in the MANTECH results. The technology-transfer objective, as defined in the program report, was as follows: "The information and data from IMW will be made available to machine-tool manufacturers and other developers of manufacturing technology." Unfortunately, the mismatch between the state of the technology and the passive technology transfer mechanisms selected for the IMW program resulted in very little technology transfer to the private sector. However, there have been some benefits. According to the Carnegie Mellon University researchers, much of their work on creating and interpreting a feature exchange language helped inform the ongoing Standard for the Exchange of Product Model Data (STEP) effort. The multiple, cooperating expert systems created in the IMW Program were each developed on different computing platforms. This greatly complicated any efforts for transfer to a commercializer, let alone implementation on the factory floor. Under a separate contract, Cincinnati Milacron is currently integrating these software systems on a single computer platform for eventual transfer to a teaching factory at Central State University in Ohio. A recent study funded by the Air Force revealed some market interest in the commercialization of the expert system software and the special fixtures developed by the IMW program, but the additional funding necessary to support these transfer activities is currently unavailable (Przybylinski et al., 1992).

Research: The NGC Program

The most recent research program, the NGC, was in part a reaction to Toshiba's 1986 sale of milling machines to the Soviet Union. This sale symbolized to the Department of Defense (DoD) that the United States was becoming dependent on foreign machine-tool suppliers who could not be trusted to withhold their technology for security reasons. It also spawned President Reagan's Machine Tool Domestic Action Plan. This effort brought together over 350 experts representing a cross section of the industry to help set a machine-tool research agenda. From June 1–5, 1987, the Air Force sponsored the Machine Tool/Manufacturing Technology Development Conference. Controls was one of the six areas of high priority identified by the conference participants. With the Air Force as champion and the National Center for Manufacturing Sciences (NCMS) providing additional support, the NGC effort began with a series of five workshops to establish technical requirements.

The goals of the NGC Program were to develop and validate a specification for an open system architecture. This open-architecture CNC system would help to make this advanced technology a commodity, off-the-shelf product. Experts pointed to "other successful open architecture strategies, such as computers and data communication" as a model for CNC. A small task force of workshop participants provided a strawman specification for developmental purposes. The next step was to create industry support to develop controllers meeting these general specifications collaboratively.

The NGC Program began with a noble goal, to provide a standard, open CNC architecture that would benefit defense suppliers and, in the end, the Air Force. However, it is important for any technology development effort to recognize the relationship between the technological goal and the existing industry structure and strategy. What is the basis of competition? Price? Features? Proprietary technology? If a technology program plans to develop and promote a new technology, ideally that technology should mesh with the existing dynamics of the industry. If the new technology will affect industry structure or firm strategy, that effect must be recognized and addressed, with time allotted to define a new status quo. This applies to the NGC Program, because U.S. CNC firms competed on closed, proprietary architectures. Thus, collaboratively developing a standard architecture was fundamentally against their existing strategy. At least in part, this prevented a cooperative industry effort from emerging. In spite of this lack of support, the Air Force and NCMS assumed program leadership and initiated a $15.4-million project that produced complete technical specifications to guide prototype development and testing. Industry experts believe that the NGC Program has provided a good technology foundation but that the business issues have kept the NGC from being fruitful to date. While NGC may work against CNC firm strategies of a proprietary technology, the firms still must satisfy their customers. Thus, a strong commercial-user pull or a DoD-standards push could determine the fate of the NGC results. To date, only a few smaller CNC firms have joined the NGC effort. An NGC team, headquartered at NCMS, will likely be seeking funding later this year to keep the effort on track.

It is important to note that none of these large research programs had very much impact on the CNC marketplace. Perhaps CAM-I's membership helped keep their effort in focus. Over the last several years, the Air Force MANTECH Program has recognized the importance of early and consistent focus on downstream technology transfer and commercialization and is currently working to address these issues, as is NCMS, although, as noted, with little success to date.

Major Issues

Supplier-Customer Relations. Machine-tool control is, as noted earlier, a relatively small market for controller firms that is also highly variable and dynamic. Controller firm sales to domestic machine-tool builders decreased throughout the 1980s because of an increase in machine-tool import penetration. Because of their position in the domestic machine industry, U.S controller and machine-tool firms were both hurt by import penetration. However, each group coped with this in different ways. The machine-tool firms found alternative sources for CNC control, while controller firms sought other market opportunities. Thus, the U.S. controller–machine-tool relationship grew more distant. As controller firms developed their alternative markets, their machine-tool CNC technology lagged behind their competitors. According to a machine-tool industry veteran, U.S. machine-tool builders typically gave domestic controller firms "the benefit of doubt if comparable on price and performance." Unfortunately, domestic firms often were not competitive. Then, as some U.S. firms improved their CNC machine-tool products, they found it difficult to win business back. As a U.S. controller manufacturer said, "once a machine-tool builder does the controls engineering integrating foreign control products, it is hard to get them to switch." These financial and technical switching costs contributed to the distance between buyers and U.S. vendors.

In response to their difficult relationship with machine-tool firms, U.S. controller firms focused their sales efforts on the machine-tool users. An end user usually selects the controls in new equipment purchases, while retrofitters often influence controller selection for retrofits.[10] For example, until 1985, some of the larger end users considered controller firms to be their primary equipment contractors. After 1985, these same firms increasingly worked more directly with machine-tool builders. This happened for two reasons. First, retrofitting existing equipment became much more important in the 1980s as manufacturers upgraded their controls, particularly in aerospace firms. Second, controller specifications became more available and were disseminated widely. According to a CNC executive, some large end users "moved away from specifying the brand of control and just wrote the feature requirements." End users could write specifications and let the machine-tool firms handle it. Since new equipment demand was soft, controller firms faced an uphill battle. It was difficult for most domestic controller firms to build a relationship with anyone, let alone nurture a close relationship.

---

[10]A retrofit can be either upgrading a machine tool from NC to CNC or replacing an old CNC controller with a newer one.

Human Resources. Regarding access to human capital, some of the CNC firms and machine-tool firms did not adequately embrace the available human resources offered by the computer industry. Computer specialists working as researchers in the machine-tool industry said, "the machine-tool industry was doing its best to reinvent computer technology without much of the necessary talent," to which a machine-tool industry respondent answered, "the early computer equipment was unreliable in our industrial settings." Thus, for reasons of quality and reliability, some of the larger machine-tool firms integrated backward and established computer-oriented research agendas. Most were unsuccessful and exited rather quickly.

There are several possible explanations for this discord between some computer people and some machine-tool and CNC people. CNC development and application require an interdisciplinary team of manufacturing people knowledgeable in metal removal, control-system design, and computer technology. Creating and coordinating such teams is extremely difficult. The NGC effort is one of the first to have taken this approach. In addition, resource constraints may have kept CNC and U.S. machine-tool firms from investing in staff development, because "they were under serious competitive pressures," said a CNC firm representative.

Customer Base for Exports. A scorecard was still necessary to keep track of all the players in the CNC market. In the late 1970s, FANUC and Siemens teamed up to attack the U.S. market. By 1986, their relationship soured, and they dissolved the partnership, allowing once-formidable CNC companies to reappear. For example, General Electric's controller business was decimated in the mid-1980s. The company then arose from the ashes by partnering with FANUC. FANUC provided the design expertise and manufactured the product, and General Electric provided U.S. distribution and support.

1990 Onward: CNC Specialty Tools (Competing in a Global Market)

Technology and Market Issues

In the late 1980s, "homegrown" or "special-purpose" controllers making use of powerful, cheap chips became popular. These were controls designed specifically for a machine or designed to produce a specific part. These controllers had advantages. They were low cost and could be readily tailored to specific functions, but they created logistical and training problems. Ideally, user firms wanted to develop support capabilities on site, using relatively low-cost in-house maintenance people. However, every new piece of equipment with a special-purpose controller required specialized maintenance training. Depending on the sophistication of the equipment, new machines may have also required expensive maintenance contracts and access to higher-priced vendor support professionals. As a result, supporting these multiple configurations became very difficult. The problems and higher costs associated with the proliferation of special-purpose controllers also made it difficult to keep machine operators trained and working effectively. Even with all of these problems, this market shift to customized CNC controllers eroded FANUC's current market share to approximately 50 percent of the global CNC market. Thus, we see a decline in NC exports to the United States and a shrinking of the "import gap" (see Figure D.5). Furthermore, as shown in Figure D.5, Japan's domination of stand-alone NC exports to the United States diminished slightly after 1990, from 96.5 to 88.7 percent of all imports.

Technological changes in CNC that are expected in the 1990s include predictive control to compensate for such factors as machine wear or ambient temperature, automated preventive maintenance scheduling, diagnostic software for accuracy and precision, and computerized machine manuals (see Appendix F).

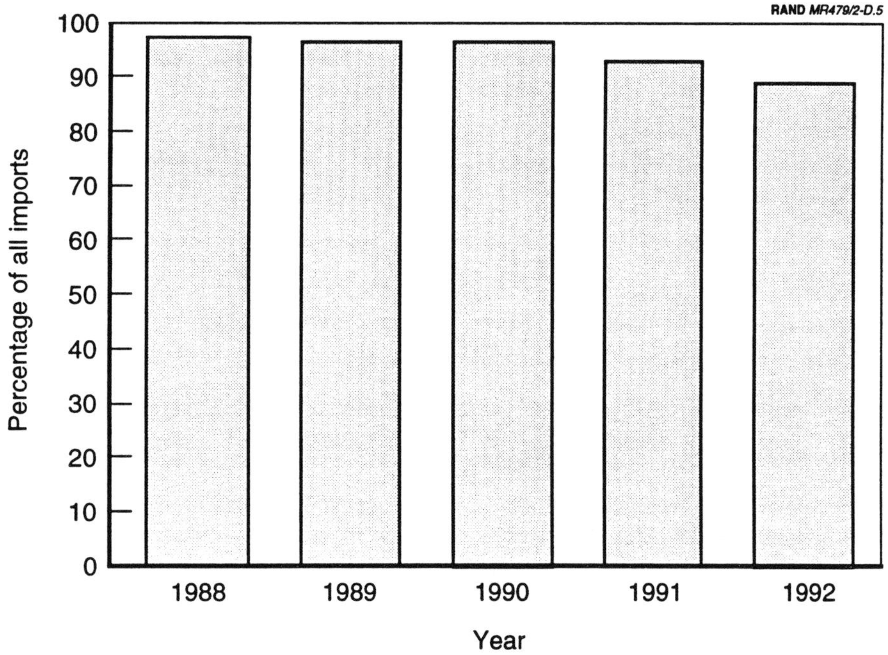

Figure D.5—Real Japanese Stand-Alone NC Exports as a Percentage of All U.S. Imports

Major Issues

Supplier-Customer Relations. Recently, CNC users have become dissatisfied with the lack of responsiveness from market leader FANUC. Once known for listening to customer needs and offering desired features, FANUC shows signs of being an aloof bureaucracy like many of its former competitors. This creates an opening for other controller firms to continue to erode FANUC's leadership position. It is unclear as of yet how this will play out.

Human Resources. The Manufacturing Technology Center (MTC) Program and efforts under way in defense conversion can have a significant positive impact in this area. Several of the MTCs are linked with community colleges and economic development agencies, organizations that have a stake in building human capital in their areas.

Capital Investment. During this period, MITI helped stabilize investment patterns by providing significant financial support to both machine-tool builders and users during this period. The following tax incentives applicable to machine-tool firms were effective until March 1993 (Ostrowiecki and Faricy, 1993):

- 7 percent of the cost of acquiring facilities for conducting R&D in fundamental technologies is deductible from corporate or personal income tax.
- 6 percent of the cost of R&D to SMEs is deductible from corporate or personal income tax.
- Special depreciation allowances are available for acquiring fixed assets used in experimental research on industrial technology.
- Donations to research corporations can be deducted as losses.
- Funds at low interest rates are available from the Japan Development Bank for the commercialization of important industrial technologies.

In addition, in 1992, the Japan Development Bank instituted a program to promote the acquisition of labor-saving machinery to help reduce working hours. Up to 50 percent of the funding needs can be borrowed for an interest rate of only 5.9 percent (Holman, 1992, p. 15). It is expected that this will help boost domestic capital investment, particularly in the machine-tool industry.

Customer Base for Exports. These structural changes put increasing pressure on CNC firms to compete in global markets, but many U.S. CNC firms were faced with learning how to be global companies (see Volume 1, Chapter Four).

Existing trade policies and the supporting infrastructure did little to help U.S. firms. Trade with the USSR and the other Eastern bloc countries was restricted for high-technology items, including CNC controls over three axes. Procedures to export CNC controls and other machine tools involved three different agencies—the Department of Commerce, the Department of Defense, and the State Department—each with its own, often conflicting, regulations. Plans to relax these restrictions were announced by President Bush in 1990, but it is unclear what was actually done. Antitrust law prohibits U.S. firms from working cooperatively. This too was modified in 1984 to allow U.S. firms to work cooperatively in bidding on international projects. CNC firms, as did many other industrial firms, began the long journey toward building global markets.

Industry consolidation and acquisitions continued. Primarily because of competitive pressures from FANUC, Texas Instruments' Control Division was sold to Siemens in 1991.

Conclusion

CNC technology has offered great opportunities to improve manufacturing productivity and flexibility. The evolution and diffusion of CNC technology provides an interesting contrast between approaches taken by the United States, Japan, and Germany to support this assimilation, as shown in Table D.3.

Of course, this is not the whole story. But as a result of these and other factors, non-U.S. firms dominate the controller market, and CNC technology has a lower level of penetration in U.S. manufacturers than in their Japanese and German counterparts.

Given the increasing capability to produce inexpensive yet sophisticated microcomputer-based "specialty" CNC developed for the lower end of the user market and given the large demand for such products, it is possible that U.S.

Table D.3

Approaches to Evolution and Diffusion of CNC Technology

	United States	Japan	Germany
Market forces	Let the market work	Rationalize the market	Use standard-setting to foster specialization
R&D support	Support general, unfocused R&D	Support specific, applied R&D	Support specific, applied R&D
Adoption assistance	Provide little assistance	*Kohsetsushi*	Fraunhofer

manufacturers will continue to experience large advances in their competitive positions, given their strengths in the core technologies for these products. However, if U.S. NC manufacturers continue the tradition of focusing on the large, sophisticated users in the transportation-equipment industry (i.e., automobile and aerospace), they may well find themselves facing an erosion in competitiveness similar to that experienced when the Japanese captured the "commodity" CNC market.

The United States is starting to address some of these issues with the NGC Program, the MTC Program, and other efforts. There may be an opening in the market. Furthermore, the United States still leads the world in computer technology. In addition, FANUC has shown some recent signs of weakness. It remains to be seen whether U.S. manufacturers can turn these opportunities into a stronger market position, but they do seem to be in a better position today than in the recent past.

References

Association for Manufacturing Technology, *1991–1992 Economic Handbook of the Machine Tool Industry*, 1992.

Bundesministerium für Wirtschaft, *Unternehmensgrößenstatistik 1989/1990: Daten und Fakten*, prepared for Institut für Mittelstandsforschung im Auftrag des BMWi, Studienreihe 68, Bonn, 1990.

Department of Commerce, Economics and Statistics Administration, Bureau of the Census, *1987 Census of Manufactures, Industry Series: Aerospace Equipment, Including Parts*, Washington, D.C.: Department of Commerce, MC87-I-37B, March 1990a.

Department of Commerce, Economics and Statistics Administration, Bureau of the Census, *1987 Census of Manufactures, Industry Series: Motor Vehicles and Equipment*, Washington, D.C.: Department of Commerce, MC87-I37A, March 1990b.

Graham, Glenn A., *Automation Encyclopedia*, Dearborn, Mich.: Society of Manufacturing Engineers, 1988.

Holman, Richard, "Japan Unveils Labor-Saving Loans," *Wall Street Journal*, April 22, 1992, p. 15.

Johnson, Chalmers, *MITI and the Japanese Miracle: The Growth of Industrial Policy, 1925-1975*, Stanford, Calif.: Stanford University Press, 1982.

MIT Commission on Industrial Productivity, "The U.S. Machine Tool Industry and Its Foreign Competitors," working paper, 1989.

Okimoto, Daniel I., *Between MITI and the Market*, Stanford, Calif.: Stanford University Press, 1989.

Ostrowiecki, Beverly A., and Timothy B. Faricy, *Competitive Analysis of the Machine Tool Industry*, Ann Arbor, Mich.: Midwest Manufacturing Technology Center, Industrial Technology Institute, 1993.

Przybylinski, Stanley M., et al., *Final Report: Technology Transfer Demonstration Project*, Wright-Paterson Air Force Base, Ohio: Manufacturing Technology Directorate, 1992.

Schmidt, Rachel, *Civil and Military R&D Spending: The Case of Numerically Controlled Machine Tools*, Santa Monica, Calif.: RAND, P-7471-RGS, 1988.

Shapira, Philip, *Japan's Kohsetsushi Program*, National Institute of Standards and Technology, U.S. Department of Commerce, 1990.

U.S. Air Force, *Intelligent Machining Workstation Initiative (IMW), Phase II*, AFWAL-TR-89-8031, April 1989.

Appendix E
Case Studies: Transfer Lines

Stan Przybylinski, Industrial Technologies Institute

Introduction

Transfer machines are a specialized combination of material handling and machining equipment used in high-precision, high-volume manufacturing. These high-value machines, sometimes referred to as "specials," are crucial to manufacturing operations in the automotive and aerospace industries, key segments of the U.S. economy. This product market was selected for a case study, because, in many respects, it is an exception to the decline of the machine-tool industry analyzed in the main report:

- The market for transfer machines is one of the few machine-tool segments that has not succumbed to foreign competition.
- These machines were some of the first to penetrate Japanese automotive transplant operations.
- Transfer machine makers have been working closely with their customers on machine design for a long time, long before the phrase "concurrent engineering" entered the manufacturing lexicon.

This case study will first provide an overview of transfer machines, their technology, and markets for the period 1978 to the present. We will then focus on two U.S. transfer machine suppliers, The Ingersoll Milling Machine Company and H. R. Krueger Machine Tool, Inc. Profiles of these firms can help provide insights on successful strategies and practices that could possibly be adopted by other U.S. machine-tool firms.

Description of the Technology

A transfer machine is a combination of individual work stations arranged in a required sequence, connected by work piece transfer devices, and integrated with interlocked controls (Society of Manufacturing Engineers, 1983, pp. 15–81). Transfer machines can be either of the rotary or in-line type.

Rotary machines transfer the holding fixtures or pallets in a circular path and are typically limited to smaller work pieces and fewer stations. In-line types transfer the work piece in a straight linear path and can accommodate larger work pieces. A rotary-type transfer machine is shown in Figure E.1. The major components of a rotary transfer machine are the indexing device for rotating the work piece fixtures or pallets and the machining heads.

There are three main types of in-line transfer machines: sliding or free transfer, walking-beam (lift-and-carry) transfer, and palletized transfer. Figure E.2 shows a palletized transfer machine. The major components of an in-line transfer machine are the wing base, platen, center base, and spindle heads.

RAND *MR479/2-E.1*

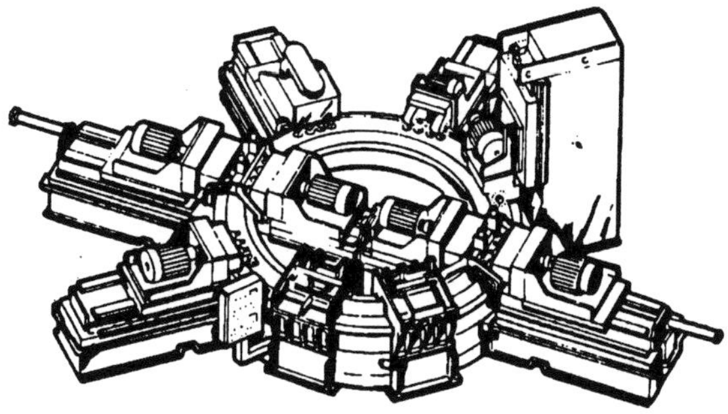

Figure E.1—Rotary Transfer Machine (Textron, Inc.)

RAND *MR479/2-E.2*

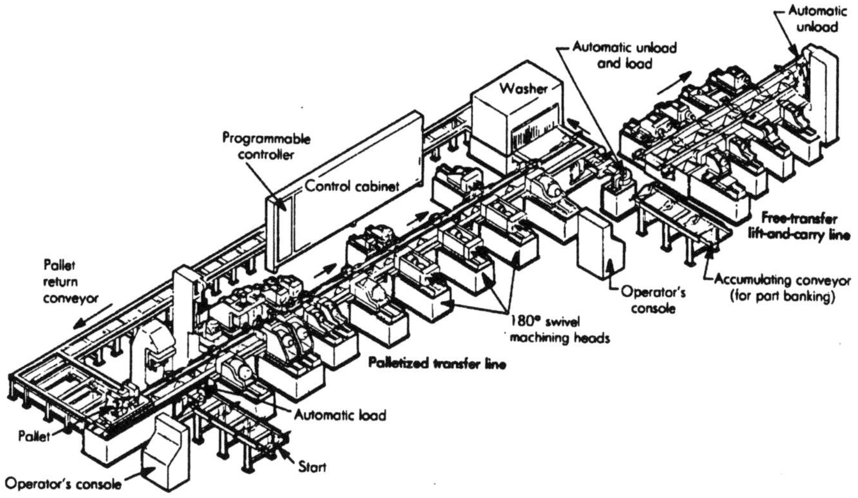

Figure E.2—In-Line Transfer Machine (Snyder Corporation)

Transfer machines provide the highest degree of automation obtainable with special-purpose machinery, machinery designed to manufacture a specific part or family of parts. Thus, the primary benefit of a transfer line is its ability to handle volume production. The industrial sectors that most use transfer machines are automotive and heavy equipment industries.

Market for Transfer Machines

The end users of transfer machines are some of the world's largest manufacturers. Because of their need to process high-precision goods at large volumes, end users tend to be very demanding during the design-build cycle. In the 1980s, most transfer machine builders were small firms that could respond quickly to the needs of their customers. However, while there were many small firms, the market was highly concentrated; large firms such as Ingersoll Milling Machines, Giddings & Lewis, and Lamb Technicon captured a large percentage of total sales in the category. The machine builders responding to these manufacturers have a well-established line of machining units that meet user needs. They typically locate their engineering staffs close to their customers to more quickly respond to user requirements.

The U.S. demand for transfer equipment peaked in 1980 and 1981; after a sharp drop in 1983, shipments remained stable through the mid 1980s, as automotive manufacturers dramatically changed their engine designs to meet the fuel economy and emission requirements the marketplace demanded. Table E.1 lists the value of U.S. shipments of station-type machines and import penetration during the 1980s (Association for Manufacturing Technology [AMT], 1990, p. A-9).[1] The increasing import penetration reflects, at least in part, transfer machine purchases by Japanese transplants.

Historically, a number of firms competed in the U.S. transfer machinery market, including The Cross Company, F. Joseph Lamb, Buhr, Snyder, La Salle, H. R. Krueger, Ingersoll Milling Machines, Greenley, W. F. & John Barnes, Place Machine, Ex-Cello, Rockford Automation, and M. L. Parker, some of which have now gone bankrupt or have merged with competitors. Most firms are located in Michigan or other parts of the Midwest because of geographic proximity to the automotive design centers. This proximity is important given the close relationship required to successfully design and install these complex machines. With increasing opportunities for global sourcing, these historical relationships

[1]Transfer machines are one category of station-type machine. AMT only has data broken out on transfer machines for a few years out of this period.

Table E.1

U.S. Shipments of Station-Type Machines

Year	Value (in millions)	Import Penetration (%)
1980	$794	1.0
1981	$896	1.1
1982	$731	1.1
1983	$274	0.6
1984	$312	4.0
1985	$406	4.9
1986	$518	6.3
1987	$300	7.5
1988	$225	24.2
1989[a]	$563	9.4

[a]Projected

between machine builders and end users will likely be scrutinized, with users always seeking higher quality and more efficient equipment.

On average, transfer machines cost between $750,000 and $1 million. Very often, builders receive no progress payments, so they must, in essence, finance the construction and purchase of these large, resource-intensive machines. As a result, builders also end up carrying large amounts of work-in-process inventory. To finance this large expense, a triangular relationship of builders, banks, and end users existed in the 1980s. Automotive end users rarely paid any money up front for equipment, so the automotive transfer machine suppliers depended on their strong relationships with their local banks for funds. Local banks willingly lent money to most equipment builders that had purchase orders from auto companies. In contrast, heavy equipment manufacturers frequently made advance payments, reducing the capital burden on firms supplying that market.

Transfer Machine Technology

In 1978, transfer machines consisted of electromechanical controls, AC motors, and proprietary drive systems to move the large multiple spindle heads in one axis. The work piece movement was mostly synchronous for cutting operations and, frequently, asynchronous for assembly. At that time, transfer machine firms were primarily concerned with the following technical issues:

- Developing proprietary gear sets for feed rate and rapid advance
- Improving methods to speed the processing of large, heavy work pieces

- Improving the stability of the base and holding fixture
- Attaining a high degree of precision.

Between 1978 and the present, the evolution of transfer machine technology can be characterized by changes in motor technology, control technology, and approaches to reliability and maintainability. Motor development took place in three distinct phases: AC motors in 1978, DC drives from 1978 to 1984, and AC servo drives from 1984 to the present. AC motors had fixed-limit switches and mechanical clutch systems that limited precision and flexibility. DC drives provided increased flexibility for multiple speeds, but were unreliable. In addition, most engineers and technicians lacked adequate knowledge of electronics to deploy DC drive technology fully. AC servo systems provided the needed flexibility and reliability. While AC servo systems also required the engineers and technicians to have knowledge of electronics, the increase in product reliability provided the added incentive to learn. A key component of the AC servo system is a resolver, a device to keep track of location.

Changes in control technology can be characterized by a transition from programmable logic control, where electromechanical relay logic is hardwired to control a given machine, to numerical control technology (NC). In some more recent applications, even computer numerical control (CNC) has been applied. Control technology for transfer machinery also benefited from additional memory. In addition to more sophisticated control, the transition to NC technology also offered increased flexibility. The added flexibility raised the cost of a transfer machine, and users discovered that a careful analysis had to be done to strike an appropriate balance between flexibility and automation.

The last major technological change in transfer machinery is the change in attitude toward reliability and maintainability (R&M). The beginning of the 1980s saw a major push by U.S. machinery builders to develop systems with diagnostic capabilities. Because of user demand and advances in machine-tool technology, transfer equipment builders began focusing on improved R&M. They decided, in effect, to build their equipment better to simplify ongoing maintenance rather than develop mechanisms to cope with faults. Today, many transfer machinery builders are involved in the R&M activities of the National Center for Manufacturing Sciences and the Industrial Technology Institute.

In the following sections, two U.S. transfer machine builders are profiled: the Ingersoll Milling Machine Company and the H. R. Krueger Machine Tool Company. After providing a company overview, the discussion focuses on each firm's market and technology strategies, how they deal with the large capital requirements inherent in this business, and what human resource policies enable them to retain good employees and prepare them to contribute to the company's success.

The Ingersoll Milling Machine Company

Company Overview

What has evolved into the Ingersoll International family of companies can trace its roots back to Winthrop Ingersoll in 1887. In 1978, Ingersoll International, Inc., was formed as a holding company for all of the Ingersoll subsidiary operations, holding 100 percent of the capital stock in the Ingersoll Milling Machine Company (IMM). About one quarter of Ingersoll International's business comes from the sale of transfer machines. As a privately held company, detailed financial information is not available.

IMM designs and builds special-purpose metal-cutting and automated metal-parts machining systems.[2] These systems involve all of the basic machining operations, including milling, boring, drilling, and tapping. These machines fit into two general categories: heavy machinery (portal-type machines) and production machinery (transfer machines).[3] The company is a major supplier of machine tools and manufacturing systems to the aerospace, automotive, farm, truck, and tractor industries. It also supplies the power generation and the primary metals industries. Ingersoll is noted for its strength in developing machines to manufacture engine blocks and other power-train components. In the last 35 years, Ingersoll International has significantly increased its presence in Europe.

Many of these holdings are subsidiaries of IMM. IMM has two U.S. subsidiaries, one in England, and four in Germany (Giesen, 1985b, p. 1):

- Ingersoll CM Systems Inc. (U.S.) was acquired in 1990. It makes crankshaft and camshaft machining equipment, crankshaft induction heating and hardening machines.
- Ingersoll, Inc. (U.S.) was chartered in 1986 to sell and service machine tools in Iowa, Illinois, and Michigan, and services products in Europe that are manufactured in the United States.

---

[2]Different sources list IMM in the following SIC code sectors: 3540, metalworking machinery; 3541, machine tools, metal cutting types; 3544, special dies, tools, jigs, and fixtures; 3545, machine tool accessories; and 3599, manufacturing industries not elsewhere classified.

[3]Fortunately for IMM, these two businesses tend to be countercyclic.

- Ingersoll Machinen und Werkzeuge GmbH (Germany) makes cutting tools and electrical discharge machines.
- Bohle Werkzeugmachinen GmbH (Germany) makes precision machining centers.
- Waldrich Siegen Werkzeugmachinen GmbH (Germany) makes large machine tools, such as heavy-duty roll lathes, roll grinders, and giant machining centers.
- Waldrich Coburg Werkzeugmachinenfabrik GmbH (Germany), acquired in 1985, produces portal-type machining centers, way grinding machines, and thread-milling machines.

The company employs approximately 4,500 worldwide, with half in the United States at their main 1,000,000-ft^2 facility in Rockford, Illinois.

Marketing Strategy

According to Edson Gaylord, Ingersoll's Chairman of the Board, IMM's success is due to two philosophies that have remained constant over the years (Weimer, 1987, p. 7):

- "Ingersoll has always had a reputation for having an honest desire to work through difficult situations to find out what seemed to be most fair and to do what's right. This attitude has gained us a good business reputation with most of the people we have done business with over these 100 years, and we have never had an interruption in our work due to a labor dispute."
- "The second and most distinguishing characteristic about Ingersoll is that we have engaged not in selling machines but in finding better ways to help customers make parts. For the last 50 years our machines have carried a guarantee of accuracy and production, a practice still not widely accepted in our industry."

IMM is regarded by the automakers as particularly strong in engine block-making and body die-making technologies. Its main U.S. competitors are Giddings & Lewis and Lamb Technicon. In Europe, its main rivals are Hüller Hilli, Grob, Excello, and Heller. The nature of IMM's automotive business required developing close relationships with its customers, often custom designing transfer machines in collaboration with customers. To help nurture close relationships, IMM expanded its Troy, Michigan operation in 1988 to allow its engineers to get involved in "before-" and "after-build" continuous improvement work in its customers' plants. According to Gaylord, "Once a system is set up and turned on, there's an opportunity that neither the customers nor we have taken advantage of yet to make adjustments here and there, and perhaps even some additions, to improve the system's performance, uptime and overall productivity" (Wrigley, 1988, p. 6).

Long-term customer-supplier relationships are essential to the vitality of many businesses. The lack of these relationships has hurt firms in many segments of the machine-tool industry. In contrast, IMM has long been successful in selling equipment to General Motors (GM) and the rest of the Big Three automakers. In 1984, IMM won Ford Motor Company's Zeta four-cylinder engine tooling program in Bridgend, South Wales—at the time a unique sale of U.S.-built transfer machines to a foreign user (Wrigley, 1984, p. 1). IMM has developed the last five Chrysler engine lines, including one in Mexico. In 1989, IMM was selected as GM's partner in the simultaneous engineering of the aluminum transmission-case machining line for the F4 transmission (Wrigley, 1989, p. 1). In 1990, IMM signed a long-term supplier agreement with GM unlike any in the history of the U.S. automotive industry. Ingersoll's agreement with GM's Buick-Oldsmobile-Cadillac (B-O-C) group assured IMM of all future B-O-C engine block machining business, as long as IMM met the provisions of the agreement and continued to want the business (Wrigley, 1990, p. 1). Both sides felt they would benefit. Long-term agreements allow for a much longer planning horizon. The close relationship early in the design cycle would help IMM better satisfy the needs of B-O-C. GM believed that involving IMM in product design and even research and development (R&D) would result in the more efficient production of higher-quality parts. According to Larry Streng, manager of manufacturing engineering for B-O-C, "The machine-tool builder's involvement in such things as R&D and continuous improvement can only benefit manufacturers like ourselves" (Wrigley, 1990). However, in a more recent policy reversal, GM placed all power-train manufacturing under GM Powertrain, making Ingersoll and others again compete for this business.

Ingersoll has aggressively marketed its equipment internationally. Consistent with its long-view strategy, IMM established a German subsidiary in 1961 that did not yield a dividend for 25 years. According to Gaylord: "We had to put back every cent we earned until we had built a viable group of companies, strong enough to be world competitive, before there was any left over for the stockholders" (Vasilash, 1989, p. 40).[4] In the 1970s, IMM was a major supplier to the Kama River automotive plant in the former Soviet Union. Located 600 miles

---

[4]Ingersoll stock is very closely held, with complete ownership by Gaylord and several Ingersoll family members.

east of Moscow, this 40-square-mile facility is the largest consolidated automotive plant in the world. IMM supplied over $20 million in transfer machinery.[5]

IMM has had good success competing in Japan. In the mid-1980s, IMM had several large orders (Vasilash, 1989):

- In 1985, IMM built the world's largest CNC machining center for Hitachi, with a second ordered. This machine can hold workpieces up to 200 metric tons (Giesen, 1985a).
- Fuji Heavy Industries ordered a composite tape-laying system.[6]
- IMM's German operations supplied giant roll lathes and grinders for companies in Japan's heavy industries.
- IMM also beat out Toshiba for an order for roll grinders from Nippon Steel.

Recently, IMM supplied Dainichi Kinzoku Kogyo Company, Ltd., a major Japanese lathe maker, with a large five-face machining center.[7]

IMM was also part of a group of companies that was the first to sell to Toyota's Georgetown plant. In 1989, IMM received an order to provide boring, milling, and drilling equipment for Toyota engine blocks. Another large order followed in 1990. U.S. suppliers are hoping that this is the beginning of a trend by the transplants, which historically have purchased their machine tools from Japan.

Ingersoll sees Eastern Europe and China as the largest future market opportunities, believing that the demand for automobiles and off-road vehicles will increase significantly, thus increasing demand for its kind of equipment. IMM is expanding its long-time presence in Europe, expanding its sales there as well as adding sales staff to serve China. AMT, the industry trade group, is helping many firms penetrate these emerging markets. Consistent with its long history, IMM will go it alone without AMT's assistance.[8]

Ingersoll has been able to ride out recessions and downturns in the U.S. automotive industry because it also supplies other industries. IMM has been designing and selling custom machines for fabricating vehicle engines since 1900 and can use this skill not only for automotive engines, but also for farm

---

[5]Interview with Jim Siebel, R&D manager at IMM.

[6]A composite tape-laying system is a multiaxis device that accurately positions tape in three-dimensional space for the construction of composite-based parts needed in aerospace and other applications.

[7]"Dainichi Kinzoku Kogyo to market Ingersoll machine tools in Japan" (1992).

[8]Interview with John Droy, Vice President of Sales for Production Machinery at IMM.

equipment and other types of engines (Vasilash, 1989). According to the company, automotive orders would ideally account for approximately 50 percent of sales (Giesen, 1988, p. 6).

IMM is a strong proponent of free, but fair, trade. In 1984, IMM dropped out of the National Machine Tool Builders Association to protest the association's stand in favor of import quotas. "The nation needs a strong machine-tool industry, and the wrong way to get that is to set up trade barriers," stated Gaylord (Brooks, 1984, p. 5). "The defense argument is just a cover for protectionism" (Donahue, 1984, p. 208). Gaylord felt this protection would just allow already "browbeaten and discouraged" builders to become "more complacent." Gaylord and IMM are also against other nations' practicing protectionism. In 1983, Gaylord spoke out against French protectionism that cost his German subsidiaries business. He also accused the French government of providing a $16-million subsidy to help French machine-tool firms penetrate the U.S. market (Brooks, 1983, p. 1). IMM complements its technology development strategy with protection of its technology rights. For example, in 1984, IMM and several other U.S. firms filed a trade complaint about Brazilian imports of tillage discs. The International Trade Commission voted 4 to 1 in their favor and imposed an 8.06 percent countervailing duty on Brazilian imports of these products (Brooks, 1985, p. 5). IMM also recently accused Pratt & Whitney of infringing on its patents for a portal-type milling machine (Sterner, 1989, p. 4).

Part of IMM's market success can be attributed to its ability to respond to customer requirements rapidly. This is dependent on its state-of-the-art manufacturing technology, the topic of the next section.

Technology Strategy

Ingersoll is clearly a technological leader, quick to acquire and implement new manufacturing technology. In 1957, the company installed two NC drills, one of the first installations of such equipment. During the early 1960s, Ingersoll adopted an automatic guided-vehicle system and an automated storage-and-retrieval system (Quinlan, 1989, p. 34). It automated its own manufacturing operations in the 1970s, well ahead of most other firms, let alone other machine-tool companies. It purchased its first NC machining center and first computer-aided design system in 1975. By the 1980s, Ingersoll's employees, who "jumped at the chance" to automate, had developed and implemented over 1,300 independent systems.[9] While each function posted gains, many "bridge"

[9]George Hess, as quoted in Quinlan (1989).

programs had to be constructed to allow communication between these islands of automation.

Thus, the 1980s became the decade of integration.[10] IMM's customized, integrated corporate database system, developed in the early 1980s, replaced these 1,300 individual systems. One five-machine flexible manufacturing system produces over 12,000 different prismatic parts each year. Of these parts, 70 percent are produced in lots of one and 50 percent will not be manufactured again (Kramer, 1984, p. 7). These modernization efforts were recognized by the Society of Manufacturing Engineers, who awarded the company the 1982 Leadership and Excellence in the Application and Development of Computer Integrated Manufacturing Award, a recognition of outstanding computer-integrated manufacturing activities.

Because it develops custom machines, Ingersoll resembles a large job shop, with a large production run considered to be three parts. The company is also vertically integrated, with 90 percent of its parts fabricated in house. Since it handles over 25,000 new parts per year, IMM has an incentive to continue its efforts to "optimize" its systems in the 1990s.

IMM partially funded the development of a system called Process Planning and Generative Numerical Control. Working from a feature-based solid model constructed by a design engineer, this system "retrieves all processes required for the part and automatically generates an NC part program" (Quinlan, 1989). In typical Ingersoll style, this technology was developed by the formation of a software development association with Automation Technology Products (now called Cimplex) (Harvey, 1988, p. 5).

On the product side, IMM is applying new technology to enhance its competitive position, routinely partnering with its customers in product development. For example, IMM teamed with Boeing in 1987 to develop a multispindle profiler machine. This $6-million contract supported the development of one machine, as well as "breakthrough" technologies, such as an advanced tool-management system and a five-axis programming language (Giesen, 1987, p. 8).

IMM pursues technology development efforts despite constraints on time and money.[11] Much of the company's R&D work is in response to specific customer requirements, and technical problems are addressed when a salesman gets an order for a machine or sells a new capability that does not really exist. Much of

---

[10]Ibid.

[11]Interview with Jim Siebel, R&D manager at IMM.

IMM's product and process R&D work is distributed, with each functional area contributing ideas and manpower. The R&D staff may draw people off the assembly floor, work right in engineering, and do tests on production machines in the middle of production schedules.

One question of interest to this study is the extent to which U.S. firms take advantage of federal and state assistance programs in technology development and deployment. Typically, IMM shuns government assistance. An exception, however, came in the case of the "Octahedral Hexapod Machine," a revolutionary new design for an eight-axis machine tool that will be able to reconfigure its hardware and software rapidly to tackle a wide variety of high-precision machining tasks. IMM has been working on this technology for a number of years, with considerable interest from potential customers. To aid in the further development of this technology, IMM applied for and was awarded an Advanced Technology Program (ATP) grant of $1.87 million from the U.S. Department of Commerce. The ATP provides matching funds to U.S. firms to develop pre-competitive, generic technologies that will improve U.S. industrial competitiveness.[12]

Capital Investments

As essentially a family-owned business, IMM views itself as having a longer time horizon than its publicly held competitors. Its long wait for a dividend from their German subsidiary is a prime example. Family control has allowed them to derive most of the needed funds from continuing operations.

IMM appears willing to commit resources when required to satisfy customer needs. For example, in 1988, IMM engineers felt that the ambient air temperature in their manufacturing facility was preventing them from meeting the necessary tolerances to satisfy customer requirements. In response, IMM air conditioned its whole plant (Giesen, 1987). This contrasts with the company's approach to incidental expenses; the executive staff, for example, occupy Spartan offices atypical of many U.S. multimillion dollar companies (Vasilash, 1989). Ingersoll's plant lacks the "old workhorse machines" seen on the floors of many major manufacturers. Of the 163 major machines on the floor, the average equipment age in 1989 was just 10.4 years (Vasilash, 1989). Like other innovative firms, such as 3M, IMM turns the tables on the cost-justification process. Most organizations place strict capital budgeting requirements on those wanting to replace

---

[12]Under ATP grants, the U.S. government supplements the funds from the individual awardee. The intellectual property from the development effort is the property of the grantee, with users of the technologies benefiting by their earlier introduction into the marketplace.

equipment. At IMM, after a machine finishes its ninth year on the floor, managers have to justify keeping it (Vasilash, 1989). In total, one manager estimates that IMM has invested $100 million over the last ten years in the Rockford facility alone.

Human Resource Policies

Clearly, IMM encourages innovation and technological change. There are many facets to the corporate culture:

- Employees have a history of participating in the planning of technological change.
- There are no time clocks at the Rockford facility. All employees are salaried.
- Ingersoll policy states that any regular salaried employee will receive 90 calendar days' notice of actual layoff.
- During an early 1980s downturn, IMM demonstrated its focus on the long term by keeping skilled people on the payroll. These staffers worked at various tasks around the Rockford complex, painting buildings and trimming bushes, much as Japanese workers do when their employers face similar circumstances.

Approximately one third of IMM's employees have college degrees, and another sixth have completed a trade school or associate program.[13] IMM fosters continuing education in several ways. First, it has a liberal educational assistance program. Employees are encouraged to continue their educations. After earning a "pass" or a "C" grade, employees are reimbursed for 75 percent of their tuition and book expenses. Second, IMM trains extensively in house. Technical courses are available three weeks out of every month, with team-building instruction available one week out of each month. Finally, IMM's small, in-house training group, referred to as the "Ingersoll Institute," has recently adopted a "Department Trainer" concept for technical and team-building training. An individual from each department is selected as the Department Trainer and receives in-depth instruction on the subject matter and how best to impart it to his or her group. For example, in 1993, IMM began selecting its managers as Department Trainers in team building, imparting to them all of the skills and knowledge necessary for the team to adopt this approach.

[13]Interview with Margaret Smith, Manager of Organization Development and Training at IMM.

Future Outlook

Continuing profitability in the face of a limited market is the major challenge IMM faces. It is facing growing pressure from the Japanese in the production of flexible transfer lines but continues to invest heavily in new products to maintain its strong position in this market.

H. R. Krueger Machine Tool, Inc.

Company Overview

The H. R. Krueger Machine Tool, Inc. (HRK) is a Farmington, Michigan-based manufacturer of automated manufacturing equipment for the production of high-volume, precision-machined parts. The present management of HRK assumed control in 1971. Over 99 percent of its capital stock is owned by its officers. In 1975, HRK acquired Elcon Systems Inc., a maker of industrial process-measurement controllers, such as test stands, calibration, gauging, and measuring systems.[14]

HRK manufactures medium-sized and small special machine tools, the average weighing about 60,000 pounds. Machine types include in-line transfer, dial index, rotary transfer, and custom drilling and tapping machines. Krueger produces 20 to 30 units per year, depending on the market and the machinery most in demand. On average, machine tools make up approximately 70 percent of its business, with the remainder coming from Elcon.[15] HRK employs 80 people at its 38,000-ft^2 Farmington facility.

HRK sells machine tools to the automobile and farm equipment industries in the United States, Canada, and Mexico. Elcon has some international sales. Table E.2 documents HRK's recent financial performance, showing a near doubling of sales and tripling of profits from 1990 to 1992.

Marketing Strategy

HRK's strength is in the development and production of machines to manufacture camshafts, crankshafts, oil pumps, water pumps, alternator housings, and other parts "you can hold in two hands," according to Moore. HRK has been a long-time supplier of U.S. auto manufacturers, as well as of

---

[14]Thus, HRK is often listed under two SIC codes: 3541, machine tools, metal cutting types, and 3823, process control instruments.

[15]Interview with Bruce Moore, HRK President and CEO.

Table E.2

H. R. Krueger Financial Information (in dollars)

	FY 1990	FY 1991	FY 1992
Sales	10,371,492	11,914,942	19,411,449
Net profit (loss)	464,956	1,142,549	1,328,720

SOURCE: Dun & Bradstreet (1992).

NOTES: Sales for the three months ended March 31, 1993, were $6,500,000. The fiscal year ends September 30.

Caterpillar and John Deere. Its main competitors are Kingsbury, Cargill Detroit, R&B Machine, and Grobe.

HRK's marketing strategy is based on its perceived strengths in manufacturing. Producing a new machine generally breaks down into two very different periods. The job begins with a long engineering cycle, characterized by close collaboration with the customer. This is followed by an intense build cycle. Like other players in the transfer machine business, such as Lamb, Ingersoll, and Giddings & Lewis, HRK designs and builds its machines using semistandard modules. Anywhere from 30 to 40 percent of each machine is based on these modular building blocks, with the rest customized according to individual customer needs. Because many of these modules can be manufactured and put on the shelf, HRK can respond quickly to customer demands. Component manufacturing helps even out the production cycle, an important factor in this business. Production time for these modules is around 2 weeks, as compared to 20 weeks for new tooling.

HRK had used this approach, which it calls "Production Centers," for some time. In the early 1980s, however, its technology could not meet all of the demands of the market, accuracy being the major concern. In 1985, HRK's engineers began developing its new machines starting with "a blank sheet of paper and questions for their customers about what they wanted in their future machining systems."[16] This led to the development of "a range of standardized machine-tool components that are faster, more accurate and more reliable than anything we've built before . . . the key advantage of the machine, we believe, will be precision and ready adaptability to production of a broad range of parts."[17] Production centers fall between traditional dedicated specials and "flexible" systems incorporating full CNC capabilities. According to HRK's Marketing Vice President, Dave Williams, "production centers deliver the advantages of

[16]Bruce Moore, quoted in Wrigley (1989). "Krueger Sells Machine-Cutting Units for Ford Auto Alternator Housings" (1989), p. 26.

[17]Ibid.

programmability without the cost and complexity of CNC. . . . On the average, we estimate an additional 10 to 15 percent invested in production centers will yield up to a 30-percent return based on increased production, precision, and the family-of-parts processing abilities."

These machines were designed with part changes in mind. According to HRK tooling engineer Bruce Chapin: "They can be programmed on the floor with a portable terminal on a station-by-station basis, from the central control console through the system's dedicated control computer, or off-line on a personal computer and then transferred to the machine via floppy disk."[18] With the programming complete, manufacturing different part configurations simply requires selecting the part number on the master control console. The machine automatically reconfigures itself to the machining requirements for the desired part.

Typical of the close working relationships required for success in the transfer machine business, HRK worked with users to validate these machines in the line of fire. In collaboration with Ford's Rawsonville division, HRK conducted extensive testing of the units in the plant. "The concept works," said Williams, "because we've done extensive prototype testing, including running the units under full load at a six-second cycle time for 1.5 million cycles. The units then met all the quality criteria we had established for the production center line. . . . We also have a production center prototype working at a beta test site for more than two years machining transmission parts. We're extremely pleased with the test results, which have been fully confirmed by the first production machines."

A good example of the "concurrent engineering" approaches employed in this market is the way that the tools and fixtures were tested. The actual tools and fixtures for the machines were tested and proven on a prototype unit at the Rawsonville plant while the machines were being built. "This substantially reduced the time required to get the machine ready for production qualifications," Williams said (Wrigley, 1989).

Moore feels collaborative product development is much more effective. It allows HRK to consider design-for-manufacturing principles, reducing its cost of manufacture, as well as reducing machine costs and the costs for end users to produce parts. About 30 percent of Moore's orders fall into this category, with the other 70 percent of his customers approaching HRK with fixed designs.[19]

---

[18]Bruce Chapin, HRK tooling engineer in "Toolholders Enhance Flexible Machines," *Tooling and Production*, Vol. 56, No. 10, January 1991, p. 67(2).

[19]Interview with Bruce Moore.

Currently, HRK focuses mainly on the North American market. However, in the 1950s and 1960s, HRK was a big exporter to Europe. European companies were expanding their manufacturing operations, and U.S. transfer machines were the best in the world. HRK had a European representative and could compete quite well. In the early 1960s, the market began to change. According to Williams, the European firms improved their technology, and import duties began to be levied on U.S. machine tools. In response, HRK licensed their technology to Thomas Ryder and Son, an English machine-tool firm. In the years that followed, HRK landed "most of the business they wanted," according to Williams, and the relationship with Ryder continued successfully until the early 1980s. At that time, Ryder was bought out by Gulf & Western. (The business was closed within a few years.) During this same period, many large transfer machine builders, such as Ingersoll and Lamb, were investing quite heavily in Europe. Furthermore, the European suppliers continued to improve. As a result, HRK found the European transfer machine market too "saturated" to compete effectively. So, while others looked to Europe for sales growth, Williams says HRK headed "south of the border," where the company has been successful in the Mexican market for transfer machines. In Europe, it competes with European firms and U.S. subsidiaries that have the home-court advantage of having facilities close to their customers. In Mexico, HRK is on an equal footing with European and Japanese firms.

HRK is also looking at other markets, with some assistance from AMT. Williams views AMT as a "specialist" that you "don't call until you need help." AMT provides services addressing the needs of the whole industry, of which HRK is one small part. Thus, HRK tries to be focused when accessing their services. To HRK, AMT is most helpful with marketing and economic issues. With the collapse of the former Soviet Union, HRK believes that a large market for machine tools has opened up to the West. In addition to its own initiatives, HRK is working with AMT to determine how best to enter the Russian machine-tool market. HRK feels it needs this assistance, because Germany is physically closer to Russia, a major consideration in transfer machine purchases, with the added difficulty that Germany may offer loans to Russia targeted for the purchase of German machine tools. HRK is also working with AMT on exports to China.

Technology Strategy

On the manufacturing floor, HRK uses a mix of CNC and manual equipment, currently about 60 percent CNC and 40 percent manual. This places them in the top 10 percent of similar machine builders, based on a recent benchmarking study of such firms.[20] HRK recently installed an advanced Swiss-built CNC precision boring machine. This equipment gives HRK the capability to completely machine all major components of its machine tools.[21] Moore says that this machine was bought more on "philosophy" than on a specific requirement. HRK felt that the use of this equipment would set a quality standard for its suppliers to follow. HRK also recently acquired a 10,000-ft^2 office building adjacent to its facilities and will use it to house a technical center and office and engineering space.

Like many small firms, HRK does not have many resources to dedicate to R&D but it feels it "can't afford not to," according to Williams. HRK's technology is one of its main competitive advantages, something it takes great pride in. However, Williams believes that trying to maintain this edge while building products is a financial burden that can also cause burnout in some of his best people. They try to do "as much as we can afford."[22]

HRK uses the patent system to help protect its market advantage. For example, they recently patented a process calibrating their production center index tables. "Using this process," Moore said, "we can obtain positioning repeatability of plus-or-minus 0.0008 inch on an 85-inch-diameter table. We use a laser alignment system to generate statistical process control data on the table's positioning capabilities, which is then used to adjust the AC servo drive system."[23]

HRK uses selected federal and state technical assistance programs to as great an extent as possible. HRK was the first firm assessed by the Michigan Modernization Service, a state-sponsored manufacturing extension service. Several years later, HRK was the first firm assessed by the Midwest Manufacturing Technology Center, one of seven manufacturing technology assistance organizations funded by the National Institute of Standards and Technology (NIST). However, for a firm like HRK, you "run out of the ability to access support programs," according to Williams. Conversely, HRK has not attempted to access federal and state programs to support R&D because, according to Williams, "we don't want our innovations to become common knowledge."[24]

---

[20]NIST/Midwest Manufacturing Center (1993). These results are based on an N=34.

[21]"H. R. Krueger Machine Tool, Inc." (1991), p. 20.

[22]Williams was unaware of the Advanced Technology Program but appeared interested once informed of the program.

[23]Moore in Wrigley (1989).

[24]Interview with Williams.

Access to Capital

Like many small manufacturing firms, HRK uses short-term bank loans, secured by accounts receivable, inventory, and equipment for operating support. Moore echoed the sentiments of many small firms that most banks do not understand manufacturing well enough to readily provide financial support in a timely fashion. If a firm's usual banker leaves his institution, it could eventually cause that firm to go under, according to Moore. Most banks are reluctant to lend money on the specialized work-in-process inventory typical of transfer machine builders. Moore considers HRK lucky to have a special relationship with a local bank. The bank has agreed not to change personnel on his account who are familiar with machine tools and particularly with the transfer machine business. HRK's part of this bargain is that the bank has access to HRK's computerized cost system so that it can stay apprised of the current status of machine orders.

Human Resource Policies

Until the last 15 years or so, HRK was typical of most machine-tool firms, and having a graduate engineer on the staff was an unusual occurrence. Since that time, however, HRK has evolved from "smokestack to high tech," according to Moore. As the technology level goes up, HRK's "ability to attract good minds goes up."[25] Overall, approximately 75 percent of HRK engineers are college graduates, with a higher percentage in the Elcon operation. In machine tools, most are mechanical engineers; in Elcon, electrical engineering degrees are more typical.

"HRK is too small to have a training department," says Moore. Common training for HRK employees includes:

- One-on-one instruction in the plant
- Vendor training on specific equipment
- Training in reliability and maintainability
- Training in quality tools and techniques.

Major Challenges Ahead

The biggest challenge facing HRK and its customers is, according to Moore, "living in a world economy." GM already competes worldwide, and he believes Ford and Chrysler want to improve their ability to be "world players." This will

[25]Interview with Moore.

place added pressure on HRK to match foreign rivals. HRK will compete by continuing the changes of the last 15 years. It plans to improve its production capabilities continuously, to upgrade its staff continuously, and then to translate these human and capital resources into new, world competitive products.

When asked about HRK's competitors, Williams stated that its main competitor is the "changing nature of the market." He believes that the days of the transfer line "may be numbered." In the past, end users felt they could justify the large expenditures on dedicated equipment. In the new math of international competitiveness, traditional transfer machines are now seen as too expensive and too inflexible. Based on his recent trip to Japan, Williams believes that the Japanese are not much further ahead in solving this dilemma. This gives HRK and its U.S. counterparts a window of opportunity to develop technologies that can meet the needs of the high-volume, high-precision machining market of the 1990s and beyond.

Conclusion

Unlike other segments of the machine-tool market, transfer machine builders have been able to hold on to a lion's share of the domestic market and to make some gains abroad. Like other machine-tool firms, IMM and HRK began as family-owned firms. Unlike them, they remain closely held today. This fact provides patient capital that is an advantage in a competitive, cyclical business. IMM and HRK have also been able to maintain a close, ongoing relationship with their major customers, a factor important to success in many businesses and vital in transfer machines. Both firms understand the importance of having a highly skilled, highly motivated workforce. HRK's workforce has evolved over the years to where a majority of employees are degreed engineers. IMM has a lower percentage of degreed engineers, but uses innovative human resource policies and practices to keep its staff motivated and up-to-date.

Participating increasingly in a worldwide market, all transfer machine builders face stiff competition. As noted by HRK's Dave Williams, the greatest competition may be not from another firm, but from the changing nature of the high-volume, high-precision manufacturing equipment market. Demand for cheaper, more flexible equipment may be the impetus for change in the 1990s and beyond.

References

"Dainichi Kinzoku Kogyo to Market Ingersoll Machine Tools in Japan," *COMLINE: Industrial Automation Industry of Japan*, September 25, 1992.

"H. R. Krueger Machine Tool Inc.," *Crain's Detroit Business*, September 29, 1991, p. 20.

"Krueger Sells Machine-Cutting Units for Ford Auto Alternator Housings," *Metalworking News*, Vol. 16, No. 733, May 1, 1989, p. 26.

Association for Manufacturing Technology, *Economic Handbook of the Machine Tool Industry: 1990-1991*, McLean, Va., 1990.

Brooks, Rosanne, "France Blocking Tool Imports," *American Metal Market*, Vol. 91, July 18, 1983, p. 1.

Brooks, Rosanne, "Ingersoll Milling Leaves NMTBA; import dispute," *American Metal Market*, Vol. 92, March 19, 1984, p. 5.

Brooks, Rosanne, "Trade Panel Decision on Brazilian Tillage Discs Aids U.S. Producers," *American Metal Market*, Vol. 93, October 7, 1985, p. 5.

Chapin, Bruce, "Toolholders Enhance Flexible Machines," *Tooling and Production*, Vol. 56, No. 10, January 1991, p. 67.

Donahue, Christine, "Winning the Hard Way," *Forbes*, Vol. 133, June 4, 1984, p. 208.

Dun & Bradstreet, report, September 30, 1992.

Giesen, Lauri, "Hitachi Has Ordered $4.5M Ingersoll Machine Center; May Be World's Largest," *American Metal Market*, Vol. 93, November 18, 1985a, p. 5.

Giesen, Lauri, "Ingersoll Buys Adolf Waldrich Tool Company," *American Metal Market*, Vol. 93, December 16, 1985b, p. 1.

Giesen, Lauri, "Ingersoll, Boeing Goal: Advanced Profiler System," *Metalworking News*, Vol. 14, May 11, 1987, p. 8.

Giesen, Lauri, "Ingersoll Prepares Management Plan; End of Family Ownership Seen as Probability," *Metalworking News*, Vol. 15, No. 695, August 8, 1988, p. 6.

Harvey, Robert E., "ATP, Ingersoll, Boeing, Chrysler Form Software Development Association," *Metalworking News*, Vol. 15, No. 708, November 7, 1988, p. 5.

Kramer, David, "Ingersoll's $20M, In-House FMS Is Aimed at One-Part Production Runs," *American Metal Market*, Vol. 92, May 21, 1984, p. 7.

NIST/Midwest Manufacturing Technology Center, "Machine-Building Performance Benchmarking Panel," May 1993.

Quinlan, Joseph C., "Beyond CIM—What?" *Tooling and Production*, Vol. 54, No. 10, January 1989, p. 34.

Society of Manufacturing Engineers, *Tool & Manufacturing Engineers Handbook*: Vol. 1, Dearborn, Mich., 1983, pp. 15-81.

Sterner, Bob, "P&W Files Lawsuit Against Ingersoll in Patent Dispute," *Metalworking News*, Vol. 16, No. 759, November 6, 1989, p. 4.

Vasilash, Gary S., "Impressions of Ingersoll," *Production*, Vol. 101, No. 2, February 1989, p. 40.

Weimer, George, "The Can-Do Country (American Manufacturing)," *Production Engineering*, Vol. 34, June 1987, p. 7.

Wrigley, Al, "Ford of Europe Orders System from Ingersoll," *American Metal Market*, Vol. 92, March 26, 1984, p. 1.

Wrigley, Al, "Ingersoll Beefs up Detroit Engineering; Seeks to Bolster Its Auto-Industry Savvy," *Metalworking News*, Vol. 15, No. 676, March 28, 1988, p. 6.

Wrigley, Al, "Ingersoll Milling Gets Engineering Contract for F4," *Metalworking News*, Vol. 16, No. 753, September 25, 1989, p. 1.

Wrigley, Al, "U.S. Automakers Make Long-Term Suppliers Pacts; B-O-C Open-Ended Agreements Signed with Lamb, Ingersoll," *Metalworking News*, Vol. 17, No. 769, January 22, 1990, p. 1.

Appendix F
Detailed Technology Ratings and Cases

Kimberly Lebrane and Prof. Galip Ulsoy, University of Michigan

Introduction

We live in an era of rapid technological change, and the U.S. machine-tool industry is no exception. After decades of relative stability, technological change was an important factor in the decline of the U.S. machine-tool industry in the 1980s. However, new technology in and of itself is not the problem. In most of the "key" technologies that we will discuss in the next section, the United States remains the world leader, or is at least competitive, in research and development. It is in technology deployment, or commercialization, that the United States lags behind its foreign competitors (e.g., Japan and Germany). All too often in the past, the United States has been the first to discover, develop, and at times commercialize a new technology (e.g., lasers, computer numerical control [CNC], robots, flexible machining systems [FMS]), only to relinquish its market leadership position to foreign competition.

Figure F.1 illustrates several important issues related to the role of technology in the machine-tool industry. In the example, the productivity of a $300,000 machine tool is increased by 10 percent by making a $30,000 investment in improved control technology. This investment in turn leads to an increase of 10 percent, or $3,000,000, in the value of parts produced by the machine during its lifetime. The example is intended to illustrate a main characteristic of the machine-tool industry: Investments in improved machine-tool technology have the potential to provide significant returns on investment for the users of these machines. Although the machine-tool industry is small in terms of total sales, leadership in machine-tool technology can have significant economic effects for the users of the machine tools (and consequently for the national economy). This fact and the importance of the machine-tool industry for national defense are the reasons the machine-tool industry has been identified as a critical technology in several recent studies (National Research Council, 1990; U.S. Dept. of Defense, 1990).

The purpose of this appendix is to explore the current status and trends of key technologies that may have a substantial impact on the future of the machine-tool

RAND MR479/2-F.1a

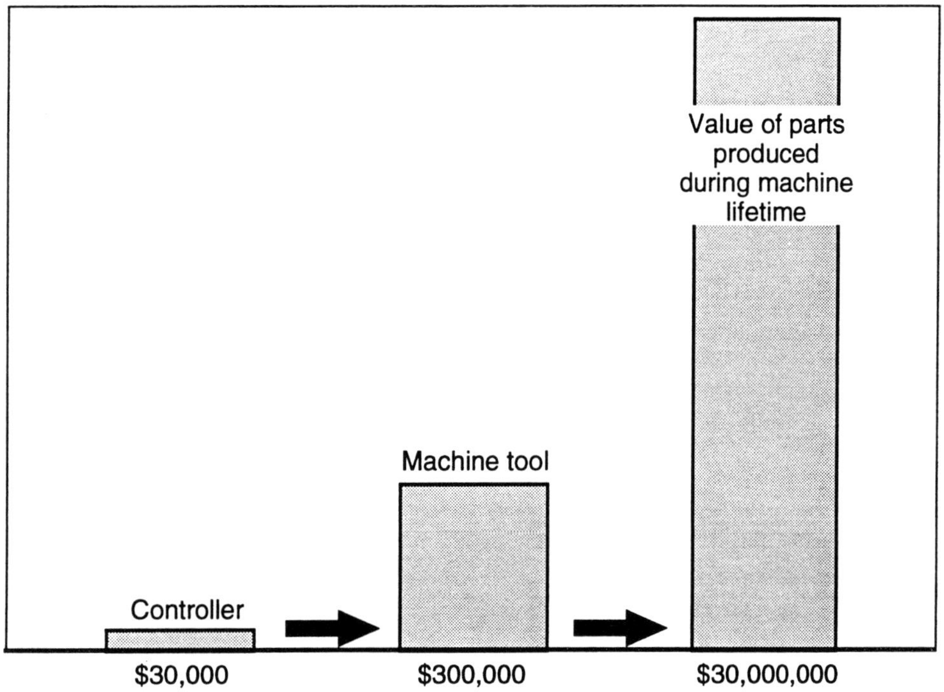

Figure F.1—Importance of Technology in Machine Tools

industry. It also includes a comparison of these "key" technologies among the United States, Japan, and Germany. The next section is a summary of the status and trends in selected "key" technologies; these are each described in more detail in the Annex. The final section provides a summary, discussion, and observations.

Technology Status and Trends

This section summarizes the material in the annex to this appendix. The annex covers 23 individual areas that we determined to be key technologies in the sense that they have the potential to lead to significant changes in the machine-tool industry.

The selections were based upon our operating definition, a preliminary review of the literature (including both trade publications and academic studies), and extensive consultations with experts in industry and academia. The chosen technologies include areas and topics that are new or have scopes broader than the machine-tool industry alone.

Operating Definition

For the purposes of this study, we have broadly defined the term *machine tools* to include metal cutting, metal forming, and joining machines, as well as new processes that might replace them. We have also included the measurement systems, sensors, computers, controllers, tooling, fixtures, and other components that are an integral part of machine-tool systems.

Specifically included in this operational definition are the following Standard Industrial Classification (SIC) codes in the following three general categories:

- Machine Tools

  3541: Metal Cutting Types
  3542: Metal Forming Types
  3549: Metalworking Machinery
  3548: Welding/Soldering Tools
  3699: Laser Cutting Tools

- Machine Tool Components and Accessories

  3544: Special Dies and Tools, Die Sets, Jigs and Fixtures and Industrial Molds

  3545: Cutting Tools, Machine Tool Accessories, and Machinists' Precision Measuring Devices

- Sensors and Controls

  3625: Relays and Industrial Controls
  3823: Industrial Instruments for Measurement, Display, and Control of Process Variables

Our operational definition includes the following specific processes:

- Traditional Machining Processes
  - Turning
  - Boring
  - Trepanning
  - Planing
  - Shaping and slotting
  - Broaching
  - Drilling
  - Reaming
  - Countersinking, counterboring, and spotfacing
  - Roller burnishing

- Tapping
- Thread milling
- Thread grinding
- Thread rolling
- Die threading
- Milling
- Gear manufacture
- Sawing
- Multiple-operation machining
- Automatic lathes
  - Machining centers
  - Transfer machines
- Flexible manufacturing systems
- Proper fixturing
- Tool condition monitoring systems

- Grinding, Honing, and Lapping
  - Superabrasives
  - Honing
  - Lapping
- Nontraditional Machining Processes
  - Abrasive jet machining
  - Abrasive flow machining
  - Waterjet/abrasive waterjet machining
  - Ultrasonic machining
  - Electrochemical machining
  - Electrochemical grinding
  - Electrochemical discharge grinding
  - Electrostream and capillary drilling
  - Shaped tube electrolytic machining
  - Electrical discharge machining
  - Electrical discharge grinding
  - Electron beam machining
  - Laser beam machining
  - Thermal energy method
  - Chemical milling
  - Photochemical machining
- High-Productivity Machining
  - High-speed machining
  - High removal rate machining

- Machine Controls and Computer Applications in Machining
  - Numerical control
  - Adaptive control
  - CAD, CAM, and CIM

Key Technology Areas

In this subsection we summarize the current status and future trends in the selected key technology areas. The material in the annex provides a list of these key technologies as organized by SIC codes, as well as short summaries of the 23 individual key technology areas.

Metal-Cutting Machines. Metal cutting is not a new industry; it has been around for centuries. The traditional methods of metal cutting (e.g., turning, milling, grinding) have changed very little over the past decades (e.g., Figures F.2 and F.3). The trends in these areas, spawned by the added capabilities of numerical control (NC) and CNC machines, are toward higher speed and greater precision. New machine configurations, such as a rotary mill or a combination milling-turning machine able to machine more complex geometries, are also being investigated. For example, the Ingersoll Milling Machine Company has developed a radical new machine-tool structure and concept that minimizes geometric and thermal errors and that relies on advances in computer and control technology to handle increased complexity in those areas.[1]

The increased usage of nonmetallic materials (e.g., plastics, composites, ceramics), particularly in the aerospace and automotive industries, has spurred the growth of nontraditional machining processes such as electrical-discharge machining (EDM) and water jet (or abrasive water jet) cutting. Although these technologies currently lack the necessary throughput to replace traditional metal-cutting methods, their impact on the industry will continue to increase. The United States is currently competitive in both of these new technologies. However, Japan is already pulling ahead of the United States in the commercialization of EDM. The keynote speaker at a 1991 conference on EDM observed that U.S. machine shops have a tendency to consider EDM last (after milling, turning, and grinding) and that this attitude has caused U.S. EDM usage to lag behind Japan where "EDM is replacing milling and grinding the fastest."[2]

---

[1]Personal communication, Dennis Bray, Vice President for Technology, Ingersoll Milling Machine Company.

[2]Hermann Rempfler of Letra SA (Asconsa, Switzerland), keynote speaker at the Modern Machine Shop EDM '91 conference (Cincinnati), as quoted in *American Machinist*, December 1991.

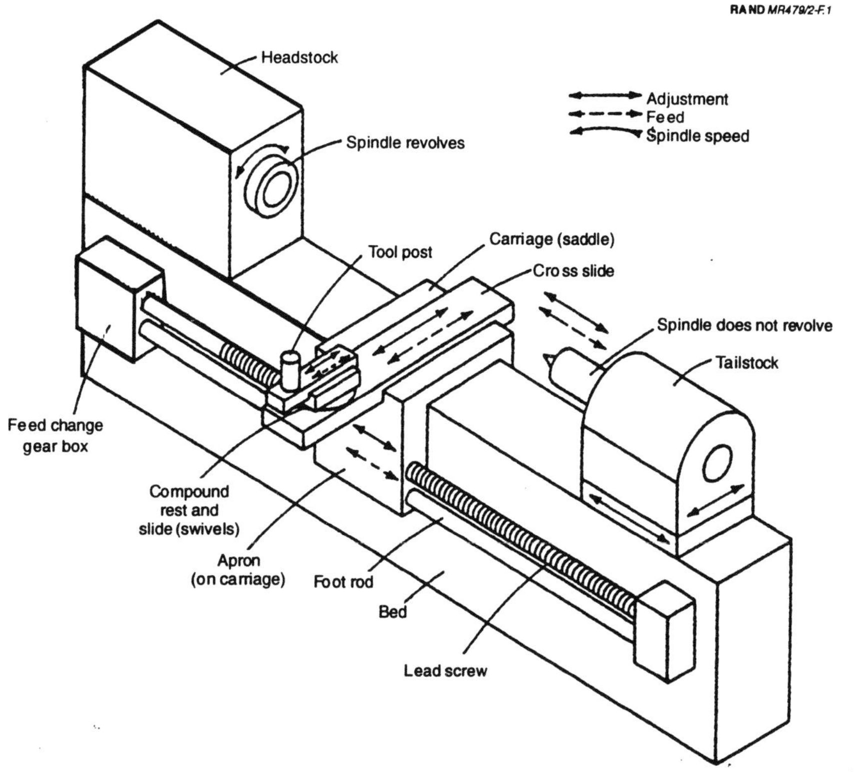

Figure F.2—Principal Components and Movements of a Lathe

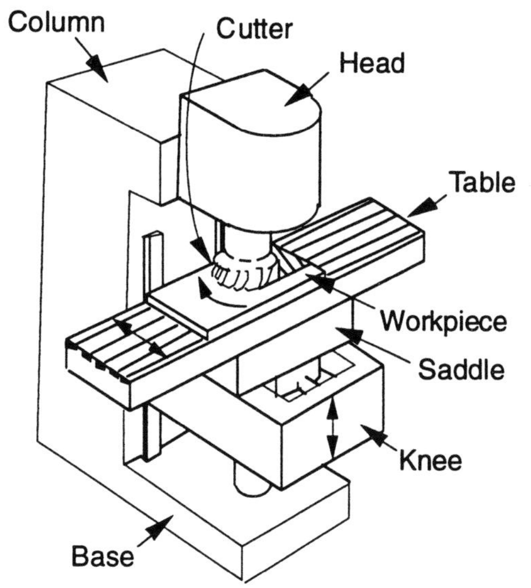

Figure F.3—A Vertical-Spindle Knee-and-Column Milling Machine

Another industry expert predicts that "many of the latest technical developments are very likely to come from the EDM equipment builders in Japan."[3]

Metal Forming Types. Metal forming is another technology that has been around in basically its current form for centuries. The main trend in this area is toward eliminating as much secondary machining as possible by forming materials to near-final shape through the use of powders and improved formability materials. Efforts are also being made to adapt processes that have been successful on other materials (e.g., injection molding of plastics) to the metal industry.

A new type of forming, layered manufacturing (also known as rapid prototyping or solid freeform fabrication), is causing quite a stir in the industry. Quips one expert, "Rapid prototyping technology is so new that a standard name to describe it has yet to appear."[4] Currently, the process allows a manufacturer to create prototype parts directly from a three-dimensional drawing of a CAD part (see Figure F.4).

RAND *MR479/2-F.3*

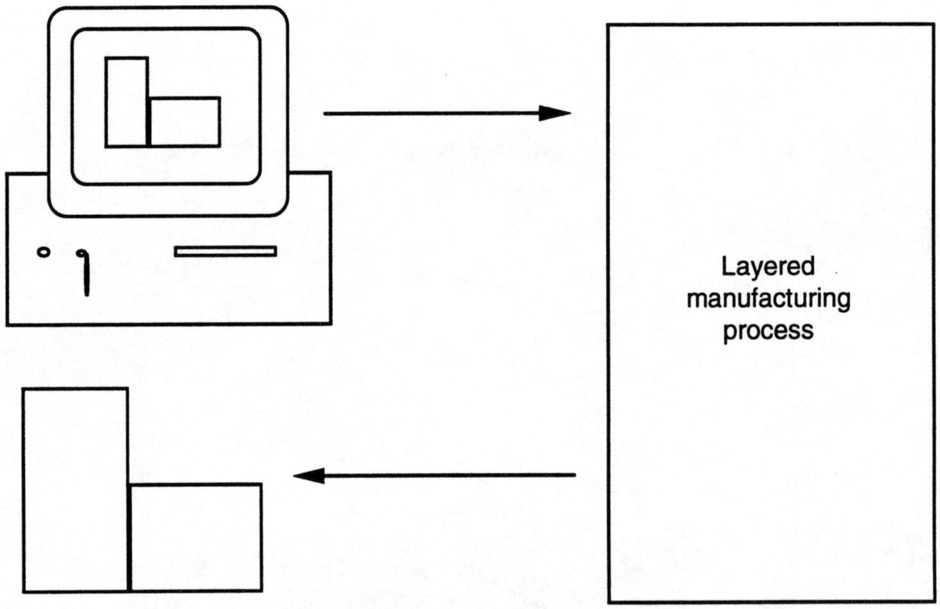

Figure F.4—Layered Manufacturing Processes Are Like Three-Dimensional Printers, Producing a Physical Part from an Electronic Description of Its Geometry

---

[3]Mark Alpert, Executive Editor of *Modern Machine Shop*.

[4]Terry Wohlers, President, Wohlers Associates (Fort Collins, Colorado).

Industry experts predict that if this process can be upgraded to produce parts with strengths suitable for production, as opposed to prototyping, it would revolutionize the machine-tool industry. Several competing processes are currently under development for possible commercialization. The United States is currently the world leader in this technology; it is of critical importance that it remain so.

Other Metal Working Machinery. The dominant trend in the area of transfer line and special-purpose equipment is the search for greater flexibility. Remaining competitive in manufacturing requires the ability to respond quickly to fluctuating market demands. Typical current production volumes in the automotive industry, for example, are around 500,000 per year, but these are expected to be reduced tenfold in the coming decade. As a result, even makers of the most historically dedicated machinery, such as transfer lines (Figure F.5), are jumping on the flexibility bandwagon through the use of modular tooling and fixturing. The major developments in the area have been the advent of flexible manufacturing cells that unite several CNC machining centers and flexible manufacturing systems that tie together discrete cells. The key issue is achievement of flexibility without undue penalties in terms of quality, production rates, and investment cost (Nagel and Dove, 1991). Because of differences between the U.S. market and the Japanese and German domestic

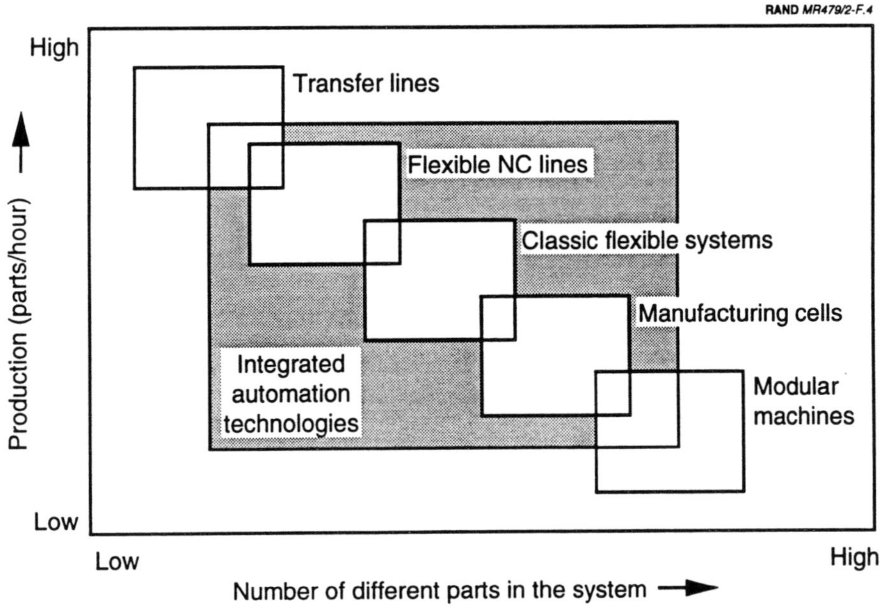

Figure F.5—Relationship Between Transfer Lines, Flexible Manufacturing Cells, and Flexible Manufacturing Systems

markets in the automotive area, the United States is about 5 to 10 years behind in flexible transfer line technologies. This is despite the fact that U.S. manufacturers are among the world leaders in dedicated transfer line technology. It is imperative that the United States strengthen its position in the area of flexible transfer line technologies.

Laser Cutting Tools. Laser cutting is another nontraditional machining area that is growing in importance as its commercially viable applications expand. Lasers are now used widely in cutting, heat treatment, and welding. Like CNC and so many other technologies, laser technology originated in the United States, but laser processing is now dominated by foreign firms, mainly in Germany and Japan. The impact of this loss will continue to be felt as the applications for laser technology continue to expand in such areas as welding and heat treatment. This is an area where investments in applied research have been very effective. The laser was invented, developed, and commercialized in the United States, which still has some strong university research programs in laser processing technology.[5] However, Germany (mainly through its Fraunhofer institutes) has been much more effective than the United States in facilitating commercialization of this technology.

Special Dies and Tools, Die Sets, Jigs and Fixtures, and Cutting Fluids. Jigs and fixtures are another area where the key trend is toward flexibility. There is growing use of flexible and modular fixturing and automated transfer systems, such as pallets and rail-guided vehicles, to help reduce machine downtime.

Cutting fluids, which are essential to effective performance of machining operations, pose a different technological challenge for the industry. Rigorous government hazardous-waste regulation, combined with pressure from environmentalists, has spurred the search for a "universal" cutting fluid that can be used in a variety of applications and is easily recycled. Traditionally a world leader in environmental technologies, such as energy consumption and waste recycling, the United States is losing ground to Germany and Japan. Japan has taken a lead in this area of environmentally-sound cutting fluids. German companies have made considerable progress in designing products for recycling and for other environmentally sound approaches to manufacturing. As "environmental consciousness" grows, these and other concerns are expected to play a greater role in the future of the machine-tool industry as well as other manufacturing industries.

---

[5]Personal communications with Professors J. Mazumder (University of Illinois) and Professor E. Kannatey-Asibu (University of Michigan).

Cutting Tools, Machine-Tool Accessories, and Machinists' Measuring Devices. Cutting tools (e.g., drills, milling cutters, turning inserts) are key elements of any machine tool. Important issues are tool wear and breakage, chip formation, and performance at high cutting speeds. There have been many incremental developments in cutting tool technology, most notably the advent of cermet (ceramic-metal matrix) inserts and diamond coatings. Advances in these technologies serve primarily to decrease tool wear and allow higher cutting speeds and better surface finish.

Accurate measurement is considered a key issue in the industry, as seen in the growing use of coordinate measurement machines (CMMs) for quality control. The trend toward higher precision has caused an industry-wide push to "close the information loop" by producing CMMs that are robust enough to withstand the rigors of shop-floor use. Additional efforts are being made to integrate the measurement devices into the actual machine tool for true in-process gauging (see Figure F.6). The United States and Germany are leaders in this area of technology, which is expected to grow in commercial significance over the next decade. Recent studies indicate that technology and industry leaders see in-process measurement and control as a key technology area for the future of the machine-tool industry (Machine Tool Task Force, 1980; Ulsoy and Koren, 1993).

Relays and Industrial Controls. The need for flexibility led the shift from dedicated machinery to increased use of CNC machining centers. Although the United States originated CNC technology and remains among the leaders in CNC research and development, a Japanese firm (FANUC) currently dominates this market. The U.S. firms that pioneered the technology have either dropped out of the market altogether or reduced their shares to a minor level.

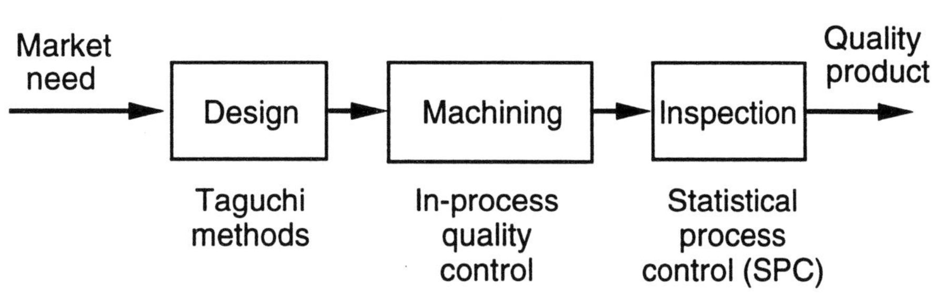

Figure F.6—Quality Control Involves Quality Assurance at the Design and Inspection Stages and in Process

This is a loss that may be felt more acutely as the trend toward computer integrated manufacturing (CIM) increases. CIM is a marriage of control (e.g., CNC), information, communication, and measurement (e.g., CMM) technologies and lacks only a highly intelligent control and communications capability for integrating machine tools, sensors, computer hardware, and software into a continuously upgradeable machining system (Ashley, 1990). FANUC's market dominance in CNC makes it well positioned to fulfill this need.

Although a great deal of research effort is being focused on standardization of open-architecture computer control systems in the United States, it appears that Europe (Germany) is leading in this area. Some machine-tool suppliers are now providing their own personal-computer–based CNC systems. However, this trend will only have significant commercial impact if accompanied by standardization. Under the leadership of the U.S. Air Force, significant efforts were undertaken to standardize open-architecture computer-control systems. Such efforts currently continue under leadership of the National Center for Manufacturing Science (NCMS), which is an industry-led technology development organization (NCMS, 1990). However, the efforts to date have not been very effective (see Appendix D). While users will clearly benefit from standardized open-architecture systems, controller vendors are concerned about sharing their proprietary software with competitors.

Information management technologies also play an important role in this area. Expert systems allow the average worker access to extensive knowledge bases, promote more informed decisionmaking, and aid troubleshooting. Among the artificial intelligence (AI) technologies, expert systems, fuzzy logic, and neural networks are likely to find widespread application in future machine-tool control systems. Fuzzy logic systems, which have found widespread use in Japanese-made consumer products, are yet another example of a technology that originated in the United States that has been most effectively commercialized by Japanese companies.[6] Fuzzy logic systems have recently begun to appear in Japanese-made machine tools.

Electronic data interchange (EDI) offers a wealth of opportunities for improved communication between machine-tool makers, users, and suppliers, providing a means to reduce product cycle time drastically. The United States leads in this research and in the creation of a national information infrastructure to link firms, but lags behind Japan and Europe in standardization of data exchange protocols

[6]The inventor of fuzzy logic, L. Zadeh, found little interest in his work in the United States but became a widely sought after and highly regarded speaker in Japan during the 1970s and 1980s. Zadeh and fuzzy logic are now being "rediscovered" in the United States. It is interesting to note that this is reminiscent of Deming.

and software for manufacturing environments. The lack of U.S. standards in this area impedes the utilization of EDI to its fullest capacity. This is an important area for not only the machine-tool industry but for manufacturing as a whole. While this technology is receiving some attention from government funding agencies, it is important that the machine-tool companies not be left out, simply because they are small, as this technology is developed.

Industrial Instruments for Measurement, Display, and Control of Process Variables. The new vision in manufacturing is that of automation that can work in harmony with and enhance the skills of the human operator. This is in contrast to the goal of unmanned factories from only a decade ago. Consequently, technologies at the man-machine interface are becoming increasingly important. Work is being done in this area to improve the interface between the operator and the machine tool through the use of touch screens and flat panel display technology. The key focus in this area of development is to make these technologies robust enough to operate in a factory environment. Japan is the world leader in commercialization in this area, which is important for many industries, including machine tools. Several recent industry-government efforts have been launched to help U.S. companies compete in this important market, which certainly has implications beyond the machine-tool industry. Broader technology development efforts, for example virtual reality and holographic displays, may also prove useful in the machine-tool industry and in the training of machine operators.

Concluding Remarks

In summary, we have considered traditional (e.g., turning, milling, grinding) and nontraditional (e.g., EDM, water jet, lasers) machine-tool technologies, as well as new technologies (e.g., layered manufacturing, net shape manufacturing) that may (to some extent) replace machine tools. Currently, most of the commercial gains in both traditional and nontraditional machining areas have been through *process* rather than *product* innovation, with the majority of technical improvements resulting from incremental changes. The key trends in the process area have been flexibility, speed, precision, integration, and robustness, with flexibility being the most critical. It is not surprising, but still important, to note that Japanese and German companies have been more effective in continually improving processes than U.S. companies (e.g., laser processing, EDM). In contrast, the majority of the product innovations have traditionally been, and continue to be, generated by U.S. labs or companies. The radical new machine-tool designs and the layered and net-shape manufacturing processes are areas in which the United States has technological leadership. Although the market for these nontraditional machines is expanding, these technologies are still more than a decade away from seriously competing with traditional machines for all but the most specialized applications.

A look at the ages of the various key technologies selected for study reveals that machine-tool technology is indeed changing rapidly (see Table F.1). Many of the technologies in commercial use today did not even exist 10 to 20 years ago. It can be expected that the high pace of technological change of the past decades will continue, and even accelerate, in coming decades. It is encouraging that the United States leads, or at least is competitive, in essentially all areas of technology in terms of research. Proper utilization of the fruits of that research could yield important advantages for the U.S. machine-tool industry in the coming years of rapid technological change.

Although all the technologies we have discussed are considered to be potentially important for the machine-tool industry, several have been further denoted as critical in Table F.1. This designation is based upon the opinion of the authors and experts interviewed about which technologies may have the most significant economic impacts on the machine-tool industry. A comparison of the technology areas shows that, in many of the more mature technologies, the United States has relinquished market control in several critical areas (e.g., EDM, FMS, flexible lines, lasers, AI, CIM, and CNC). There are other technologies in which the United States is on the verge of falling behind its foreign competition (e.g., high-speed machining, precision machining, CMMs, EDI, and micromachines). This does not bode well for the future of the industry. It is imperative that the United States remain competitive in these key technologies, particularly those denoted as critical.[7]

The United States, however, remains a leader or is at least competitive in most areas of current research relevant to the machine-tool industry. Thus, technology research and development is not currently the most important issue. However, technology commercialization is a serious concern. The reasons the United States lags behind in this area are extremely complex and are discussed in some detail in Volume 1 of this report. These include such factors as shifts in product demand. Our assessment of the technology relevant to the machine-tool industry provides additional evidence for some of these problems: emphasis on product innovation rather than process improvements (e.g., lasers, EDM), weak supplier-customer relationships (e.g., flexible transfer lines), poor standard setting (e.g.,

---

[7]It is perhaps not coincidental that the United States lags, or is being challenged, in the areas we have identified as critical. Strategic planning on the part of Japanese companies has likely targeted many of these technology areas.

Table F.1

Summary of Technology Areas Relevant to the Machine-Tool Industry

Key Technology Area	Critical?	Age (years)	Research Leaders	Market Leaders
Electro discharge machining	Y	20	U.S., J	J
High speed machining	Y	15	U.S., J	U.S., J
New machine configurations	N	10	U.S.	U.S., J
Precision machining	N	10	U.S., J	U.S., J
Waterjet machining	N	10	U.S.	U.S.
Improved formability	N	10	U.S.	U.S.
Layered manufacturing	Y	5	U.S.	U.S.
Net shape manufacturing	N	5	U.S.	U.S.
Flexible machining systems	Y	10	U.S., J	J
Flexible transfer lines	Y	10	G, J	G, J
Laser welding	N	20	G, J, U.S.	G, J
Laser cutting	N	20	G, J, U.S.	G, J
Automated transfer	N	20	G, J	G, J
Cutting fluids	N	10	J	J
Flexible fixturing	N	5	U.S., G, J	G, J, U.S.
Coordinate measuring machines	Y	15	G, U.S.	G, U.S.
Cutting tools	N	10	U.S., J	J
Artificial intelligence	Y	10	U.S., J	J
Computer integrated manufacturing	Y	15	G, U.S.	G
Computer numerical control	Y	30	U.S., J	J
Electronic data interchange	N	10	U.S., J, G	U.S., J, G
Micromachines	N	5	U.S., J	U.S., J
Display technology	N	10	U.S., J	J

NOTE: G = Germany; J = Japan.

CNC, EDI), lack of vision by users (e.g., EDM, AI), and poor contacts between machine-tool makers and researchers (e.g., fuzzy logic).

Based on the research conducted for this appendix, presented in more detail in the ensuing annex, the following observations can be made:

- It is important that the United States *maintain its lead in research* relevant to the machine-tool industry; technology is changing quickly, does have significant impact, and may have even greater impact in the future because of the accelerating pace of technological change:
  - The rapid progression of technology in the machine-tool industry opens many opportunities for U.S. machine-tool companies. For example, the current U.S. research lead in layered manufacturing technologies could become a very important commercial advantage if fully utilized.

- Technological change also creates opportunities for lost markets to be recaptured. The changes in computer, communication, sensing, and control technologies make it possible for FANUC's dominance in the CNC market to be reversed. A standard open-architecture system that is widely accepted by control makers would greatly facilitate such a U.S. comeback.

- It is equally important that the United States *find ways to translate its lead in research into a lead in rapid commercialization*; this is currently a weakness, and various measures should be taken to reverse this trend:
  - In many cases, the race for commercialization of technology is won through process improvements (e.g., laser processing, EDM). The U.S. companies and U.S. educational institutions at all levels need to emphasize process engineering, as well as product innovation.
  - The technology deployment phase, between research and commercialization, is very resource intensive and requires excellent cooperation among different organizations. The United States needs to benchmark and emulate successful models from across this country as well as Germany, Japan, etc.
  - Rapid standard setting can be critical in many areas for effective technology deployment (e.g., CNC, EDI). Effective collaboration among technology users, suppliers, government, and researchers is needed.

Annex
Key Technologies

These technologies are described below, grouped by SIC code. Each description includes a brief summary of the technology and a discussion of current status, trends, and an international comparison.

SIC Code 3541: Metal-Cutting Types—Electrical Discharge Machining (EDM)[8]

Current Status

Although the fast-growing acceptance of EDM worldwide has caused many to herald its emergence from the category of nontraditional machining, it is far from conventional. EDM (Figure F.7) uses a shaped electrode (usually graphite or copper) to emit a series of rapid electrical discharges ("sparks") that melt and vaporize metal, producing a cavity that is a mirror image of the electrode itself.

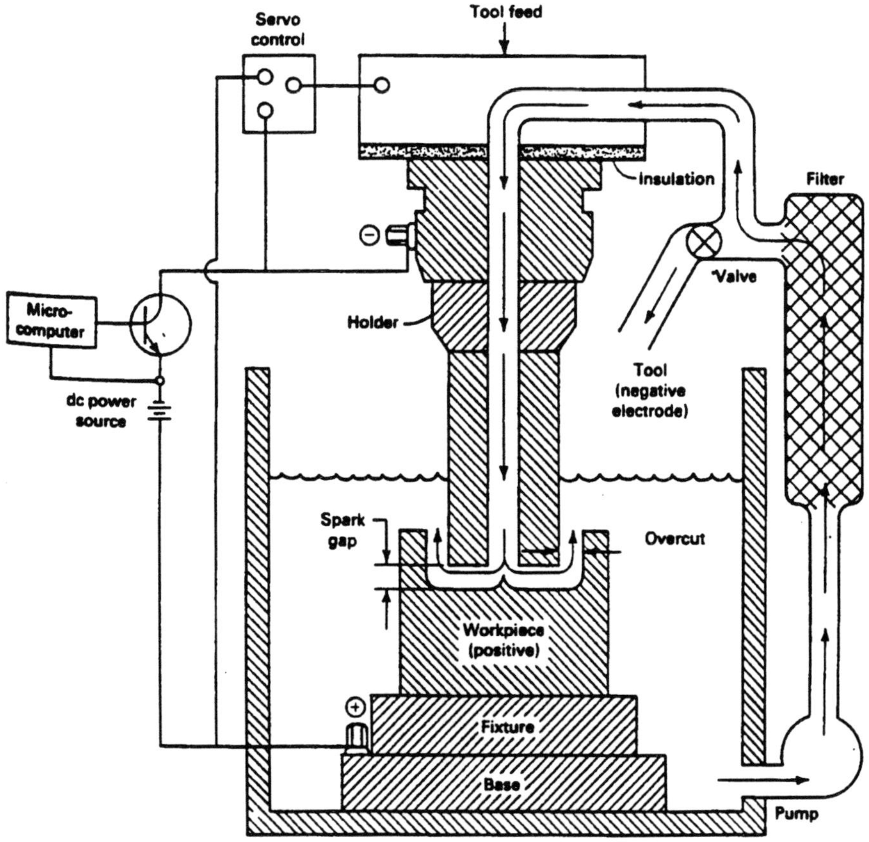

Figure F.7—Typical Setup for EDM

---

[8]The following material is based on Albert (1991), Fuller (1989), Mason (1993), Noaker (1991a), "Technology Trends" (1991a, b), and interviews with Manrong Miao and Elija Kannatey-Asibu.

The sparks travel to the work piece via a dielectric fluid (typically deionized water or a petroleum-based oil) that serves as a conductor, coolant, and medium for removal of excess metal chips (swarf). The amount of metal removed is a function of both the energy of the sparks and the area of the electrode. Both the electrode and the work piece must be electrically conductive.

A newer form of EDM uses a continuously spooling conducting wire (usually brass) instead of an electrode. In this process, a numerically controlled table is used to move the wire with respect to the work piece. The capabilities of wire EDM include maximum cutting speeds of 30 $in.^2/hr$ and accuracies of 0.0001 in. Both EDM and wire EDM are used primarily to make molds and dies. Wire EDM is also used to make electrodes for EDM and prototype parts.

EDM is rapidly gaining in popularity, because it offers many advantages over traditional forms of machining:

- It is easier to machine parts with difficult geometries; it is unaffected by material hardness and therefore can cut materials that were traditionally considered to have poor machinability (e.g., hardened tool steel, cemented tungsten carbide); and
- It eliminates severe cutting forces, because there is no direct contact between the electrode and the work piece.

Trends

The main trends in EDM are moving in two different directions: (1) faster cutting speeds and (2) greater accuracy and better surface finish. In an effort to adapt EDM to production work, the United States has focused the majority of its attention on increasing cutting speeds; EDM currently remains much slower than most traditional machining processes. In Japan, the focus is on more efficient management of the process variables and greater accuracy. To this end, two Japanese leaders in CNC technology (FANUC and Mitsubishi) have added fuzzy logic control to EDM units. For greater accuracy, Japanese wire EDM builders have increased their use of submerged cutting, wherein the wire, work piece, and fixtures are contained in a tank filled with dielectric fluid.

Country Comparison

Although the United States is competitive in this area, Japan is quickly pulling ahead in the arena of commercialization, especially where advanced technologies are concerned. Japanese machine-tool makers have been helped by large domestic demand. In 1991, Japan accounted for approximately 33 percent of worldwide EDM consumption. Although the United States uses as many wire EDM machines as Germany, France, Italy, and the United Kingdom combined, Japan still purchases twice that number. In addition, Japanese builders have many advanced automation features (e.g., slug removal systems, automatic wire threading) that they do not market in the United States where low-cost, low-tech machines are more popular. U.S. job shops are perceived to have an "attitude of a less than wholehearted embrace of advanced technology." ("Technology Trends," 1991a.)

SIC Code: 3541: Metal-Cutting Types—High-Speed Machining (HSM)[9]

Current Status

The exact definition of HSM in terms of cutting speeds varies widely depending on the type of machining and the material being machined. Therefore, HSM is generally characterized by its "small chip loads." This reduced chip size causes a corresponding decrease in the generated cutting forces and their resultant surface deformations, allowing chip removal rates to be increased without sacrificing consistency or accuracy. As removal rates increase, more of the heat generated by the process is carried away by the chips, reducing the temperature in the cutting zone. This provides for better surface finishes and longer tool life. The increased chip removal rates contribute to the high efficiency of the process; HSM cells can often process parts three to five times faster than conventional machining at 30 to 40 percent lower cost.

Improvements in cutting-tool technology, combined with the growing number of applications that use nontraditional materials, have greatly increased the demand for HSM. More robust cutting tool materials and coatings have led to the use of smaller diameter tools (less than 2 in.), most notably end mills. The spindle-rotation speeds required to attain high surface-cutting speeds with these smaller tools are much greater than those conventional machines offer. Also, nontraditional materials often have high "strength-to-weight" ratios (e.g., plastics, fiber-reinforced composites, aluminum alloys, super alloys) which require high tool-surface feeds (which translate into higher spindle speeds) to achieve the desired surface finishes and dimensional specifications. HSM in the United States is used most often in the aerospace industry. In milling, the

[9]The following material is based on ASM (1989), "Cover Story" (1993a, b, c), Gallist (1989), Gettelman (1990), and Miao (1993) and an interview with Dr. Miao.

primary use of HSM, spindle speeds of up to 100,000 rpm have been achieved. The typical range for high-speed milling is 15,000 to 50,000 rpm, while the top conventional speed is 6,000 rpm.

Trends

High-speed spindle technology, essential to HSM, is critically linked to bearing technology. Therefore, a variety of possible bearing technologies, including ceramic, magnetic, and airless bearings, are being investigated. Investigations are also being made into the use of HSM as an alternative to casting. The extremely high metal-removal rates make machining parts from solid stock a viable alternative, and the elimination of preprocessing saves both time and cost. Some areas related to HSM where future growth is also needed are integrated sensing techniques for monitoring and control of all conditions affecting the spindle (lubrication, cooling, bearing load) and sensors and diagnostics capable of detecting actual and/or incipient tool breakage linked to control systems.

Country Comparison

Japan and the United States are the technology leaders in this area.

SIC Code 3541: Metal-Cutting Types—New Machine-Tool Configurations[10]

Current Status

"Live tooling," the most exciting new development in CNC turning, entails the addition of a second spindle to an existing machine. This allows both ends of the part to be machined at one time, so the part can be finished on a single machine. This increases accuracy and reduces changeover time. The concept of "back-end turning" is not new; it has existed on non-NC machines for decades. What is new is the application of this concept to CNC machines. In some cases, the addition of live tooling has reduced processing time by 20 to 40 percent. Costs and manufacturing space can also be greatly reduced, because live tooling can often eliminate the need to purchase additional machinery.

Live tooling configurations fall primarily into one of two categories: twin-spindles or subspindles. In twin-spindle machines, the added spindle is usually

[10]The following material is based on Albert (1991), Mason (1992a), Miller (1989), Miska (1990a), and "Universal Concept Gaining Ground in U.S." (1992).

equal in both size and power to the main spindle. In this configuration, the spindles are usually oriented coaxially, each with its own separate turret, to allow simultaneous machining operations. This configuration is used primarily when both ends of a part are of the same complexity and involve milling and cross-drilling operations. In subspindle configurations, the added spindle has only a fraction (generally one-fifth to one-half) of the capacity of the main spindle. This configuration is used primarily when one end of a part is markedly less complex than the other. Approximately three-fourths of turned parts fit in this category. Subspindle machines come in both single- and dual-turret configurations.

Trends

The main trend is toward the use of twin-spindle "mill-turns" that combine live tooling with part handling to form turning cells. The newest and fastest of these machines is from Japan. A new machine configuration that uses a frame structure to support an inverted prismatic robot-type structure is under development by a leading U.S. machine-tool company. Another new machine configuration that departs from the traditional three Cartesian and two rotary axes in milling is the rotary mill (see Figure F.8). In subspindle machines, the

RAND *MR479/2-F.7*

Figure F.8—Example of a New Machine-Tool Configuration—A Rotary Mill

trend is toward more power; newer subspindles tend to have at least one-half the capacity of the main spindle. Live tooling is also being added to nontraditional machining processes such as EDM.

Country Comparison

The United States is competitive in research and development in new machine-tool technology. However, Japan (Miyano) currently has the largest U.S. market share in subspindle machines.

SIC Code 3541: Metal-Cutting Types—Precision Machining[11]

Current Status

Precision machining is not only concerned with the accuracy of a single measured position; it is also concerned with the repeatability with which that accuracy can be imparted to the work piece. In milling, this repeatability is affected by three general factors: mechanical design, manufacture, and CNC servo technology. A machine whose design lacks rigidity will have too much spindle vibration for efficient high-precision machining. Also, if care was not taken during manufacturing to ensure the proper alignment and surface finish of parts that have relative motion, vibration from friction will prevent efficient high-precision machining. Lags in CNC servo control also affect positioning accuracy.

Current positioning accuracy levels for high-precision machining are 0.003 mm for midsize machines and 0.002 mm (with 0.001 mm repeating accuracy) for compacts. Some "super accuracy" configurations can reach positioning accuracies of up to 0.0015 mm. Current acceptable vibration amplitudes are 1 μm for high precision and 0.05 to 0.025 μm for superhigh precision.

Trends

The key trend in this area is toward increasing the rigidity of the machine and the robustness of the control technology. More emphasis is being placed on the careful design and manufacture of precision machines. Improvements in related technologies (e.g., CNC, spindles, bearings) will enhance this process. In addition to improving machine precision through the mechanical design, sensing

---

[11]The following material is based on Chatterjee (1988), Koelsch (1991b), Mason (1992b), Winski (1992), and Miao (1993).

and software compensation are also used. In particular, compensation techniques for geometric and thermal errors can improve machine accuracy significantly. Similar compensation techniques can also be used to overcome errors introduced by friction and backlash.

Country Comparison

The United States and Japan are the technology leaders in this area.

SIC Code 3541: Metal-Cutting Types—Waterjet/Abrasive Waterjet Machining[12]

Current Status

Although the concept on which waterjet machining (WJM) is based (harnessing the erosive power of one of the earth's most plentiful resources) has been around for centuries, the first waterjet for industrial use was not developed until 1961. Today's WJM process (Figure F.9) uses a narrow jet of water (3–14 mils) traveling

RAND *MR479/2-F.8*

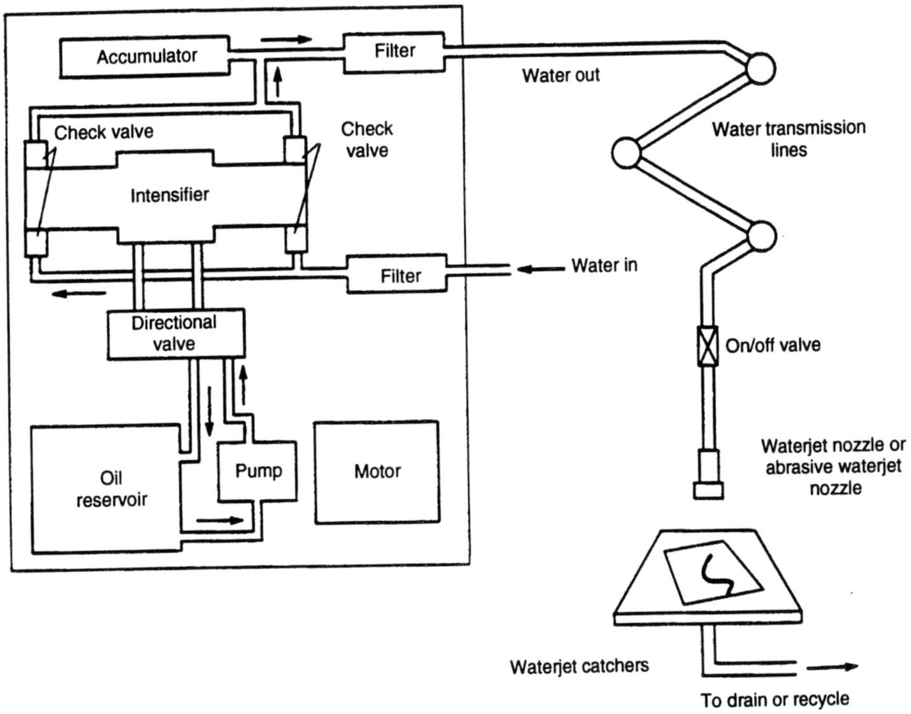

Figure F.9—Schematic of a WJM System

12The following material is based on Geskin and Gordon (1993), Johnston (1989), and Koelsch (1991a).

at supersonic velocities (750 to 850 m/s) to erode the work piece material. WJM is mainly effective for cutting nonmetallic materials.

In an effort to expand the capabilities of the process, abrasive waterjet machining (AWJM) was developed in 1981. The addition of fine abrasive particles into the jet stream allowed machining of harder and denser materials (e.g., titanium, ceramics, composites). Current AWJMs have jet diameters around 20 mils and velocities ranging from 350 to 550 m/s.

Extremely complex technologies, such as high-pressure pumps, timing valves, pressure intensifiers, and piping and nozzles for stream containment and definition, are necessary to attain jet velocities of 750 to 850 m/s, about twice that of a bullet. Nozzle pressures usually stay around 50,000 psi, but can sometimes go as high as 150,000 psi, while jet kinetic power ranges upward from 10,000 watts.

Since the mechanism for material removal is erosion, as opposed to the melting or vaporization used in most other methods, WJM and AWJM have the advantage of a much smaller (or nonexistent) heat-affected zone. This allows simultaneous cutting of parts from multiple layers of thin material, while maintaining a high quality of cut for all layers.

Trends

The main research goal in this area has been to develop sufficient understanding of the underlying physical and chemical aspects to accurately model the process. Currently, the process relies heavily on empirical data; erosion rates are a function of material properties and cannot be predicted easily.

Other work is being done to improve the efficiency of pure waterjet cutting to eliminate the environmental concerns that stem from using abrasives and to allow the use of higher velocities and smaller-diameter jets. One area being investigated is the use of ice particles in the jet.

Several additional areas in WJM and AWJM have been targeted for improvement:

- The process is extremely loud, often reaching harmful decibel levels.
- The material removal rate is lower than other nontraditional machining processes, which as a group are much slower than conventional machining.
- The range of applicable materials is limited.

Country Comparison

The United States is the world leader in this technology.

SIC Code 3542: Metal-Forming Types—Improved Formability Materials[13]

Current Status

Components produced by semisolid materials (SSMs), often called "slurries," are beginning to replace traditional liquid castings and forgings. Processing with SSMs has many advantages. Because alloys are more viscous in semisolid form than when fully liquid, their flow is closer to laminar; this allows them to fill die and mold cavities more evenly. The viscosity of SSMs can even be tailored (through stirring) to a specific die geometry. In addition, SSMs tend to have lower temperatures than liquids. This, combined with the preexistence of solid particles, decreases total solidification time, shrinkage, and die wear. SSMs that have a very large solid content can also be processed using traditional forming processes for solid materials (e.g., forging, extrusion, rolling) but with much lower loads. If desired, they can be returned to their semisolid state after casting (through reheating) for additional processing.

Although a wide variety of metal alloy systems have been investigated for semisolid processing (e.g., steels, superalloys, aluminum alloys, copper, zinc, magnesium), the majority of commercial applications use "light-alloy" systems, such as aluminum or magnesium.

Trends

Key areas targeted for future study are

- adapting semi-solid processing techniques to ferrous alloys (popular in Japan)
- composing an alloy specifically for semisolid processing
- altering die design for better semisolid processing.

---

[13]The following material is based on Brown and Fleming (1993) and interviews with A. Ghosh and M. Haghi.

Country Comparison

The United States is leading in this technology.

SIC Code 3542: Metal-Forming Types—Layered Manufacturing[14]

Current Status

Layered manufacturing, also referred to as rapid prototyping, solid freeform fabrication, three-dimensional printing, or desktop manufacturing, involves the creation of parts directly from computer memory. This is achieved by electronically dividing a three-dimensional CAD model of the part into a series of thin horizontal cross sections, which are then used, layer by layer, to fabricate a physical model. Although the actual prototyping methods may vary, they generally fall into one of three categories: (1) a liquid or solid is chemically altered by a laser or other form of light energy (e.g., stereolithography), (2) a powder is sintered by a laser or other form of light energy (e.g., selective laser sintering), (3) particles or layers of material are added to a surface in select areas (e.g., laminated object manufacturing). A sample process from each category is described below.

Stereolithography (Cubital, Quadrax, 3D Systems) uses a focused ultraviolet laser to create cross sections on the surface of a bath of liquid polymer. The polymer solidifies wherever it is touched by the laser, thereby forming a pattern on the surface. An elevator then lowers the part so that the newly fabricated solid layer is just below the surface of the bath. A wiper blade passes across the liquid surface to speed leveling, and the process is repeated until the part is finished. Excess material is removed from crevices by ultrasonic cleaning, while unused polymer is stripped off in an alcohol bath. A major drawback to the process is that parts with overhangs and undercuts require a support structure for fabrication, which must be removed by subsequent machining. The most commercially advanced stereolithography system is produced by an American firm, 3D Systems, Inc.

Selective laser sintering, developed at University of Texas at Austin and commercialized by DTM Corp., uses a high powered CO_2 laser to fuse layers of powder. As the process begins, a thin layer of heat-fusible powder is deposited

---

[14]The following material is based on "Applicatons" (1992); Sachs et al. (1992), pp. 481–484; "Production Lines" (1991); Toth-Fejel (1992); Wohlers (1991); and an interview with Prof. Dutta at the University of Michigan.

into a workspace container and is heated to just below its melting point. A laser traces an initial cross section of the object under fabrication on the thin layer of powder. The laser beam causes the powder temperature to rise to the point of sintering, forming a solid mass. The container lowers slightly, and the process repeats. Each successive layer fuses to the underlying layer, and additional layers of powder are deposited and sintered until the object is complete. Laser intensity is modulated to sinter the powder only in the areas defined by the object's design geometry. In areas not sintered, the powder remains loose and serves as a natural support for the next powder layer. An advantage over stereolithography is that no support structure is necessary during fabrication.

Laminated object manufacturing uses a laser to cut foils or sheets, stacks them, then glues or welds them together.

Stereolithography is a commercial (but expensive) technology for rapid prototyping; the other technologies are still under development. None are currently suitable for actual part fabrication on a commercial scale.

Trends

The key trend in this area is developing a process that produces structural parts (with properties suitable for use in actual parts) at production speeds suitable for industry. One step toward this aim is fused deposition modeling (FDM). Developed by Stratasys, this process uses investment casting wax for direct output to the investment casting process. The wax pattern quickly dewaxes from the ceramic shell when the shell is fired using normal investment casting processes. The modeler is capable of running multiple parts at one time, as well as thin walled parts for casting; typical models are built from CAD data in less than one hour. FDM uses no lasers or polyphotomers so it is environmentally safe. The success of this modeling technology coupled with the investment casting process is illustrated by Biomet Inc., which has used it to produce products for orthopedists.

Another new process is three-dimensional printing, which is similar to selective laser sintering, except that it uses an "ink-jet" printing of a binder material to selectively join the powder instead of a laser. Parts can be fabricated using a wide variety of materials, including ceramics, metals, cermets, and polymers.

Work is also being done to develop methods to use the prototype parts to create negatives for tooling in such areas as injection molding and metal casting and to be able to use multiple colors to highlight strategic sections.

Country Comparison

The United States leads, with most research and development based in universities, but some work is going on in Germany and Japan.

SIC Code 3542: Metal-Forming Types—Net Shape Manufacturing[15]

Current Status

Metal injection molding (MIM) is one of the most promising areas in powder metallurgy. In MIM, extremely fine (10 to 20 μm) metal powders (elemental or prealloyed) are blended with an organic polymer and injected into molds using equipment in a fashion similar to plastic injection molding. Molded (green) parts first go into a low-temperature oven for initial debinding (removal of the binder polymer through heat), then are transferred to a high-temperature furnace for final polymer removal and complete sintering.

While many aspects of the MIM process are similar to that for thermoplastics injection molding, there are some significant differences. For example, shrinkage rates in MIM are up to 20 percent, compared to 2 to 3 percent in thermoplastic molding. Therefore, MIM requires tighter tolerances and higher precision in the injection and clamping units to prevent part flaws from being magnified in the debinding and sintering processes. Also, the greater abrasiveness of metal powders causes more wear and tear on the barrels than in thermoplastic molding.

The advantages of MIM include

- three-dimensional design flexibility
- the ability to process complex parts
- highly uniform density and high strength of resulting parts, for better corrosion resistance and mechanical integrity
- material properties approaching those of wrought materials.

There have been many recent improvements to the process that are still currently only available from a few companies. One such company (AMAX) has developed a process for rapid debinding (without oxidation or damage to the

[15]The following material is based on Miska (1990b), "Tech Update 1990," and "Technology Update" (1990).

part) that is compatible with current sintering processes. Parts are chemically leached before sintering, which removes residual binder by thermal evaporation. This speeds up the process, thereby increasing throughput. Another company (Alcan Powders and Pigments) has developed ultrafine copper powders with average particle sizes in the 3 to 10 μm range. Several other companies are using existing robot technology to automate the process.

The powders used in MIM are more expensive than the ones used for conventional powder metallurgy parts. As a result, the advantages of the process apply mostly to small parts, especially ones with complex geometries.

Trends

The key trends in MIM are toward decreasing the cost of the powders, so as not to limit part size; increasing the binder removal rates before sintering, so as not to limit production capability; increasing the choice of alloys (currently limited by oxidation during binding or by initial choice of binder); and lessening the shrinking.

Also, many of the developments that are currently applied only in a few leading companies (e.g., automation, decreased particle size in powders) will spread throughout the industry.

Country Comparison

The United States leads in this technology. Commercial production, once exclusively the domain of U.S. companies, has just recently begun in Japan and Europe.

SIC Code 3549: Metalworking Machinery—Flexible Manufacturing Systems[16]

Current Status

FMSs successfully combine machine tools, material-handling systems, and computers to meet a wide variety of manufacturing requirements (Figure F.10). They are designed to machine parts in "families" based on common work-piece

[16]The following material is based on ASM (1989), Gettelman (1991a, b), Koelsch (1990), Poeth (undated), and Shapira (1990).

features, such as being parts of an assembly or representing generic part class, size, or machining requirements. FMSs typically use automated material handling systems, such as pallets and rail-guided vehicles, to transfer work pieces between cells.

Trends

In the past, FMSs have only been applied to middle volume, midlevel-variety manufacturing, but with the advent of increased sophistication of all components, FMSs are becoming a viable solution to high-production applications and high-variety conditions.

Japanese manufacturers, once high users of FMSs, are now breaking down their systems into separate arrangements of flexible cells.

Country Comparison

The United States was the first to develop this technology, but the Japanese have taken the lead in commercialization.

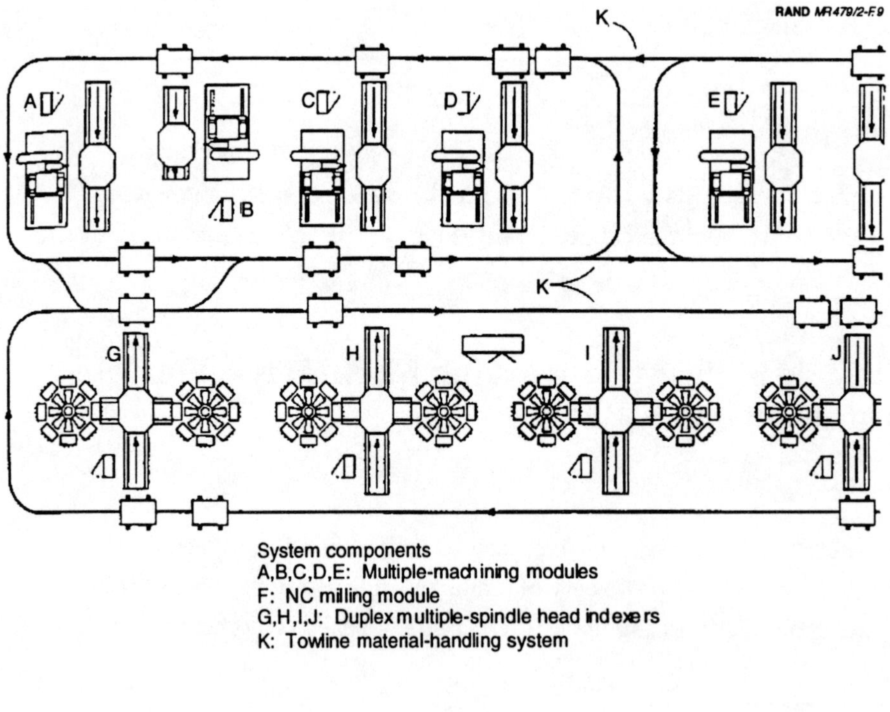

Figure F.10—A Flexible Machining System

SIC Code 3549: Metalworking Machinery—Flexible Transfer Lines[17]

Current Status

In the past, transfer lines were considered "rigid production systems" and were used primarily for mass production. A traditional transfer line consists of a series of highly specialized single or multiple operation machine tools that are connected by a material handling system and controlled by a programmable controller or relay network. Transfer lines are designed to process a specific part (or part family with minor variations). If the part is phased out, the transfer line must be scrapped or rebuilt, because the cost for retooling for another part is approximately 90 percent of the original total cost of the machine. However, where production volume and part longevity are high enough to justify their use, transfer lines provide the highest levels of productivity and repeatability.

Transfer Lines can be classified as being either synchronous or nonsynchronous. Synchronous or "index-type" transfer lines usually have a series of machines arranged in line or around a rotary or circular index. When all the stations have competed their work, the parts in the circuit are simultaneously advanced to the next station, beginning the cycle anew. Cycle time depends on the slowest operation; therefore, the highest efficiency is obtained when machining times are uniformly minimized. In a nonsynchronous system, each machine is supplied by a bank of parts, permitting it to continuously operate at its fastest rate.

Changes in market demand are requiring high-volume automotive manufacturers to provide more variety and faster model changeovers. This requires agility, that is, flexibility without undue penalties in terms of costs, quality, or throughput. Figure F.11 illustrates the cost of flexibility by comparing a fixed transfer line to a flexible line. The initial investment cost is 100 for the flexible line and 70 for the fixed line. However, a model changeover requires a new investment of 15 percent of the initial cost for the flexible line and 60 percent for the fixed line. Thus, the flexible line is more cost effective than the fixed line after the second model changeover. As model changeovers become more frequent (e.g., every five years instead of every 15 years), the flexible transfer line technology becomes more attractive.

---

[17]The following material is based on Beard (1990), "Multiple Operation Machining" (1989), Nagel and Dove (1991), and meetings with machine-tool suppliers in Ann Arbor, Michigan, May 1993.

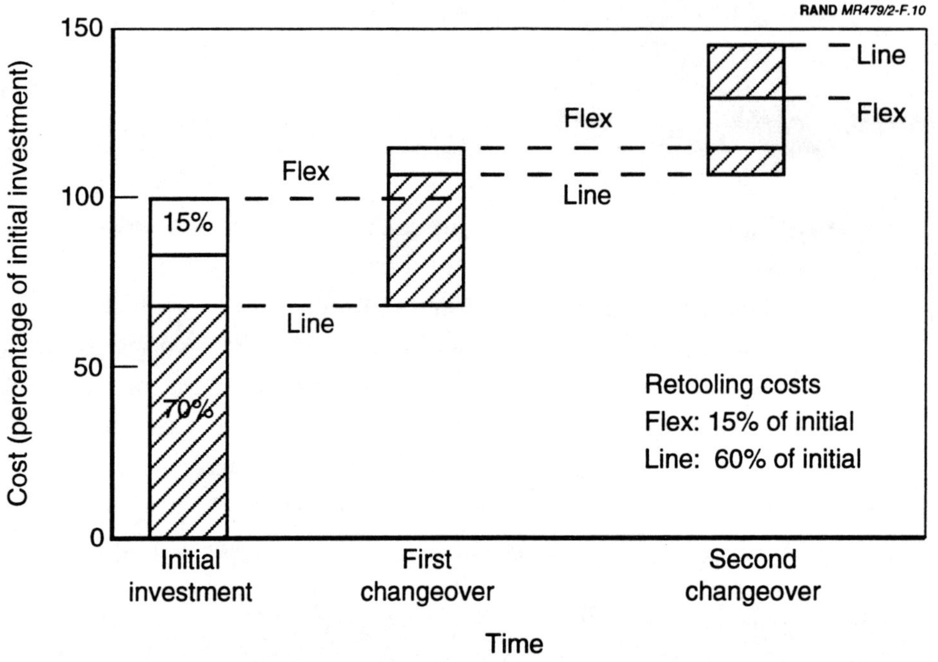

Figure F.11—The Cost of Flexibility

Some flexibility is being designed into new transfer line production facilities for automotive components. Mainly this is being supplied by German (e.g., Heller, Alfing, Ex-Cell-O) and more recently Japanese (e.g., Honda) supplier companies rather than the U.S. companies (e.g., Giddings & Lewis, Ingersoll, Lamb) that have traditionally supplied transfer line equipment.

Trends

A common trend in transfer line design is to make systems more versatile so that they run varieties of parts and/or smaller batches economically. This can be done by using modular machines, interchangeable tool heads for different parts, flexible fixtures, etc.

Several critical technological developments are needed to ensure agility (i.e., increased flexibility without undue quality or cost penalties). These include programmability (CNC machines), flexible and modular machine-tool designs, and flexible and modular fixturing and tooling. These will be evolutionary advances, rather than technological breakthroughs. However, the technical (engineering) challenges are considerable and should not be minimized. Agility goes beyond flexibility by accounting for market, technical, and business issues in responding to changes in market demand.

Country Comparison

German and Japanese transfer line machine suppliers have had 5 to 10 years of experience with flexible transfer line technology serving the early demand from their domestic customers. Thus, the German and Japanese machine-tool makers have a technological edge over the U.S. transfer line machine suppliers, who are not in a good position to move ahead in this area without assistance; the end users are likely to turn to Japanese and German machine-tool companies.

SIC Code 3699: Laser Cutting Tools—Laser Welding and Heat Treatment[18]

Current Status

From the standpoints of heat input and accuracy, laser welding offers a level of quality that cannot be achieved with other forms of welding. The automotive industry is currently the biggest market for laser welding. Neodymium-doped yttrium-aluminum-garnet (Nd:YAG) lasers, which are considered cheaper and more flexible than their $C0_2$ counterparts, are often used to fuse large automotive bodies.

Trends

Despite a lack of control of the beam diameter when using fiber optics, 90 percent of Nd:YAG welding applications use fiber optics. Improvements in fiber optics technology will greatly enhance this area. Many new applications for laser welding and heat treatment are continually being developed by process engineers in industry.

Country Comparison

Japan and Germany are leaders in this technology. However, the United States is still competitive.

---

[18]The following material is based on Irving (1992) and Sciberras and Payne (no date).

SIC Code 3699: Laser Cutting Tools—Laser Cutting[19]

Current Status

The two most common types of lasers for cutting are Nd:YAG and carbon dioxide (CO_2). Both cut by heating the material until it melts or vaporizes. CO_2 lasers use oxygen as the assist gas; it is directed coaxially with the laser beam into the work piece, thereby ejecting molten material through the back of the part. Because oxygen is a reactive gas, it creates a radial combustion front ahead of the beam. This allows increased cutting speeds. Nd:YAG lasers are used for cutting materials with high thermal conductivity and reflexivity. These lasers typically have outputs around 100 W, but outputs can range as high as 800 to 1,600 W.

Lasers are rapidly gaining in popularity, because they

- are able to process hardened alloy metals without difficulty
- can cut complex shapes and drill difficult holes
- avoid tool cost and wear
- have economical setup times
- can produce prototypes or small lot sizes that are not cost effective to make using other methods.

However, because the metal removal rate is slow, laser-cutting tools are not yet economical for high volumes.

Trends

High-pressure fusion cutting uses an inert gas as an assist gas to eliminate oxidation of cut surfaces. This process has been tested on stainless steel and aluminum; however, many metals and thicknesses still await testing.

Eximers are pulsed gas lasers that emit ultraviolet light. The gases used are a mixture of a noble gas (e.g., Ar, K, Xe) and a halogen gas (C_lF_2). Photon energy of the absorbed light breaks chemical bonds and causes molecule fragments to expand explosively away from the machined area (ablation). Very little heat

[19]The following material is based on Beard (1991), Irving (1992), Schreiber (1991a), Sciberras and Payne (no date), and an interview with Manrong Miao.

goes into the surrounding material, because most of the laser energy is carried away by ejected fragments (no melting). This leads to high-quality edge definition, high precision, and the ability to remove small amounts of material (micromachining).

Country Comparison

Japan and Germany are the leaders in this technology. However, the United States is still competitive.

SIC Code 3544: Special Dies and Tools, Die Sets, Jigs and Fixtures, and Industrial Molds—Automated Transfer Systems[20]

Current Status

Automated transfer systems, such as pallets and rail-guided vehicles, can boost the capacity of practically any machine. An automated pallet-shuttle system smoothes the machining cycle by minimizing downtime caused by work piece setup, part changeovers, tool changes, and part loading and unloading. By using a pallet-system, the operator can focus all of his or her attention on the machining process (manually or through CNC) while the automated system performs the previously manual tasks of loading, positioning, and unloading parts at the machining center. All of the operator's remaining tasks are off line, involving setup and removal of finished parts from pallets, and can be done while the machine is busy.

To accommodate a wide variety of work pieces/fixtures, pallets can be round, rectangular, or square and can range in size from 12 to 120 in. Pallet receivers are mounted onto the machine tables; at the appropriate time in the cycle, the receiver grips the pallet and locks it in the precise positioning for machining. A pallet loader (usually a floor-mounted, motorized device) is used to transfer pallets from the loading station to the receiver. When a work piece has been completed, the loader retrieves the pallet from the machine and shuttles it to an unloading station. The loader can function manually or via CNC control.

[20]The following material is based on Geppert (1990).

For added flexibility and capacity, a basic pallet system can be upgraded with a rail-guided vehicle (RGV) or an automated guided vehicle (AGV) and additional park stands. These vehicles transport pallets from floor-mounted park stands and deliver them to a pallet loader. An RGV or AGV can also off-load machined pallets and transport them to measuring stations, wash stations, or inventory areas.

Future Trends

Attention should be given to the need for some type of pallet standardization. Standardization is important to ensure that all pallets in a shop connect and that each pallet is able to handle loaders and receivers of different makes.

Country Comparison

While the United States remains competitive, Germany and Japan are the technology leaders.

SIC Code 3544: Special Dies and Tools, Die Sets, Jigs and Fixtures, and Industrial Molds—Cutting Fluids[21]

Current Status

Increased government regulation of hazardous waste disposal is encouraging companies to explore process substitution (e.g., dry machining) and invest in material recovery, recycling, and treatment. Lubricants typically used in the metal-stamping process (e.g., petroleum, soap, animal fat) often require aggressive cleaning techniques that use acidic or chlorinated compounds. These substances require disposal as hazardous waste. To avoid this, many companies are replacing oil-based compounds with synthetic, water-based fluids that clean easily and do not create hazardous waste disposal problems. Others are changing their cleaning process from vapor degreasing to water-based or alkaline cleaning. Switching to water-based coolants can reduce liability in metal cutting as well. However, such coolants are harder to maintain, because exposure to tramp oil degrades their ability to protect metal against rust, inhibits wetting and cooling, and reduces tool life. A high-speed disc-bowl centrifuge

---

[21]The following material is based on Koelsch (1991) and Arter (1990b).

(which separates different liquids) is the only effective way to remove these oils. Regular cleaning and maintenance of machines, clean operating conditions, and adding only pure, softened water to the coolant concentrate can eliminate part of the contaminated coolant problem and extend coolant life.

Trends

As environmental concerns become more pressing, being "green" is becoming more important. Manufacturers are searching for cutting fluids that are useful in a wider variety of applications and that can be easily recycled. More companies are also installing in-house coolant-and-lubricant recycling facilities. The increased use of high-efficiency lubricants (based on fatty alcohols found in vegetables) as a substitution for traditional coolants is another sign of the growing "greenness"; these lubricants are usually nontoxic, nonallergenic, and biodegradable. Also, since these fluids are applied in extremely small amounts, the metalworking process consumes all the lubricant, so there is no leftover coolant to treat, filter or dispose of. Chips come off dry without sticking together, and air jets or vacuum systems can collect them for recycling. A detergent and water rinse or conventional degreasing agent can remove any slight amount of residue.

Another trend is toward elimination of lubricants entirely through the use of dry processing. One such method is the Toyota Diffusion (TD) process (also called thermal diffusion), which diffuses vanadium carbide into and onto a metal. Successful applications of the process includes surface treatments of tooling for sheet metal, cold forging, and powdered metals. A TD-coated die can be used (without lubricant) in six to eight stamping runs of 50,000 hits each without needing to be recoated, depending on the application. This process has been widely used in Japan since the late 1970s, with Japanese automakers being some of the largest users. Arvin Industries (Columbus, Indiana) is the sole North and South American licensee of the process.

Country Comparison

Australia, Great Britain, France, and Spain had all used TD technology before U.S. manufacturers tried it. The United States is losing ground to other industrial countries, which are implementing this advanced technology more rapidly.

SIC Code 3544: Special Dies and Tools, Die Sets, Jigs and Fixtures, and Industrial Molds—Flexible and Modular Fixturing[22]

Current Status

Modular fixturing is not a new idea; people have been building fixtures out of mix-and-match components for years. In high-mix, low-volume applications, modular fixtures increase flexibility and save money by eliminating the need to purchase, build, and store large quantities of dedicated fixtures. Modular fixtures can often be designed and built in a few hours (this is often less than the time it takes to locate a dedicated fixture) and can be modified in seconds. Modularity in fixturing may be an essential element of the flexible transfer line technology that the automotive manufacturers are seeking.

Trends

The cost of modular tooling needs to be reduced to make it more affordable for smaller shops, where the technology would be the most beneficial because of the variety of jobs they handle. Many ideas and concepts from CNC machine tools can be utilized to create "CNC fixtures." Some breakthrough concepts, such as fluidized beds for fixturing, are also being investigated.

Country Comparison

The United States is competitive in this area; however, Japan and Germany are also technical leaders.

SIC Code 3545: Cutting Tools, Machine Tool Accessories and Machinists' Precision Measuring Devices—Coordinate Measurement Machines (CMM)[23]

Current Status

With the advent of CNC machines, measurement of the machining process was pushed outside the ability of the operators themselves, thereby creating

---

[22]The following material is based on Beard (1991b).

[23]The following material is based on Bosch (1992), Stevens (1991), and "Quality in Production" (1990).

the need for the three-dimensional flexible measuring capability of the CMM. In the past, the complexity of the measuring task and the need for a clean, controlled environment prevented CMMs from being located on the shop floor, thereby interrupting the feedback path. The recent industry-wide push is to close the loop by producing CMMs robust enough for a factory environment. Essentially, these machines can give the "feel" back to the machine operator and can restore the pride of craftsmanship despite a high level of automation.

The new generation of shop-floor CMMs offer linear velocities ranging from 250 to 635 mm/sec and acceleration and deceleration from 2 to 3.2 m/sec. Inspection of complex work pieces typically requires dozens to hundreds of short, quick moves, and how fast a CMM stabilizes after moving is as critical to its inspection throughput as its acceleration and deceleration are. The best test of a CMM's capability is its inspection-point-per-second speed.

Trends

Mechanical CMMs suffer from low throughput. Thus, considerable effort has been aimed at increasing CMM operating speeds without losing accuracy. Error compensation methods, very similar to those used in machine tools, can be used to improve CMM accuracy. The rapid improvements in the cost and performance of computer and optical technology have contributed to the emergence of the optical CMM as an alternative to the touch-probe model in a growing number of three-dimensional measurement applications. Although each retains certain areas of exclusivity (optics is best at analyzing flat surfaces, while touch systems exceed at probing depths and interiors), optical CMMs are getting better at depth. In the future, these two methods may combine into some sort of hybrid optical–touch-probe design. Purely optical measurement systems may also be developed, and these could overcome the throughput problems associated with mechanical CMMs.

Country Comparison

European countries (including Germany) and the United States lead in this technology.

SIC Code 3545: Cutting Tools, Machine Tool Accessories and Machinists' Precision Measuring Devices—Cutting Tool Technology[24]

Current Status

The two major areas of cutting-tool technology that are having the most impact today are inserts and coatings.

Indexible inserts decrease tool wear through their ability to change worn cutting edges and also provide chip removal guides. The most common insert material in the United States is tungsten carbide, but cermets are rapidly challenging that position. Cermets are ceramic particles dispersed in a metal matrix (oxide or carbide-based). Cermets combine the high-temperature resistance of ceramics with the toughness and ductility of carbides. Cermet inserts come in all shapes and sizes, can be uncoated or coated, have outstanding performance, and are usually cheaper than the alternatives. For example, carbides cannot compete with cermets in high-speed finishing and semifinishing of steel, stainless steel, and cast iron. In threading and grooving, cermets outperform carbide tools in wear resistance, chemical stability, and edge strength.

Diamond coatings are added to tooling through a process called chemical vapor deposition (CVD). CVD diamond has different physical properties than natural single-crystal or polycrystalline sintered diamond. CVD has a hardness close to that of natural diamond but higher than sintered diamond. However, since the CVD material is polycrystalline, it has no anisotropy (the hardness caused by the crystalline direction) that exists in natural diamond. Unlike polycrystalline sintered diamond, CVD diamond is binderless and therefore gives the same fusing resistance on cutting tools as natural diamond does, thus limiting the formation of built-up edges and improving abrasion resistance. Silicon-nitride ceramic inserts coated with thin-film diamond have been found to compete with sintered-diamond tools in some aluminum-alloy turning applications. The use of CVD diamond on small-diameter end mills (a difficult application for polycrystalline diamond because of its thickness) also looks promising.

Interlocked titanium carbon nitride (TiCN) coatings are not common in U.S. machine shops. This new-generation, wear-resistant coating, built on multiple interlocked layers with a total thickness of 0.0001 in. (0.002 mm), is significantly harder than titanium nitride (TiN). TiCN also couples maximum protection

---

[24]The following material is based on Owen (1991b), "Tech Update" (1991), and "Production Lines" (1991b).

against abrasive wear with excellent thermochemical stability and superior lubricity.

Trends

Cermet use is predicted to grow tremendously and in direct proportion to the drop in carbide usage. The use of diamond coatings will also become more widespread.

Country Comparison

Today, Japan buys 71.5 percent of all cermet cutting tools, and cermets have captured over 30 percent of the Asian hard-metal cutting-tool market (which includes coated and uncoated tungsten carbide and ceramics), in contrast to 7 percent of the markets in North and South America and 5 percent in Europe.

The United States and Japan share technology leadership in the area of coatings.

SIC Code 3625: Relays and Industrial Controls—Artificial Intelligence (AI)[25]

Current Status

As research in AI accelerates, expert systems, neural networks, and fuzzy logic are playing important roles in meeting the technological sophistication required in today's competitive world. These AI technologies are likely to find widespread use in machine-tool controllers over the next decade.

An expert system consists of a series of computer algorithms that use facts and "rules of thumb" to simulate the reasoning process of a human expert. They are used by many companies to allow new or inexperienced employees access to the wisdom of a seasoned expert. Currently, these systems are limited by the information in their knowledge bases (which may be incomplete or outdated) and their narrow operating parameters. Expert systems also lack mechanisms for catching errors (e.g., in data entry) or for assigning certainty factors to values.

Fuzzy logic allows the use of subjective concepts to emulate the human decisionmaking process. This new logic is expected to be well suited to a variety

---

[25]The following material is based on Luxhoj (1992), Schreiber (1991c), and "Computer Hardware and Software" (1990).

of AI applications. Fuzzy logic is based on the theory of fuzzy sets. Fuzzy set elements are not classified as extremes, such as 0 and 1 or on and off, but instead are assigned a value, thereby allowing programmers to model imprecise concepts. Fuzzy logic also has the ability to observe its own performance and treat some rules as more important than others.

Artificial neural networks are being used to model and control nonlinear systems. They are based upon complex connections of simple nonlinear elements called "neurons." Artificial neural networks are named after neural networks found in biological systems and represent a simple approximation of the way the brain functions. Neural networks have a learning, or adaptive, capability that makes them attractive in many applications. They are finding use in conjunction with fuzzy logic controllers. They are used to "train" or "tune" complex fuzzy logic controllers using data.

Trends

Technology advances in graphical user interfaces, window environments, and high-million-instructions-per-second computers will have large effects on expert systems. Other promising related technologies are parallel processing and speech recognition.

Fuzzy logic has already begun to appear in the control of machining processes, such as EDM. This trend toward the use of AI methods in supervisory-level control of machining processes will continue.

Country Comparison

The United States leads in research (mostly university based), and Japan leads in applications. Fuzzy logic is a good example of a technology that was developed in the United States but that has achieved commercial success through a variety of Japanese-made consumer products. Japanese companies have recently made progress in extending the capabilities of fuzzy logic control by marrying it to neural net technology.

SIC Code 3625: Relays and Industrial Controls—Computer Integrated Manufacturing (CIM)[26]

Current Status

A marriage of CNC and CMM technology, CIM lacks only a highly intelligent computer-control network capable of integrating machine tools, sensors, computer hardware, and software into a continuously upgradeable machining system to be more effective. Standardization efforts in this area (e.g., manufacturing automation protocol [MAP]) have only been partially successful. The National Institute of Standards and Technology (NIST) has been a research leader in this technology for some time. However, commercialization has not been widespread.

Trends

Developments in the individual technologies of CIM (CNC and CMM) will enhance this area. Advances in controller technology (standard open architecture), graphical user interfaces, standard hardware interfaces, and communication protocols are especially important.

Country Comparison

Although a great deal of research effort is being focused on CIM research in the United States, it appears that the European Union (e.g., Germany) is leading in this area. Because of its lead in CNC markets, the Japanese company FANUC may be well positioned to play a significant role in this market as well.

SIC Code 3625: Relays and Industrial Controls—Computer Numerical Control (CNC)[27]

Current Status. Although CNC is now a mature control technology, it is still evolving. The major benefits of CNC are versatility, speed, accuracy, increased uniformity, and lower tooling costs. Over the last decade, much research has been done to improve CNC control on the following three levels (see Figure F.12):

---

[26]The following material is based on "Controller Integrates Machining Systems" (1990).

[27]The following material is based on Ashley (1990), Ulsoy and Koren (1993), and Appendix D of this report.

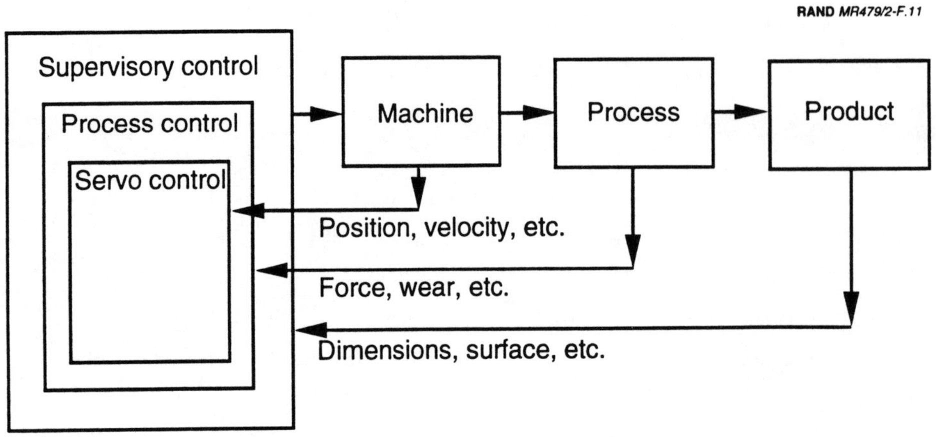

Figure F.12—A Controller for a Manufacturing Process, Showing the Servo, Process, and Supervisory Control Levels

- Servo control, which controls the motion of the tool relative to the work piece
- Process control (also referred to as adaptive control), which controls process variables, such as tool wear and cutting forces, to maintain high production rates, improved part geometry and surface finish, and good part quality
- Supervisory control, which controls both product-related variables, such as part dimensions and surface roughness, and process-related variables, such as chatter and tool and machine status; can also be used to compensate for factors not explicitly considered in the design of servo- and process-level controllers.

The majority of research has focused on improvements on the servo and process levels. On the servo level, efforts have been made to compensate for geometric and thermal errors, elimination of which can improve accuracy of the machine by a factor of 5 to 10. On the process level, several different control approaches are being taken. Adaptive control optimization, developed in the 1960s by Bendix, offers adaptive control along with optimization. The major obstacle to its adoption by industry was its requirement for an on-line measurement or estimate of tool wear. Although much research has been done since its inception, there is still no reliable tool-wear measurement method that can operate in an industrial environment. Two more-practical approaches developed in the same era, adaptive control with constraints (ACC) and geometric adaptive control (GAC), are suboptimal processes that are based on maximum cutting forces.

Until recently, ACC, which is based on force and torque requirements, was used more often than GAC, which is based on dimensions and surface finish, because of the greater reliability of force and torque sensors. However, improvements in optical sensing technology are leading to increased usage of GAC.

Trends

In the future, more research efforts will focus on the supervisory level of control. There will also be more implementation of research findings from the 1970s and 1980s, which because of the technological limitations of the time, have had little commercial impact thus far.

Efforts to develop standard open architecture computer control platforms are key. Past government efforts in this area were not successful, and current efforts are primarily under industry leadership with some government support. Many personal-computer–based CNCs are being developed as alternatives to CNCs from FANUC, Allen-Bradley, Hurco, Dynapath, and others. These systems must be open, upgradeable, modular, interconnectable, etc., for this trend to have a significant impact beyond the job-shop environment.

Sensor technologies are improving rapidly (e.g., force sensors, optical measurement devices for the parts and tools, and measurement of surface finish). These developments are very significant and will continue over the next decade. Developments in sensor technology and AI will dovetail nicely with future commercial developments in CNC.

Country Comparison

CNC technology was developed in the United States, and the United States still leads in research and development. However, Japan and Europe are also active in R&D.

The market is now dominated by one Japanese firm (FANUC), and U.S. companies (e.g., GE, Allen-Bradley, Hurco, Dynapath) have either dropped out or have reduced their market shares to very minor levels. There is also some European (mostly German) presence in the market. Europe has its own open systems and standardization efforts, based upon similar successful efforts in vehicle electronics.

SIC Code 3625: Relays and Industrial Controls—Electronic Data Interchange (EDI)[28]

Current Status

EDI is defined as "the movement of business documents electronically between or within firms in a structured, machine-retrievable, data format that permits data to be transferred, without rekeying, from a business application in one location to one in another location." EDI strives to eliminate paper from business transactions, allowing them to take place faster (no mailing delays) and with more accuracy (no rekeying errors) than ever before possible.

The development of EDI within and across industries could be facilitated by standards. These standards could lower the cost of an EDI system by eliminating the competitive advantage of a company having a proprietary system, thus making EDI more affordable to smaller businesses.[29] Value added networks (VANs) allow buyers to use multiple suppliers despite the current lack of industry standards. VANs are third-party networks that convert information between EDI systems with incompatible formats. It should be noted that VANs are more costly to a company than industry standards, as standards are free once developed, and translator services charge a fee.

Although many companies use EDI technology, few use electronic graphic interchange (EGI) technology. EGI transfers massive graphic or geometric design files between CAD systems. EGI has the same benefits as EDI (speed and accuracy), but is not yet as robust as EDI; for EGI to work, both the CAD systems and the modems of the designer and vendor must be able to be interfaced.

Trends

To compete globally, the United States must either develop or adopt international standards for EDI. The Organization for Data Exchange through Teletransmission in Europe (ODETTE) has announced it will adopt a uniform standard developed by the United Nations Committee on EDI for Administration, Commerce, & Transport (EDIFACT) by 1994. Japan is also considering EDIFACT as an option. Meanwhile, NIST has formed a task force to

---

[28]The following material is based on DeFosse and Barr (1992), Gupta and Neel (1992), and "ANSI and STEP, Meet ODETTE and EDIFACT" (1991).

[29]Some suppliers try to block adoption of universal standards to maintain their edge and buyer dependence.

develop Standards for the Exchange of Product (STEP) model data which should be ready to use by 2001.

Country Comparison

The lack of standardization in the U.S. EDI system, while not currently a problem, may eventually cause the United States to lag behind its foreign competitors.

SIC Code 3625: Relays and Industrial Controls—Micromachines[30]

Current Status

Micromachines are small enough to operate on the surface of a microchip. The problem they face is generating power. Early silicon-based systems, just a few micrometers thick, used technology common to the microelectronics industry, but produced barely enough power to overcome friction. Generating necessary torque demanded thicker components made with rare specialized equipment. In conventional microelectronic lithographic techniques, patterns of motors, gears, or other components are placed on a photosensitive polymide. Cavities are chemically etched, then filled with copper or nickel with standard electroplating technology. Secondary etching removes the polymide mold to expose a finished component. Components are well defined (aspect ratios of up to 8 to 1) because the photolithographic process creates straight edges in the polymide. The primary process used for micromechanical system fabrication is sacrificial silicon etching (or a related technique called bulk micromachining), which leaves a silicon (or doped silicon) single-crystal surface (although polycrystalline methods are being explored).

In April 1992, Japan began a $190 million, ten-year project to develop both a medical and an industrial micromachine prototype. The industrial prototype will be used to seek out and mend small cracks within nuclear power plants or in jet engine turbines. The project encompasses 27 companies and institutions, two of which are U.S. firms.

The micromachines technology is approaching commercialization in some areas, but is still 10 to 20 years away from any commercial impact on the machine-tool

[30]The following material is based on Brendley and Steeb (1993), Normile (1992), Studt (1990), and "Tech Update" (1991).

industry. The sensor aspect of the technology is not far away from being useful in machine tools, but the actuation aspect of the technology is.

Trends

This technology is most likely to impact sensor development (e.g., reliability, on-board signal processing, and cost), which could be important for in-process gauging in machining processes. Micromachines could also affect machine tools through the development of microactuators with similar benefits. The benefits of micromechanical systems are still years away (e.g., 5 to 10 years) from utilization in the machine-tool industry for such applications as in-process force and/or temperature sensing.

Other future applications for micromachines include

- positioners operating on a microchip's surface that work as stages for scanning tunneling electron microscopes
- platforms for positioning lasers to fiber optic cable
- coating devices that place a diamond film on surfaces in machine tools or on the cutting edge itself
- small sensing/measurement devices
- small motors.

Very far into the future (20 to 50 years), molecular manufacturing may become commercially viable. Objects would be "grown" one molecule at a time, very much like biological forms (e.g., firewood, hay, potatoes). The engineering challenges are wide open.

Country Comparison

The United States leads this field, but research is active in Japan and Europe. Japan seems to have a better strategic (commercial view) as opposed to the research orientation in the United States.

SIC Code 3823: Industrial Instruments for Measurement, Display, and Control of Process Variations—Display Technology[31]

Current Status

The two key areas for display technology are flat-panel displays and touchscreens. Many unsuccessful attempts have been made to replace the bulky cathode ray tube (CRT) monitor with more manageable flat-panel display devices; the "venerable" CRT is still the de facto standard. Of the three existing forms of flat-panel displays—liquid crystal, plasma, and electroluminescent—industry experts believe active-matrix liquid-crystal displays (AMLCDs) have the most potential to dominate the flat-panel market. In terms of overall viewing criteria, AMLCD performance exceeds or compares favorably with other flat-panel technologies. The biggest drawback to its inception is cost. Color AMLCDs can cost up to 12 times as much as a color CRT and from 5 to 10 times as much as other flat-panel technologies.

Studies show that touch screens are more efficient than even voice commands in such applications as factory control. Compared to the myriad of lights and switches on conventional control panels, touch screens can greatly simplify manufacturing, assembly, and retooling. Perhaps the biggest advantage of touch screens is that they provide the flexibility to reconfigure machines in software. There are several types of touch screen technologies, categorized by the way they detect touches; common types include resistive, infrared, capacitive, surface acoustic wave, and piezoelectric. No technology is superior for all applications.

Trends

A key trend in both flat-panel display touch screen technology is making these technologies robust enough to operate in a shop-floor environment, while reducing their cost.

Country Comparison

The United States is competitive in research in both these technologies, but Japan dominates the commercial market. Several industry-government joint initiatives were launched in the United States during 1993 and 1994.

---

[31]The following material is based on Leonard (1992), Berardinis (1993), and Shandle (1993).

Bibliography

Albert, Mark, "EDM in Japan," *Modern Machine Shop*, February 1991.

American Society for Metals, *Metals Handbook:* Vol. 16, *Machining*, 9th ed., Materials Park, Ohio: ASM International, 1989.

"ANSI and STEP, Meet ODETTE and EDIFACT," *Manufacturing Engineering*, Vol. 107, No. 2, August 1991.

"Applications: Rapid Prototyping a Strategic Tool in Concurrent Engineering," *Industrial Engineering*, Vol. 24, No. 11, Nov. 1992, p. 22.

Arter, Richard, "At USCTI Roundtable: US. Toolmakers Race to Keep Pace with Technology," *Tooling & Production*, Vol. 56, No. 6, September 1990a, pp. 52–57.

Arter, Rich, "Japanese Technology Finds a Home in Indiana," *Tooling & Production*, Vol. 56, No. 7, October 1990b.

Ashley, S., "A Mosaic for Machine Tools," *Mechanical Engineering*, September 1990, pp. 38–43.

Beard, Tom, "Rotary Transfer Gets Flexible," *Modern Machine Shop*, April 1990.

Beard, Tom. "Laser Takes On a New Dimension," *Modern Machine Shop*, February 1991a.

Beard, Tom, " Managing Modular," *Modern Machine Shop*, May 1991b.

Berardinis, Lawrence, "Touch and Go," *Machine Design*, Vol. 65, No. 7, April 9, 1993, pp. 48–53.

Bosch, John A., "The Changing Role of Coordinate Measuring Machines," *Industrial Engineering*, Vol. 24, No. 11, November 1992, pp. 46–48.

Brendley, K. W., and R. Steeb, *Military Applications of Micromechanical Systems*, Santa Monica, Calif.: RAND, MR-175-OSD/AF/A, 1993.

Brown, Stuart B., and Merton C. Fleming, "Net-Shape Forming Via Semi-Solid Processing," *Advanced Materials and Processes*, January 1993, pp. 36–40.

Business Trends Analysts, Inc., *The U.S. Machine Tool Industry*, Commack, New York, March 1991.

Chatterjee, S. K., "Increased Domestic Demand Ups Japan's Machine Tool Orders," *Modern Machine Shop*, April 1988, pp. 122–124.

Cohen, S. S., and J. Zysman, *Manufacturing Matters*, New York: Basic Books, 1987.

"Computer Hardware and Software: Fuzzy Logic vs. Digital Logic," *Tooling & Production*, Vol. 56, No. 8, November 1990, p. 100.

"Controller Integrates Machining Systems," *Tooling & Production*, Vol. 56, No. 8, November 1990.

Costello, R. B., and M. Ernst, *Regaining U.S. Manufacturing Leadership*, Indianapolis, Indiana: Hudson Institute, 1992.

Council on Competitiveness, *A Competitive Profile of the Machine Tool Industry*, Washington, D.C., March 1991.

Council on Competitiveness, *Gaining New Ground: Technology Priorities for America's Future*, Washington, D.C., March 1991.

"Cover Story: High-Speed Machining: It Takes More Than a Fast Spindle," *Tooling & Production*, Vol. 60, No. 5, August 1993a.

"Cover Story: High-Speed Machining from Solid Stock," *Tooling & Production*, Vol. 60, No. 5, August 1993b.

"Cover Story: Small but Fast Tools Get New Machine," *Tooling & Production*, Vol. 60, No. 5, August 1993c.

DeFosse, Stephen F., and Teresa D. Barr, "Implementing EDI/EGI Will Reduce Time to Market," *Industrial Engineering*, Vol. 28, No. 8, August 1992, pp. 30–31.

Dunn, John, "Germany Forges a New Future," *The Engineer*, Vol. 275, No. 7121, October 15, 1992, pp. 22–23.

"The Focus of National Attention: Manufacturing," *NJIT Research*, Vol. 1, No. 1, March 1993, pp. 2–9.

Fuller, John, "Electrical Discharge Machining," in American Society for Metals, 1989, pp. 557–564.

Gallist, Rudolf, "High-Speed Machining: Where It's Headed," *Modern Machine Shop*, October 1989, pp. 67–78.

Geppert, Hans, "Increased Flexibility Through Palletizing," *Tooling & Production*, Vol. 56, No. 8, November 1990, pp. 36–40.

Geskin, Ernest, and Eugene Gordon, "Waterjet Machining," *NJIT Research*, Vol. 1, No. 1, Spring 1993, pp. 10–15.

Gettelman, Ken, "World Machine Tool Review: Europe," *Modern Machine Shop*, April 1990.

Gettelman, Ken, "Japan: Elegant Simplicity," *Modern Machine Shop*, March 1991a.

Gettelman, Ken, "Second Round for FMS," *Modern Machine Shop*, December 1991b.

Gupta, Yash P., and Gia A. Neel, "The Origin of EDI And Changes Associated with Its Implementation," *Industrial Engineering*, Vol. 24, No. 8, August 1992, pp. 25–29.

"High-Productivity Machining: High-Speed Machining," in American Society for Metals, 1989, pp. 597–606.

"Injection Molding Benefits Metals," *Tooling & Production*, Vol. 56, No. 8, November 1990.

Irving, Bob, "Lasers: Made in the U.S.A," *Welding Journal*, June 1992, pp. 67–73.

Johnston, C. E., "Waterjet/Abrasive Waterjet Machining," in American Society for Metals, 1989, pp. 520–527.

Koelsch, James R., "Flexible Cells Take Control," *Manufacturing Engineering*, Vol. 106, No. 3, September 1990.

Koelsch, James R., "Use the Beam for Better Cutting," *Manufacturing Engineering*, Vol. 106, No. 7, January 1991a, pp. 51–55.

Koelsch, James R., "Got the Shakes?" *Manufacturing Engineering*, March 1991b.

Koelsch, James R., "Knee Deep in Liability?" *Manufacturing Engineering*, Vol. 107, No. 2, August 1991c, pp. 28–33.

Leonard, Milt, "Reducing Flat-Panel Display Costs, " *Electronic Design*, Vol. 40, No. 1, January 9, 1992, p. 18.

Luxhoj, James T., et al., "Using Prototype Expert Systems for AGV Selection," *Industrial Engineering*, Vol. 24, No. 9, September 1992, pp. 44–48.

Machine Tool Task Force, *Proceedings of the Machine Tool Task Force Conference*, Chicago: Lawrence Livermore Laboratory, 1980.

"Manufacturing Update: US vs Foreign Machine Tools," *Tooling & Production*, Vol. 55, No. 2, May 1989, p. 10.

Market Intelligence Research Company, *U.S. Metal Cutting Machine Tools Markets*, Mountain View, Calif., 1990.

Market Intelligence Research Company, *U.S. Metal Forming and Special Machine Tools Market: Technology Shifts and Niche Applications Impact Growth*, Mountain View, Calif., 1990.

Mason, Burt, and Addis L. Harvey, "Digitizing: Printless Part Programming Comes of Age," *Tooling & Production*, Vol. 56, No. 6, September 1990, pp. 188–189.

Mason, Frederick, "Double Double Your Turning Power," *American Machinist*, May 1992a, pp. 34–41.

Mason, Frederick, "MCs for Small, High Precision Parts," *American Machinist*, September 1992b, pp. 65–68.

Mason, Frederick, "Fuzzy Logic Steers EDM with Finesse," *American Machinist*, June 1993, pp. 31–34.

Miao, Manrong, *An Overview of the Machine Tool Industry: Current Status and Future Progress with Special Emphasis on the United States and China*, Ann Arbor, Michigan: University of Michigan, NSF Center for Dimensional Measurement and Control in Manufacturing, July 3, 1993.

Miller, Paul C., "Lathes Turn to Other Tasks," *Tooling & Production*, Vol. 54, No. 12, March 1989, pp. 54–60.

Miska, Kurt H., "Driven Tools Turn on Turning Centers" *Manufacturing Engineering*, Vol. 105, No. 11, May 1990a, pp. 63–66.

Miska, Kurt H., "Merits of Metal Injection Molding," *Manufacturing Engineering*, Vol. 106, No. 1, July 1990b, pp. 87–89.

"Multiple Operation Machining: Transfer Machines," American Society for Metals, 1989, pp. 395–397.

Nagel, R. N., and R. Dove, *21st Century Manufacturing Enterprise Strategy*, Bethlehem, Penn.: Lehigh University, November 1991.

National Center for Manufacturing Sciences (NCMS), *Next Generation Workstation/Machine Controller (NGC): Requirements Definition Document (RDD)*, prepared for the Air Force Systems Command, August 1990.

National Science Board, *Science and Technology Indicators*, 10th ed., 1991.

National Science Board, *The Competitive Strength of U.S. Industrial Science and Technology: Strategic Issues*, August 1992.

Noaker, Paula, "Kill the Arc, Tame the Spark," *Manufacturing Engineering*, Vol. 106, No. 12, June 1991a, pp. 53–56.

Noaker, Paula, "Turning Out Faster Setups," *Manufacturing Engineering*, Vol. 107, No. 1, July 1991b, pp. 43–46.

Noaker, Paula, "Pressed to Reduce Setup?" *Manufacturing Engineering*, Vol. 107, No. 3, September 1991, pp. 45–49.

Normile, Denise, "Japan Launches Big Micromachine Effort," *Research & Development*, June 1992, pp. 22–24.

Office of Science and Technology Policy, *Science and Technology*, March 1992.

Owen, Jean V., "CMMs for Process Control," *Manufacturing Engineering*, Vol. 107, No. 2, August 1991a, pp. 39–41.

Owen, Jean V., "Are Cermets for Real?" *Manufacturing Engineering*, Vol. 107, No. 4, October 1991b, pp. 28–31.

Owen, Jean V., "Teaming UP for CIM," *Manufacturing Engineering*, Vol. 107, No. 4, October 1991c, pp. 57–59.

Poeth, Dean, "The Manufacturing Technologies for the 1990's Are Here Today," Association for Manufacturing Technology, no date.

"Production Lines: Flexible Tooling for Flexible Turning," *Manufacturing Engineering*, Vol. 107, No. 1, July 1991, p. 72.

"Production Lines: Prototypes Pronto," *Manufacturing Engineering*, Vol. 107, No. 4, October 1991a, p. 88.

"Production Lines: Tougher Tool Coating," *Manufacturing Engineering*, Vol. 107, No. 4, October 1991b, p. 78.

"Quality in Production: A Fresh Look at Optical Gauging: The Optical CMM," *Tooling & Production*, Vol. 56, No. 7, October 1990, pp. 76–78.

Sachs, E., et al., "Three Dimensional Printing: Rapid Tooling and Prototypes Directly from a CAD Model," *ASME JEI*, November 1992, pp. 481–484.

Schreiber, Rita R., "Focus: Lasers (part I)," *Manufacturing Engineering*, Vol. 106, No. 7, January 1991a, pp. 41–44.

Schreiber, Rita R., "Focus: Lasers (part II)," *Manufacturing Engineering*, Vol. 106, No. 8, February 1991b, pp. 39–43.

Schreiber, Rita R., "Making Workholding Work," *Manufacturing Engineering*, Vol. 107, No. 4, October 1991, pp. 43–45.

Schreiber, Rita R., "On-Line Oracles," *Manufacturing Engineering*, Vol. 107, No. 5, November 1991c, pp. 83–88.

Sciberras, E., and B. D. Payne, *Machine Tool Industry Technical Change and International Comptetitiveness*, London: The Technical Change Centre, no date.

Shandle, Jack, "A Revolution Is in Store for Flat-Panel Displays," *Electronic Design*, April 15, 1993.

Shapira, Phillip, "Japan's Kohsetsushi Program," National Institute of Standards and Technology, October 1990.

Sprow, Eugene, "Off-the-Shelf Cell Control," *Tooling & Production*, Vol. 56, No. 8, November 1990, pp. 64–66.

Stevens, Larry, "Coordinate Measuring Machines: Putting on Muscle," *Manufacturing Systems*, April 1991.

Studt, Tim, "Micromachines: Miniature Devices Come of Age," *Research & Development*, December 1990.

"Tech Update: Manufacturing Micromachines," *Manufacturing Engineering*, Vol. 107, No. 4, October 1991, p. 26.

"Tech Update: New CO2 Laser for Cutting and Welding," *Manufacturing Engineering*, Vol. 106, No. 1, July 1990, p. 42.

"Tech Update: Powder Injection Molding Update," *Manufacturing Engineering*, Vol. 106, No. 1, July 1990, p. 46.

"Tech Update: Thin-Film Diamond Coatings in Action," *Manufacturing Engineering*, Vol. 107, No. 4, October 1991.

"Technology Trends: EDM Promises Faster, Finer Cuts," *American Machinist*, December 1991a, pp. 11–12.

"Technology Trends: U.S. EDM Use Below Japan, Europe," *American Machinist*, December 1991b, p. 11.

"Technology Update: Controller Integrates Machining Systems," *Tooling & Production*, Vol. 56, No. 8, November 1990, pp. 22–23.

"Technology Update: Injection Molding Benefits Metals," *Tooling & Production*, Vol. 56, No. 8, November 1990, p. 22.

Toth-Fejel, Tihamer, "Analysis of Critical Technologies: Machine Tools: Substitute Technologies," Industrial Technology Institute Draft, September 1992.

Ulsoy, A. G., and Y. Koren, "Control of Machining Processes," *ASME Journal of Dynamic Systems, Measurement, and Control,* June 1993, Vol. 115, No. 2B, pp. 301–308.

Ulsoy, A. G., and Y. Koren, *Review of the Research on the Control of Machining Processes*, University of Michigan, Department of Engineering and Applied Mechanics, July 13, 1993.

"Universal Concept Gaining Ground in U.S.," *Modern Machine Shop*, May 1992, p. 140.

"What's This Ceramics Craze?" Manufacturing Engineering, Vol. 107, No. 2, August 1991, p. 46.

Winski, Dennis, "Modern Requirements of Precision Milling Machines," *Modern Machine Shop*, October 1992, pp. 61–69.

Wohlers, Terry T., "Make Fiction Fact FAST," *Manufacturing Engineering,* Vol. 106, No. 9, March 1991, pp. 44–49.

Appendix G
Focus Groups

Max Nelson, RAND

Why Focus Groups?

During the initial stages of our exploratory research, it became increasingly clear that, although the literature was replete with policy recommendations, there was little understanding of how key decisionmakers in the machine-tool industry view such policy changes. Consequently, we felt it critical to gather information on the industry's perceptions toward current and potential policies and the reasons behind those perceptions, to gauge the impact of potential changes. Although some information was gathered through interviews and site visits, it was felt that these efforts were too limited to gain a deep insight into the industry. Reliance on a sole survey instrument to gather this information would be too restrictive and could not be completed in the time limits for our study. Given the nature of our interest, it was felt that open-ended questions were more conducive to our needs. We then chose to pursue a series of focus-group discussions to gather this information. In his text on this subject,[1] Richard A. Krueger describes focus groups as follows:

> Focus groups are increasingly being used by researchers .... The focus group discussion is particularly effective in providing information about *why* people think or feel the way they do. Focus groups have been a mainstay in private sector marketing research. More recently, public sector organizations are beginning to discover the potential of this procedure .... A focus group is typically composed of seven to ten participants who are unfamiliar with each other. These participants are selected because they have certain characteristics in common that relate to the topic of the group. The researcher creates a permissive environment in the focus group that nurtures different perceptions and points of view, without pressuring participants to vote, plan, or reach consensus. The group discussion is conducted several times with similar types of participants to identify trends and patterns in perceptions. Careful and systematic analysis of the discussions provide clues and insights as to how a product, service, or opportunity is perceived .... Focus groups offer several advantages, including:

---

[1]Richard A. Krueger, *Focus Groups: A Practical Guide for Applied Research*, Sage Publications, Newbury Park, Calif., 1988.

(1) That the technique is a socially oriented research method capturing real-life data in a social environment;

(2) it has flexibility;

(3) it has high face validity;

(4) it has speedy results;

(5) it is low in cost.

Focus groups have limitations that affect the quality of the results. Limitations include:

(1) focus groups afford the researcher less control than individual interviews;

(2) data are difficult to analyze;

(3) moderators require special skills;

(4) differences between groups can be troublesome;

(5) groups are difficult to assemble;

(6) the discussion must be conducted in a conducive environment.

Methodology

To structure the focus groups' discussions, we developed a framework that asked participants to rate policies along two dimensions: (1) the importance to the machine-tool industry of the policies and (2) the government's potential to change these policies to assist the industry. We selected sixteen policies in five broad categories because our research indicated these to be potentially important for the machine-tool industry (Table G.1).

Participants were asked to rank the two policy dimensions on a scale of one ("not very important") to four ("very important"). We plotted their responses and used these graphs to select some of the 16 policies for discussion. We used the discussion to explore the reasons behind the participants' responses to gain a more in-depth understanding of why certain policies were considered important to the industry and why the government's potential to change certain policies was felt to be strong in some cases and weak in others. These discussions also allowed us to elicit new information regarding the issues and the policies addressed (i.e., we were able to gain concrete examples of the effects of export controls on certain firms and heard stories of catastrophic liability suits).

This approach served several functions: (1) It provided quantitative ratings across the two dimensions; (2) it allowed us to gain industry feedback on the implementation of various policies (i.e., what has and has not worked in the past); (3) it demonstrated perceptions on potential policy options not previously considered; (4) it standardized input on the importance of each policy for the

Table G.1

Policies Examined in Focus Groups

Issue Category	Policy
Trade	VRAs
	Export promotion and assistance
	Level trade playing field
	Reduce export restrictions
Technology	Process technology/management assistance
	Standards setting
	Technology development/transfer
Regulatory	Liability laws
	Anti-trust laws
	Government procurement
Capital	Investment tax credits
	Improve access to capital
	Macroeconomic policy
Education	General education
	Apprenticeships
	Engineering training

industry, and government's potential to change various policies; (5) it provided information on the general role that government has had in the industry; and (6) it gathered information on the perceived status of the industry and provided industry feedback on our analysis and findings.

Given the structure and geographic distribution of the U.S. machine-tool industry, we decided to carry out our focus groups at four geographically dispersed sites of machine-tool activity (Los Angeles, Detroit, Pittsburgh, and Wichita). We also included four different types of participants involved with machine tools (machine-tool makers, distributors, users, and service providers and the government) from a mix of small- and large-scale organizations. In all, we had 37 participants. The breakdown of participants and locations is shown in Table G.2 and Figure G.1.

Overall Analysis

Although we understand the difficulties associated with generalizing from focus group data (i.e., nonrandom sampling, small sample size, etc.), our focus groups have provided a larger sample size than many previous studies that have relied on interviews, testimony, or small-sample surveys. This fact, along with our

Table G.2

Focus Group Participants and Locations

Location	Makers	Distributors	Users	Government	Total
Los Angeles, Calif.	5	3	2	—	10
Pittsburgh, Pa.	3	4	1	—	8
Wichita, Kan.	1	1	5	2	9
Detroit, Mich.	5	—	1	4	10
Total	14	8	9	6	37

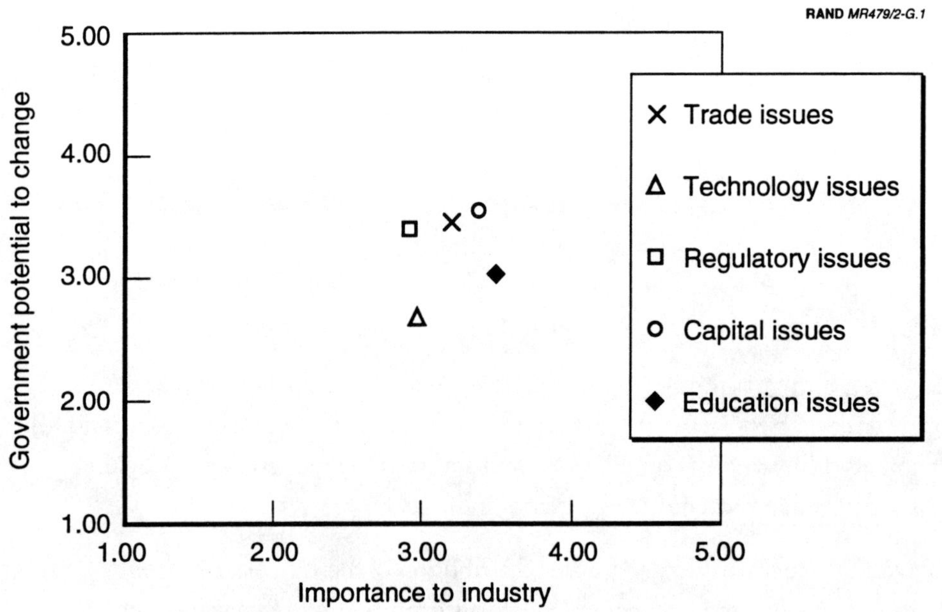

Figure G.1—Focus Group Responses by Issue Category

inclusion of a wide array of participants across organizations, geography, and industries, has increased our confidence in these findings relative to many previous data-gathering efforts. The focus groups were only one element of our overall analysis of the machine-tool industry, and they represent a small fraction of our total interviews. The groups were used as tools to help inform the study on industry perceptions of its "demand" for government services.

A number of cautions should be observed in interpreting the focus-group results. Although industry representatives may have a certain perception about a policy, this perception may be inaccurate, either with regard to the past effectiveness of the policy or its potential future impact. Also, it must be remembered that government policy serves a number of constituencies besides the machine-tool industry (i.e., consumers, workers, taxpayers, etc.).

As shown in Table G.3, our focus-group participants felt that, overall, education issues were the most important to the industry but that the government had the most potential to change capital issues. The table also presents the average response for these issue categories by the various organizational groupings. The results for the total group are presented in Figure G.1. As can be seen, capital issues were considered the most important across both variables, with trade issues ranking second, and education issues a close third.

Perhaps the most interesting finding was that technology issues ranked far below the other categories. Participants felt that technology issues were neither as critically important to the industry nor as amenable to government action as the other issue categories. However, it must be remembered that a lower ranking does not indicate that a policy is considered unimportant, only that it is considered less important than the others. As demonstrated in Table G.3, in total, technology issues were ranked almost as a three on a scale of one to four for their importance to the industry, and ranked a 2.67 on a scale of one to four for the government's potential to change these policies.

Detailed Analysis

This section provides detailed data on the quantitative and qualitative information gathered for each of the specific policies. The importance of each policy across both variables (i.e., distance from the origin) is shown graphically

Table G.3

Average Responses by Issue Category

Policy	Total	Makers	Distributors	Users	Government
Importance to industry					
Trade issues	3.20	3.16	3.42	3.16	3.25
Technology issues	2.97	2.74	3.33	3.08	3.10
Regulatory issues	2.92	2.88	2.78	3.00	2.94
Capital issues	3.39	3.40	3.33	3.33	3.50
Education issues	3.51	3.38	3.67	3.53	3.72
Government potential to change					
Trade issues	3.45	3.46	3.42	3.41	3.50
Technology issues	2.67	2.38	3.00	2.78	2.99
Regulatory issues	3.39	3.45	3.33	3.39	3.28
Capital issues	3.54	3.67	3.56	3.42	3.50
Education issues	3.03	2.83	3.56	2.94	3.39

in Figure G.2. Clearly, investment tax credits (ITCs) are perceived to be significantly more important than other policies; roughly equivalent importance is placed on most capital, trade, and education issues, except for engineering training and voluntary restraint agreements; most regulatory and technology issues are considered relatively less important. The industry's preferences are in stark contrast to recent government efforts, which have emphasized technology and regulatory issues. These efforts include the Technology Transfer Act and Cooperative Research and Development Agreements (CRADAs), cooperative research and anti-trust laws, the Next Generation Controller and standards setting, and the NIST Manufacturing Technology Centers and process technology and management assistance efforts.

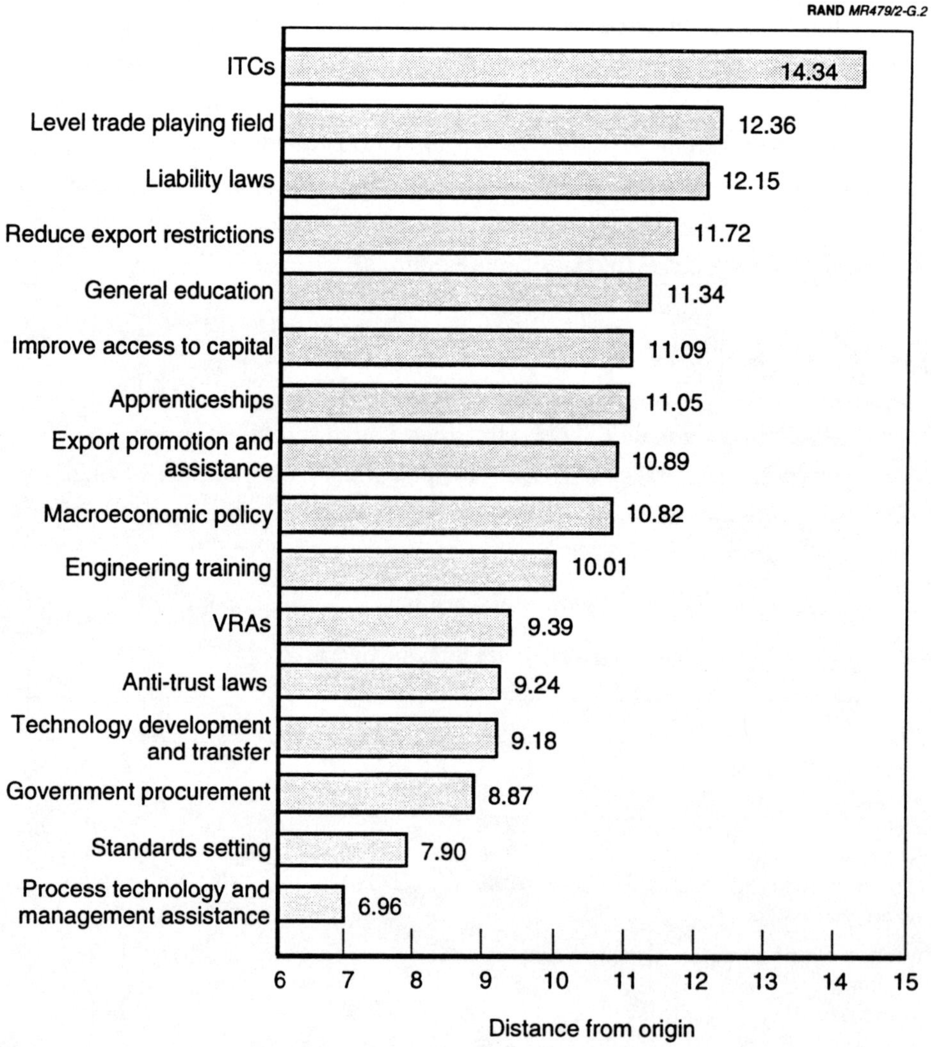

Figure G.2—Overall Ranking of Policies

Capital Issues

Capital issues were the highest-ranked issue category across all respondents. This overall importance was primarily a result of the high ranking of ITCs. While improved access to capital and macroeconomic policy were considered important by all groups, they were overshadowed by ITCs. All organizations (makers, distributors, users, and government) ranked ITCs as the most important policy.

ITCs. ITCs were felt to have had a beneficial effect in the early 1970s—having been used historically as an investment stimulus during downturns—and were considered to be the "least bad thing government can do" to foster the industry. One of the greatest virtues of ITCs is their simplicity—a factor that is critically important for machine-tool makers, 80 percent of whose customers may be small firms without major accounting departments to handle burdensome tax laws. Though previous ITCs had short-term effects, which altered the pattern of orders, respondents felt a strong need for a consistent, long-term ITC or accelerated depreciation policy to encourage investment. The newer machine-tool base in Japan was felt to be one result of an accelerated depreciation schedule that leads to faster product turnaround than in the United States, although there is little or no evidence to support this contention. It was also believed that there is a need to spur investment among U.S. customers; ITCs were felt to have "universal support" among machine-tool user firms. Though ITCs were heartily endorsed, it was felt that their implementation should not exclude foreign purchases, because the risks of a trade war did not warrant whatever benefits might flow from a "buy-American" contingency attached to any ITCs. Figure G.3 shows the distribution of responses on ITCs.

Access to Capital. The primary concern over access to capital was not the availability of money or the interest rate but the belief that lenders do not understand manufacturing—that credit is more available to other types of business investments, because bankers "selectively understand parts of business." It was felt that banks cannot earn enough on relatively small loans to warrant their hiring specialists in machine tools, and this lack of expertise leads to difficulty in acquiring capital. A suggested solution to this problem was to change banking regulations to allow bank managers to sit on machine-tool company boards as they do in Japan and Germany. Another solution was the establishment of specialist banks with an understanding of a particular industry—such as machine tools—a trend that is already under way. Furthermore, it was felt that banks are generally hesitant to loan to SMEs and, given the preponderance of machine-tool firms in this category, that the

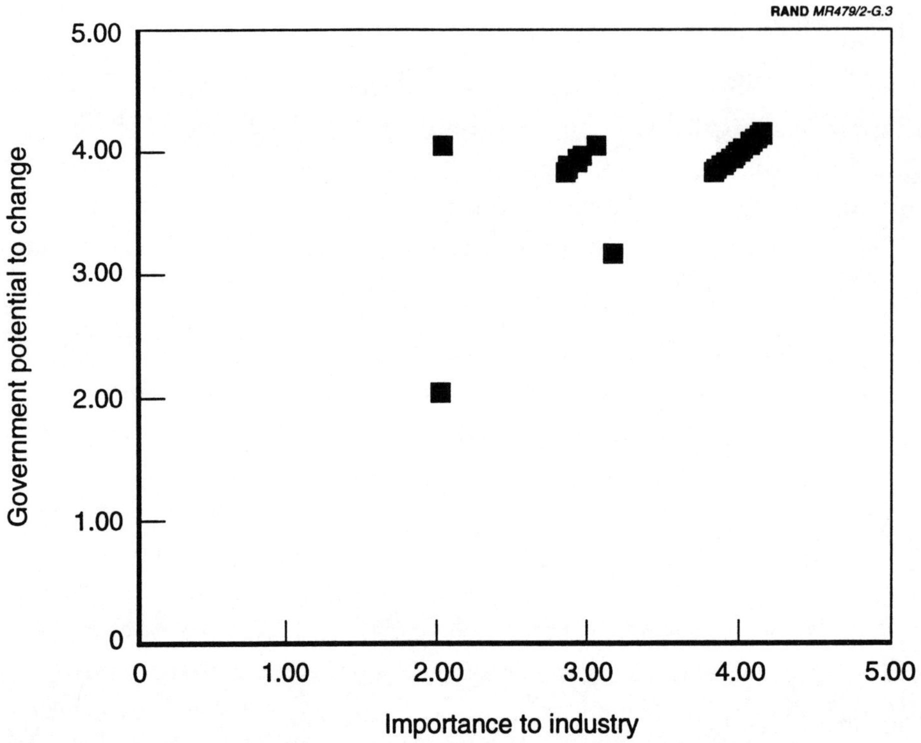

Figure G.3—Distribution of Responses on ITCs

machine-tool industry was selectively harmed by this bias. The cyclical nature of the machine-tool industry makes this situation even worse; it was believed that banks are biased toward steady growth and shy away from cyclical industries. These factors, combined with new banking reserve requirements following the savings and loan crisis, have led to a situation in which even firms with good relationships with banks are having problems. Export finance was seen to be a particular problem in acquiring capital. In Japan, export financing is provided through large trading companies, and banks provide tide-over financing for makers completing an order. However, U.S. machine-tool makers no longer even receive in-progress payments. Furthermore, U.S. banks are seen to be uncomfortable with foreign exposure and to prefer equivalent risk in other areas. Finally, it was felt that, even with freely available cheap capital, firms themselves cannot risk the uncertainty in investment. These situations lead to a catch-22 for machine-tool firms. Many are not profitable enough to finance the major new investments needed to restore their profitability; as a result, they become less profitable. Thus, the issue of access to capital is wound up in the nature of the industry structure and profitability. Figure G.4 shows the distribution of responses on "improve access to capital."

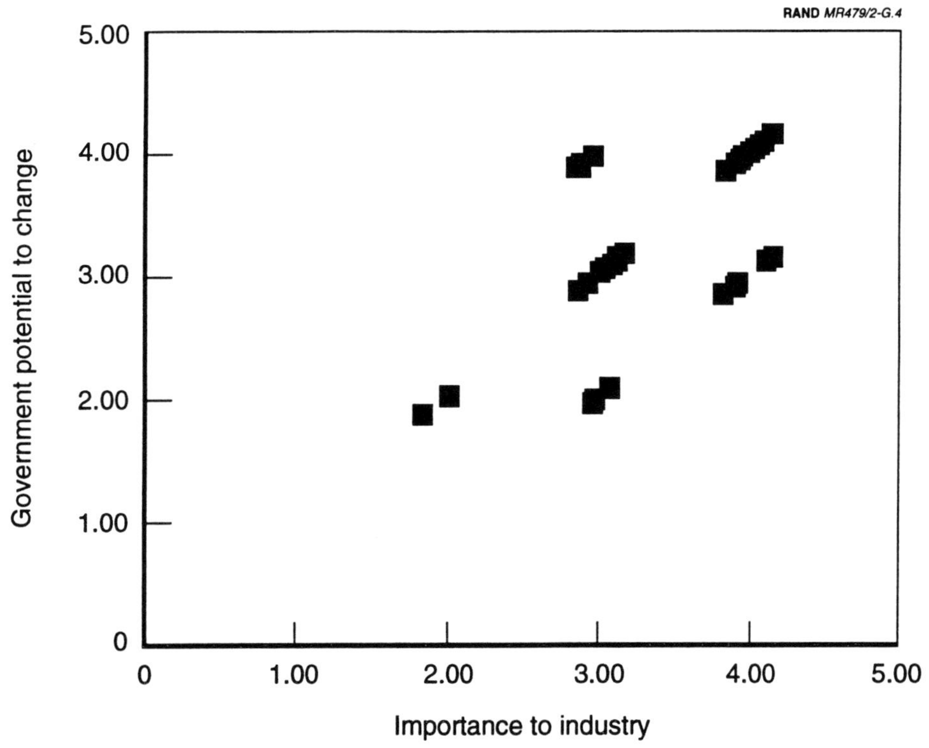

Figure G.4—Distribution of Responses on Improve Access to Capital

Macroeconomic Policy. Macroeconomic policy (i.e., exchange and interest rates) was considered to be the least important capital issue among all respondents, although it was felt that there was a higher potential for the government to change this issue than the access to capital issue. Interestingly, makers ranked this issue as more important than did the other organizations, perhaps because they felt that a decline in the dollar should create opportunity for export to Japan and elsewhere. Figure G.5 provides the distribution of responses on macroeconomic policy.

Trade Issues

Trade issues were ranked the second highest overall, with a level trade playing field considered the most important policy. However, this ranking was dominated by the high importance placed on this issue by government and user participants; makers and distributors did not rank it as highly. In fact, makers felt that "reduce export restrictions" was more important than a level trade playing field, while distributors felt that "export promotion and assistance" was the most important policy in trade issues. These findings are likely due to the various personal experiences of the organizations. For instance, users have direct

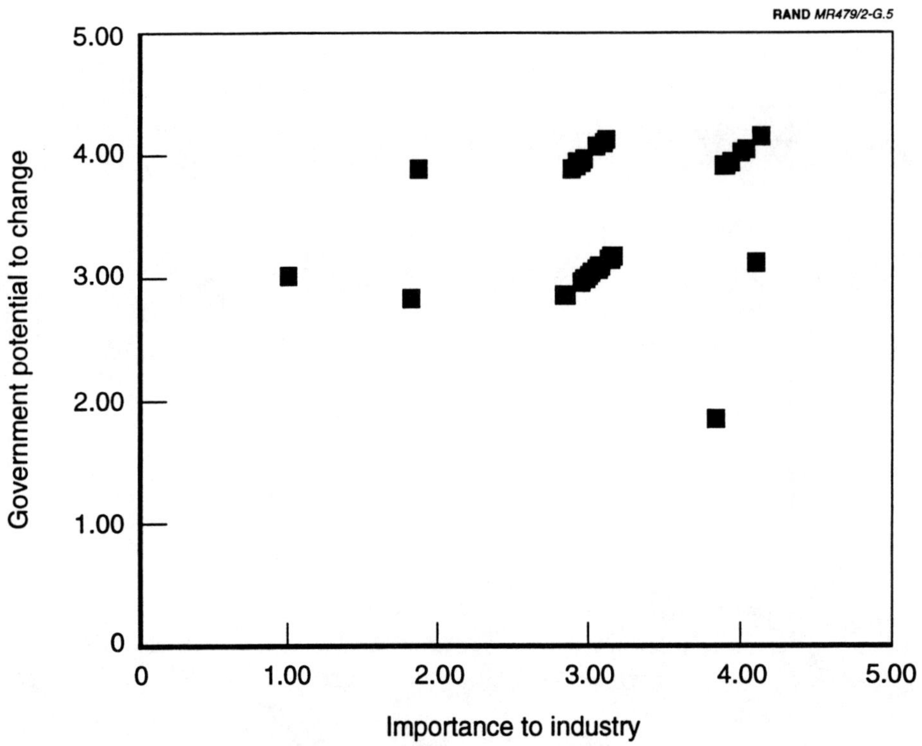

Figure G.5—Distribution of Responses on Macroeconomic Policy

experience with foreign trade practices leading to concern over a level trade playing field, while makers have direct experience trying to get export licenses, and distributors have experience with international export promotion policies.

Level Trade Playing Field. By a large margin, the vast majority of concern centered around the Japanese market. It was felt that the Japanese market was "mysterious" and hard to penetrate. Although participants found it hard to identify any particular block, they felt that, somehow, exporting to Japan "never seems to work," and that, consequently, it was "not worth the effort." It was believed that there is strong "cultural pressure" in Japan, as in other countries, to buy domestic products, and that this might be one cause of the mysterious blockage. Participants believed that the closed nature of Japanese markets made it hard for U.S. firms to take advantage of the fall in the value of the dollar. Similarly, the high yen value was cited as increasing the costs of setting up sales operations in Japan, so that the benefits were often not justified by the costs. Some participants disagreed, arguing that the United States can sell in Japan if firms have the right products. In fact, several respondents remarked that they had actually turned down Japanese orders, while others said that although they sell throughout Asia, they exclude Japan. Though there was a strong desire for a level trade playing field, implementation of policies was felt to be important, as shown by the general agreement that Super 301 antidumping statutes were difficult and expensive to enforce. Figure G.6 shows the distribution of responses on level trade playing field. As can be seen, there is a wide distribution in responses. There may be two reasons for this: First, a few of the firms participating have successfully penetrated the Japanese market and attribute the overall lack of success in exporting to Japan to other firms' strategies and not to government policies; second, many respondents expressed concern over potential recriminations resulting from international trade policies.

Reduce Export Restrictions. Participants provided a number of anecdotes related to efforts to get export licenses. The consensus was that export licensing is a "nightmare." One respondent stated that "one guy in [the Department of] Commerce reviews applications . . . and I'd like to strangle him." Participants felt that the system was arbitrary, and that it is biased in favor of some firms. The restrictions were seen to be particularly onerous for the large machine-tool markets in the former Soviet Union and China. One participant contended that it takes a minimum of six months to get a license to export to China, and then there is only a 10-percent chance of approval. Others remarked on the huge Soviet market, which enabled Germany, with its large exports to the former Soviet

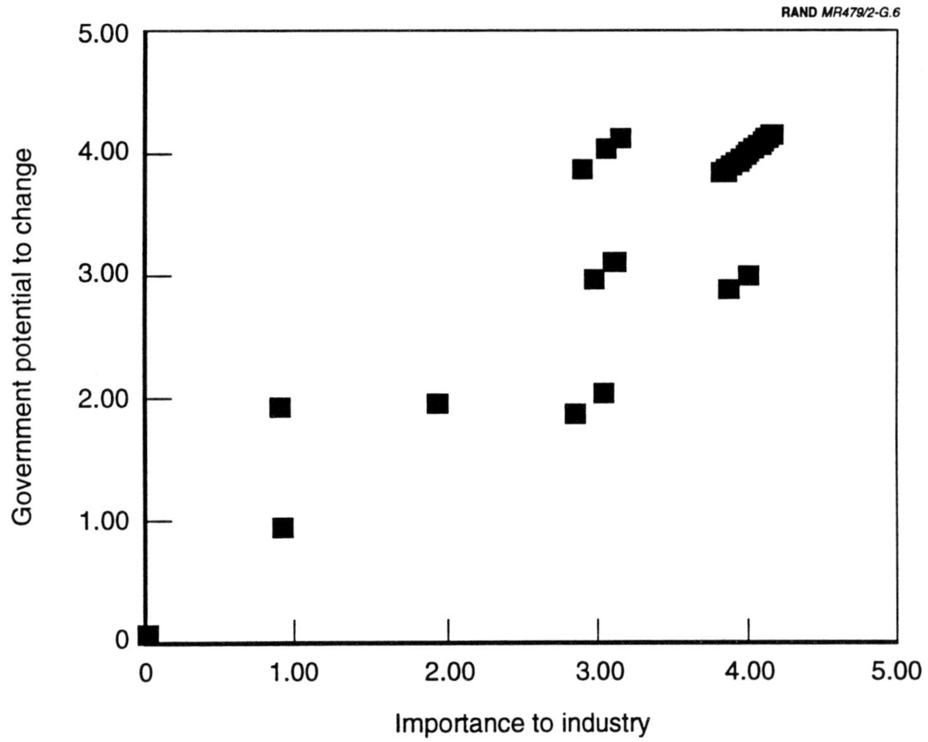

Figure G.6—Distribution of Responses on Level Trade Playing Field

Union, to weather Western business cycles. Participants remarked on their belief that Germany and Japan regularly flaunt COCOM restrictions, particularly with respect to China, and that this provided them a significant edge. However, Japan actually trails U.S. and German exports into the Chinese market. As one participant said: "They remember Nanking." It was felt that stringent export restrictions in the United States dissuade makers from trying to market worldwide and that, consequently, U.S. firms fail to achieve economies of scale found by firms in other nations. Figure G.7 shows the distribution of responses on reduce export restrictions.

Export Promotion and Assistance. Respondents felt that the government could, in fact, provide useful export assistance. While the Department of Commerce had helped some respondents locate distributors overseas, no other government export programs were described as very useful. In particular, implementation of financial assistance at the Export-Import Bank was found to be of little utility. One participant commented that although he had been involved in the bank, "we don't use them." Participants felt that the government could play a useful role by funding U.S. firms at foreign trade shows, or by having embassies provide more informed assistance. Furthermore, it was stated that foreign users of machine tools, particularly those in Mexico, cannot get access to capital to purchase U.S. machine tools. The Association for Manufacturing Technology

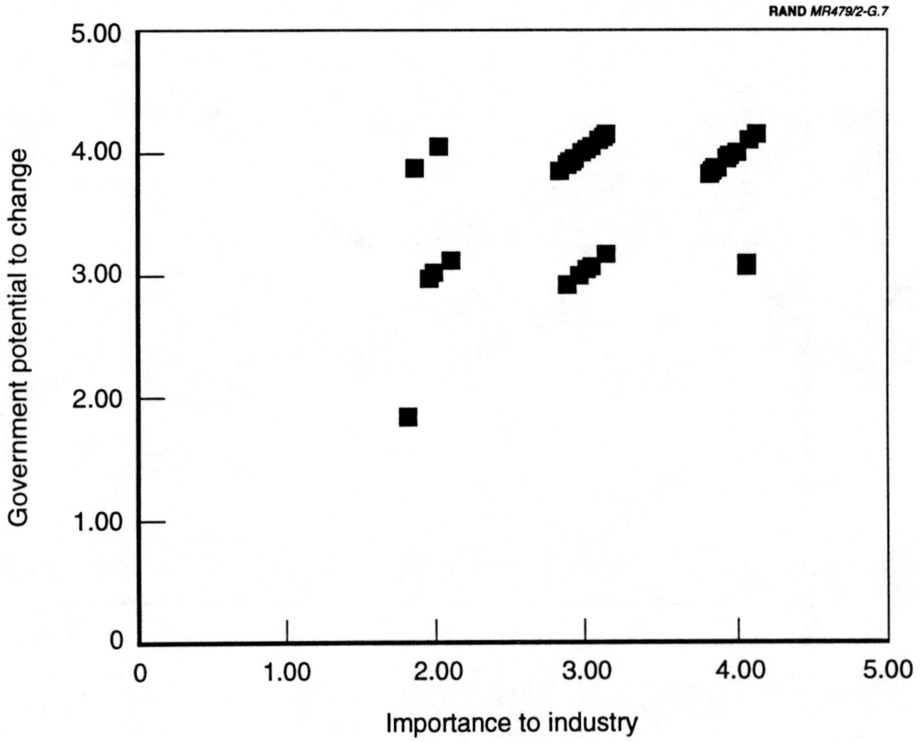

Figure G.7—Distribution of Responses on Reduce Export Restrictions

(AMT) was felt to be of particular help in facilitating exports. AMT created the first U.S. trading company to promote U.S. exports, and they got the first umbrella policy through the Export-Import Bank. Figure G.8 demonstrates the distribution of responses on export promotion and assistance. Similarly, certain state-level programs were felt to be useful through development of cooperative sales arrangements to South and Central America.

VRAs. The responses to VRAs were mixed. Most participants were against the idea of protectionism, but many saw VRAs as a crude way to level the trade playing field. The firms that benefited most directly from VRAs believed they could now compete on quality and efficiency when the VRAs expire. They recognized the unintended consequences of VRAs, which pushed the Japanese into the upscale markets and convinced Taiwan to build facilities in Thailand to get around the restrictions. Second, participants believed that the benefits flowed selectively to certain U.S. firms and not to others, i.e., it was felt that they had helped the low-end U.S. niche producers and had convinced new firms to get into the machining-center market. Third, it was acknowledged that VRAs cut both ways; although they may have a positive impact on some suppliers, they have a negative effect on machine-tool users. Fourth, participants believed that, by the time VRAs were implemented, U.S. commodity producers were already

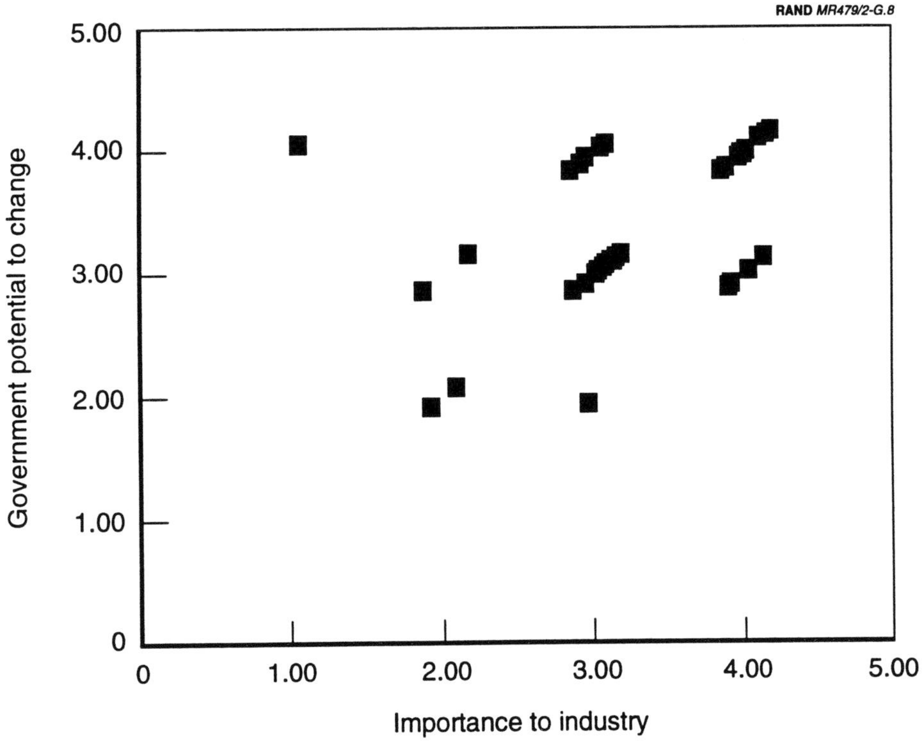

Figure G.8—Distribution of Responses on Export Promotion and Assistance

gone, and the United States had become a niche industry. Some respondents felt that VRAs should be used as a political bargaining lever to help open Japanese markets to U.S. imports. Figure G.9 shows the distribution of responses on VRAs.

Education Issues

Within education issues, general education was the highest ranking issue, with apprenticeships a close second and engineering training trailing a somewhat distant third. While makers felt general education was important, they ranked both apprenticeships and engineering training significantly lower, primarily due to their perception of a fairly low ability for government to change these policies. They wanted employees with good basic communication and problem-solving skills, whom they could then train to more specific firm-oriented tasks. Distributors felt that all education issues were important, but that apprenticeships were the most important issue for the industry. While users ranked all the issues lower than did distributors, users also felt that apprenticeships were the most important education issue. Finally, the public

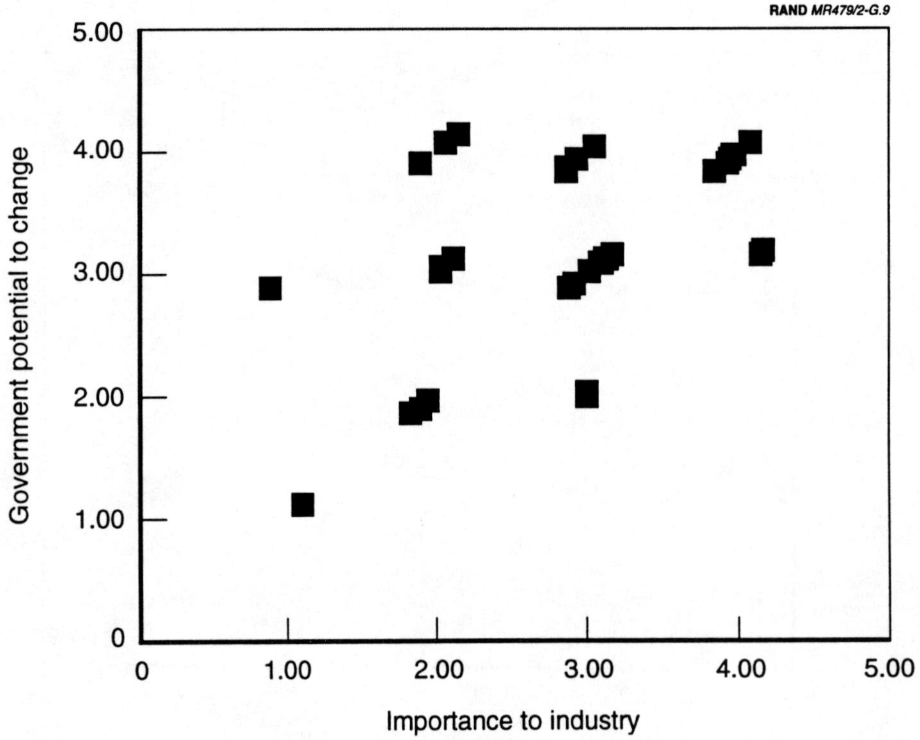

Figure G.9—Distribution of Responses on VRAs

sector participants ranked all education issues quite high, but felt that general education was the most important to the industry and the most amenable to change. Thus, makers and the government felt that general education was the most important education issue, while distributors and users felt that apprenticeships were the most important issue. These results are not surprising, since the cost of educating end-users of machine tools is increasingly borne by distributors and users; thus, they would significantly benefit from apprenticeship programs.

General Education. Concerns over general education focused on three points: the lack of new employees' basic skills; the changing skill requirements for machine-tool producers, given technology shifts; and the negative perception of manufacturing in the education system of the United States. Participants felt that many workers in the industry operate at only the 5th or 6th grade level, with little or no English ability. This lack of basic skills is becoming an increasing problem as computer numerical control technology shifts skill requirements away from machining to general problem-solving and communications skills. There was a general belief that the education system does not understand and, therefore, maligns manufacturing employment; it was felt that teachers equate manufacturing work with an antiquated "blacksmith shop." Emphasizing the firm-specific nature of many skills, many participants felt that, given an individual with basic skills, firms can "make" a worker. The distribution of responses on general education is provided in Figure G.10.

Apprenticeships. Participants felt that a lot more applied training is going on in the industry than is generally acknowledged but that there has been a decline in formal apprenticeships. The belief was stated that there were a number of local-level initiatives between firms and community colleges, although many of the more traditional apprenticeship programs (such as Cincinnati Milacron's) were dead or dying. Among the problems cited with apprenticeships were unions' resistance to youth apprenticeships and the risk that firms will lose their investment as new trainees are poached by rivals. Participants agreed that entry-level personnel are of much higher quality in Germany than the United States, primarily because of the German apprenticeship system. Although participants felt that, if the government led in defining a program, "firms would participate," they also felt that such a program would probably attract a low quality of student, citing past experience with federal policies of training the socially disadvantaged. Participants remarked that, although some historical

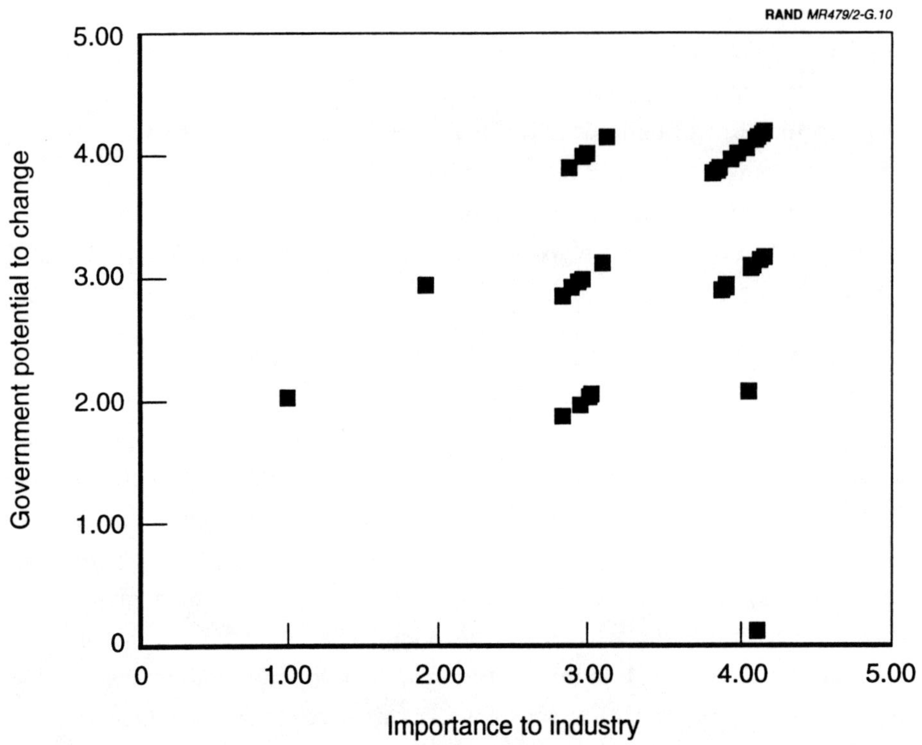

Figure G.10—Distribution of Responses on General Education

apprenticeship programs led to regional development by allowing a geographically dense pool of highly qualified machinists, federal funds are not currently available for local initiatives. Furthermore, since machinists are now more like computer operators than skilled craftsmen, it is uncertain such benefits would still flow from such a program. Figure G.11 shows the distribution of responses on apprenticeships.

Engineering Training. Participants remarked on the lack of production engineers in the United States. They agreed that U.S. engineering graduates lack problem-solving skills, industry experience, and applications focus. Contrary to this U.S. experience, German engineers "know the floor," and thus it is easier to introduce new technology in a German than in a U.S. machine-tool firm. It was felt that the United States needs two types of engineers: some who can generally assimilate new technology, and others who are specifically trained in a particular field of expertise. Consequently, it was felt that engineering courses should incorporate more shop-floor experience. The distribution of responses on engineering training is shown in Figure G.12.

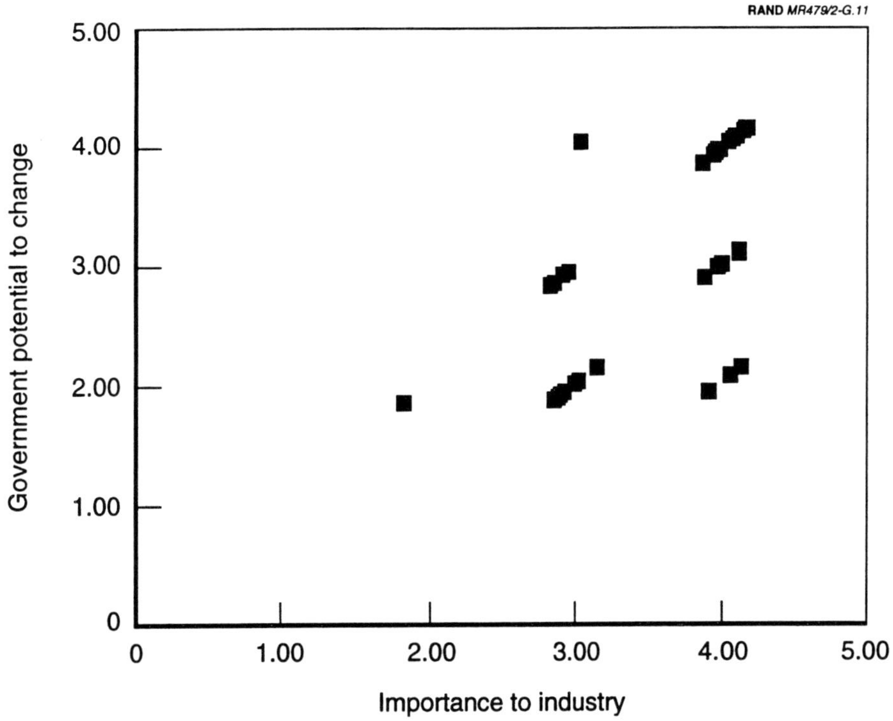

Figure G.11—Distribution of Responses on Apprenticeships

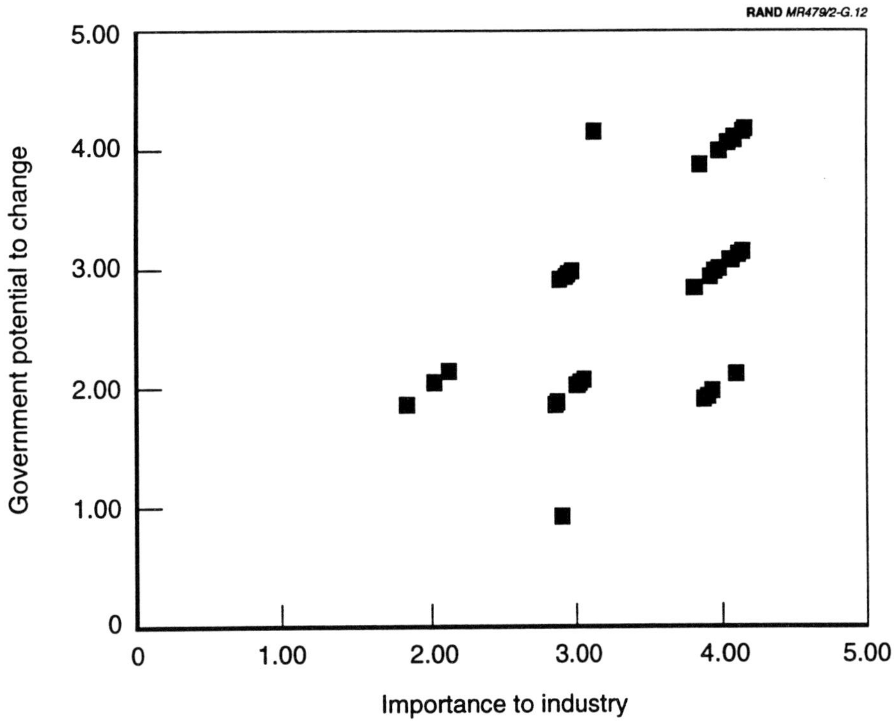

Figure G.12—Distribution of Responses on Engineering Training

Regulatory Issues

Within the category of regulatory issues, liability laws were considered to be significantly more important than either antitrust or government procurement. While participants felt government had a fairly strong potential to change all three policy areas, they felt that government procurement was significantly less important to the industry than liability laws, and that antitrust laws were slightly less important to the industry than government procurement.

Liability Laws. Participants felt that the current U.S. product liability system "defies logic." Most liability suits are at the state, not the federal level, and participants argued that the large variation in laws from state to state increases the burden; firms, for example, often need to find and hire local attorneys to manage such cases. Participants felt that, although large costs are associated with preventive measures to avoid claims (which can be much larger than a firm's total R&D expenses), liability laws in general have been beneficial by forcing firms to consider safety. However, U.S. firms can get sued even if the user removes the installed protective devices from a machine. Furthermore, participants related stories in which firms were named in suits for a type of machine that they sold 25 years ago, which was then resold four times before the actual accident. Liability suits were considered particularly worrisome, because one bad case could "destroy a firm." The problem, as measured by the dollar value per suit as well as by the number of suits, was thought to be increasing. Because the wild fluctuations in premiums make it impossible for many firms to seek insurance, participants estimated that one-quarter of U.S. machine-tool makers have no liability protection. Some participants said liability forced them into defensive product design, like doctors practicing defensive medicine, while users complained that machines were now made so safe that they were then forced to modify the machine to run it efficiently. Participants also felt that industry restructuring may be hindered because the potential liability load of U.S. firms makes acquisitions uneconomic. Also, participants argued that liability laws affect U.S. firms much more than their international competitors, because U.S. firms have a much larger and older base of tools installed in this country. Furthermore, participants felt that plaintiffs might not name foreign firms in their suits, given the difficulties involved with pursuing foreign legal actions. Finally, participants felt that the less onerous laws in foreign home markets provided a significant advantage to foreign competitors. The distribution of responses on liability laws is provided in Figure G.13.

Antitrust Laws. Participants felt that the low level of cooperation within the U.S. machine-tool industry was less a result of antitrust laws and more due to the

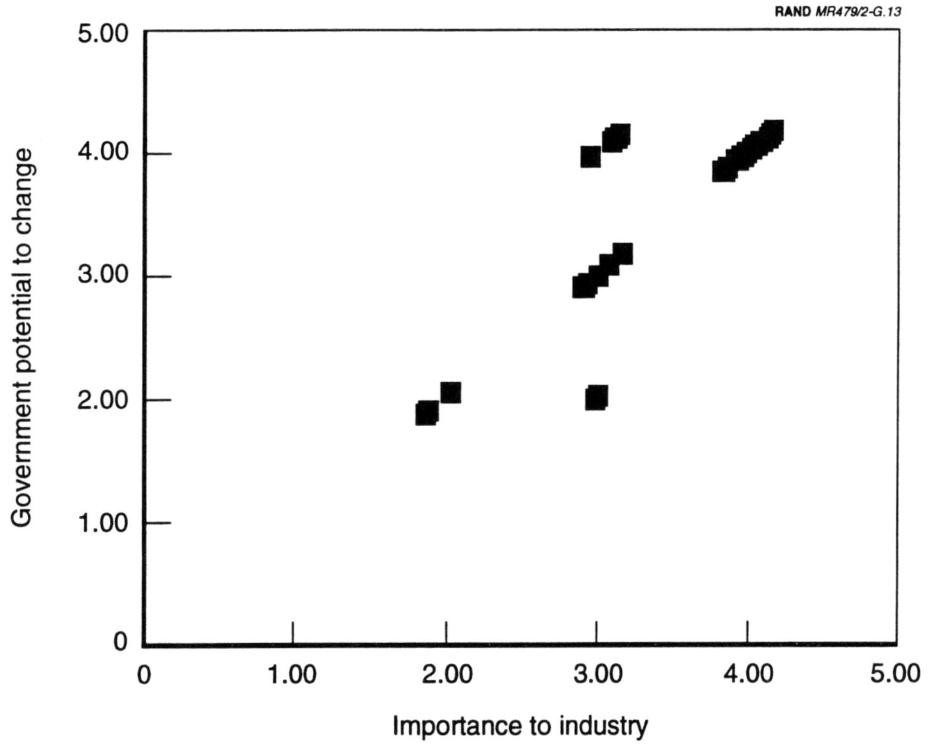

Figure G.13—Distribution of Responses on Liability Laws

competitive culture of the U.S. industry. One respondent stated that, although cooperation could help in the future, his firm would still choose to "go it alone." Owners of machine-tool firms were viewed by participants as rugged individualists who do not collaborate. The problem of cooperation is exacerbated by the inconsistent relations with suppliers. Given this inconsistent relationship between users and makers, there are few joint ventures. Thus, participants felt that industrial culture and structure were significantly more important in determining cooperative behavior than antitrust laws were. Although it was believed that networking "could" prove useful, participants felt that U.S. machine-tool makers were more likely to cooperate with a foreign firm than a domestic one. Figure G.14 shows the distribution of responses on antitrust laws.

Government Procurement. In general, participants viewed government demand as unimportant except for a few "captive" firms that relied on government contracts almost exclusively. Consequently, there was little discussion on the importance of procurement to the industry. Figure G.15 provides the distribution of responses on government procurement.

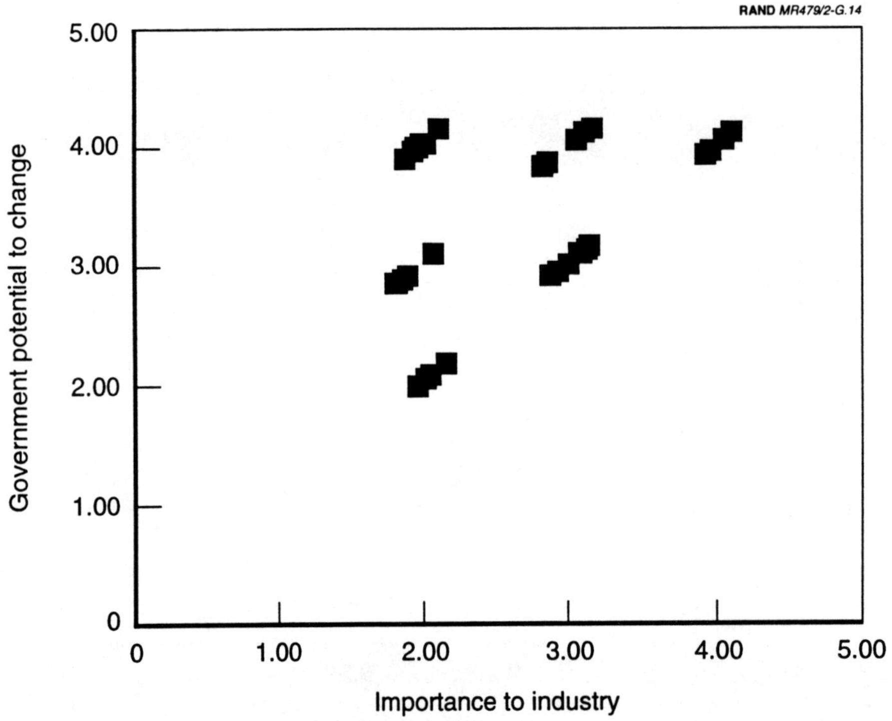

Figure G.14—Distribution of Responses on Antitrust Laws

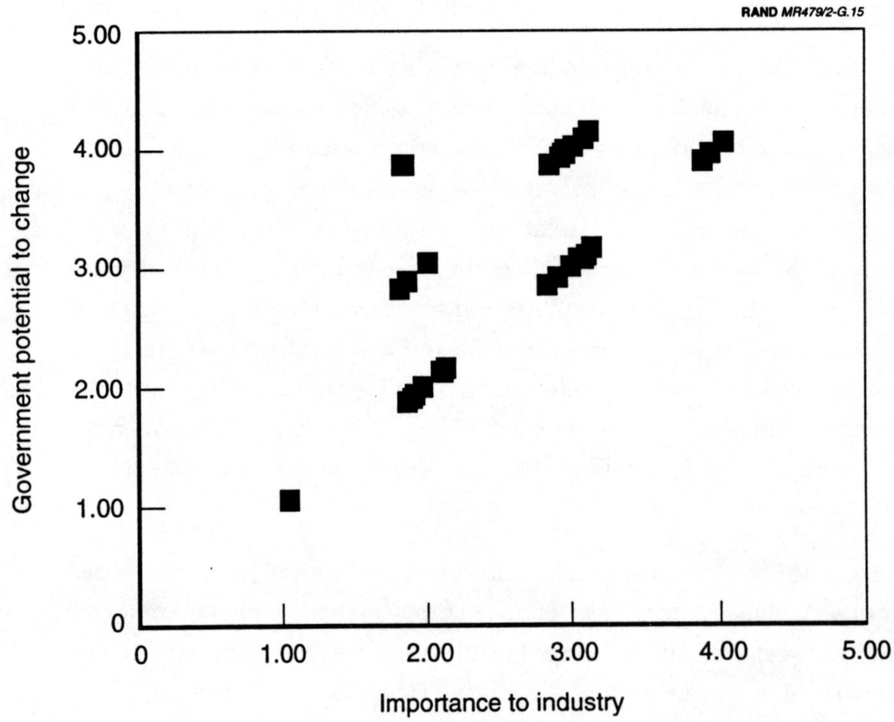

Figure G.15—Distribution of Responses on Government Procurement

Technology Issues

The technology issues category was ranked significantly lower than the other policies by all the respondents. Interestingly, makers ranked both the importance of technology issues to the industry and the government's potential to change lower than all other participants. Within the category, technology development and transfer was the highest ranked by all participants, with standards setting ranking a distant second, and process technology and management assistance ranking slightly below that. Interestingly, distributors ranked standards setting the highest. This may be due to the wide range of product types that distributors must deal with in their business. Also interestingly, public-sector individuals ranked technology development and transfer much higher than the other two policies in the category. This reflects the recent government emphasis on such efforts as embodied in the manufacturing technology centers (MTCs) and CRADAs.

Technology Development and Transfer

Discussion of technology development and transfer centered around issues of applicability and accessibility. In general, participants felt that both government and university researchers do not "ask firms what they need," and this leads to a "fundamental mismatch between research and the needs of manufacturers." Participants stated that national labs focus on narrow problem areas unrelated to manufacturers' needs, and that "universities gave up on manufacturing 30–40 years ago." There was little knowledge among participants of extant policy efforts (i.e., CRADA, NCMS, ARPA). Participants stated that the national labs are hard to access, and that the costs and difficulty in applying for government programs exceed the meager benefits of participation. It was felt this was a significant problem in the machine-tool industry since "government programs ignore SMEs," and most machine-tool firms are "not big enough to handle the paperwork." This belief that government programs emphasize large firms led to a feeling that government program benefits go to the "well connected." Participants stated their preference for a government program providing seed money to let industry "run the show" in lieu of the more traditional government technology development and passive transfer programs. Participants felt that the skills are not generally available and that the needs of firms are too disparate to make it viable for private consultants to provide technology transfer and process technology and management assistance. Figure G.16 shows the distribution of responses on technology development and transfer.

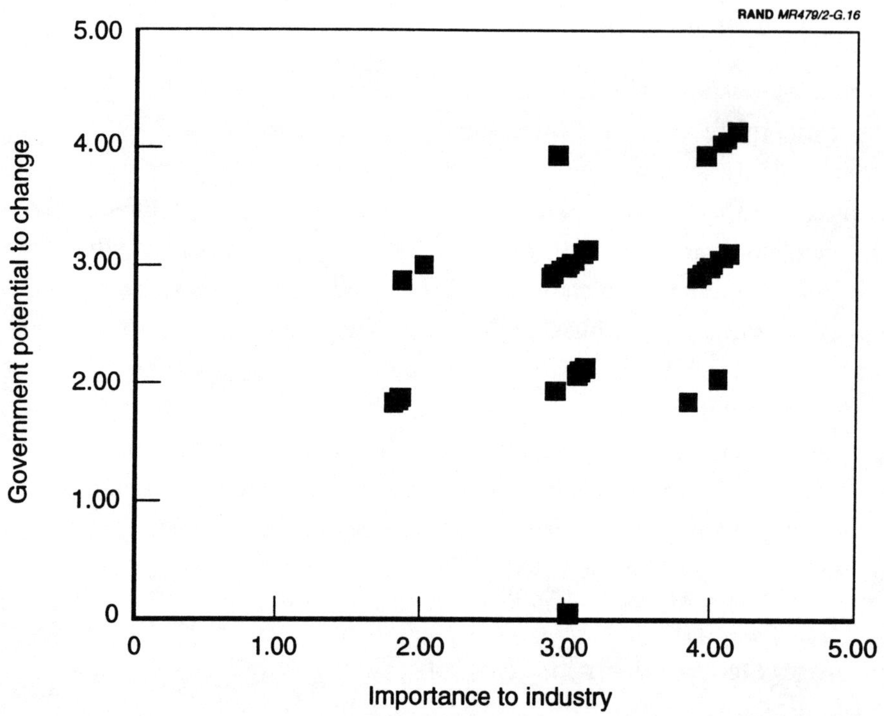

Figure G.16—Distribution of Responses on Technology Development and Transfer

Standards Setting. Although participants ranked standards setting over process technology and management assistance, time permitted little discussion of this issue. The distribution of participant responses to standards setting is provided in Figure G.17.

Process Technology and Management Assistance. There was some ambiguity toward process technology and management assistance policies among the participants. While it was felt that such services could provide some value, it was generally felt that such efforts are without focus and have thus far had little impact. This situation was contrasted with successful agricultural extension centers: "If you're a farmer with a problem, you know where to go; in manufacturing there are a plethora of programs without focus."

Furthermore, the value of such services was often felt to be minimal. Participants felt that government could add little to enhance firm productivity. One participant stated that he didn't think a government bureaucrat could "know my shop floor better than me." In general, participants were skeptical and were reminded of the adage, "we're from the government, and we're here to help you." Figure G.18 shows the distribution of responses on process technology and management assistance.

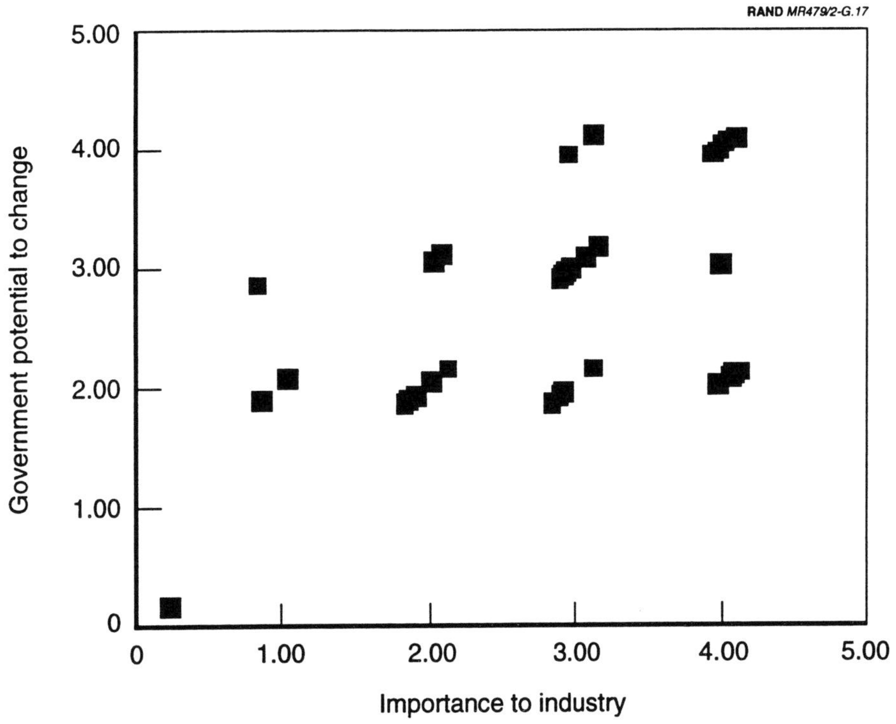

Figure G.17—Distribution of Responses on Standards Setting

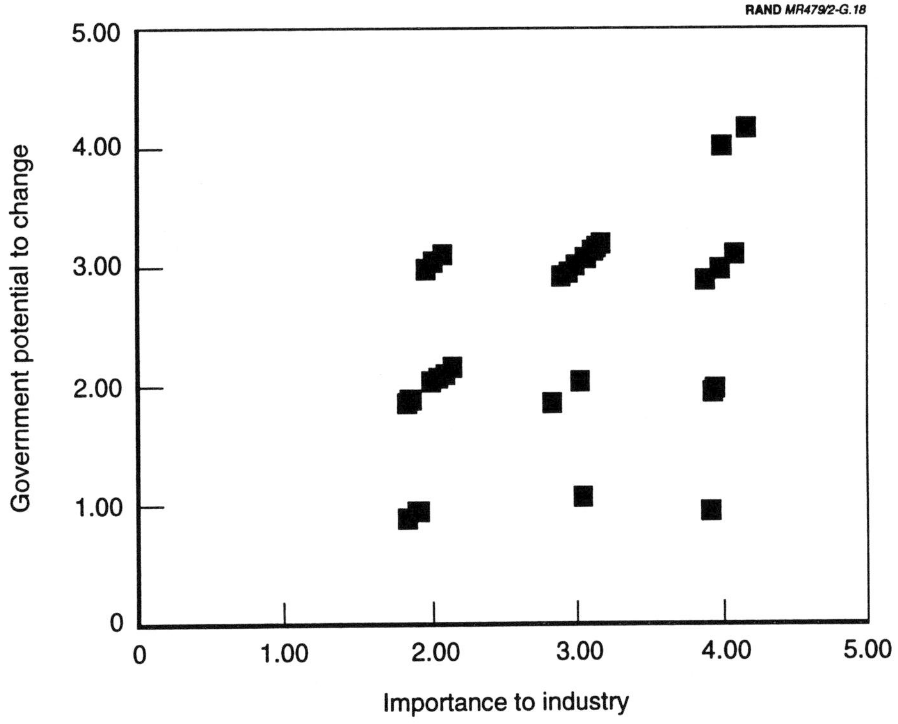

Figure G.18—Distribution of Responses on Process Technology and Management Assistance

Conclusions

Our focus groups suggest that there is a mismatch between where government has been focusing its policy initiatives and the desires of the industry. Eight policy initiatives stand out as those most favored by the industry:

1. Adopt permanent ITCs to spur domestic consumption;
2. Level the trade playing field to ensure access to foreign markets;
3. Enact liability law reform to limit catastrophic exposure, equalize domestic and foreign risk, and increase accessibility and affordability of insurance;
4. Reduce export restrictions to open up the large Chinese and former Soviet markets to which U.S. competitors have access;
5. Improve general education to ensure young people have adequate problem-solving and communication skills and encourage them to enter manufacturing;
6. Expand apprenticeship programs to provide a well-trained workforce while avoiding the free-rider problem associated with private efforts;
7. Improve access to capital by fostering an understanding of manufacturing in lending institutions and reforming the availability of capital for exporting; and
8. Promote exports to facilitate the access to foreign markets for small and medium sized firms who lack the "soft infrastructure" to penetrate these markets on their own.

The industry may also benefit significantly from efforts to increase interfirm collaboration, technology development and transfer, government demand, industrial standards, and the state of current process technology and management. The focus group results suggest, however, that policymakers will need to take into account the industry's lower perception of these efforts, particularly since many rely on employer involvement for their success.

Appendix H
Data Problems

Max Nelson, RAND

In studying data on the machine-tool industry, we encountered a number of data problems that hinder the ability to perform industrial and technology policy analysis. Though these problems are beyond the scope of this study, some discussion of the experiences gained in our efforts may be useful. We group the issues surrounding the data under seven headings: (1) categorization, (2) firm data, (3) domestic comparability, (4) international comparability, (5) reliance on trade associations, (6) accessibility, and (7) on-line availability. Each of these issues will be discussed below.

Categorization

Government industrial data are perhaps of most use to historians, of somewhat less use to economists, and even less use to technology policy analysts. The usefulness to historians results from the categorization. Data on older industries, either technologically obsolete or in the latter stages of the product cycle, are quite good. Data on industries constituting the bulk of the economy are perhaps adequate. Data on cutting-edge technologies are often nonexistent or less than helpful. For example, one can easily find aggregate patent data in such categories as stoneworking, horseshoeing, coopering, telegraphy, and brush-, broom-, and mop-making. Finding data in meaningful biotechnology categories is nearly impossible. It is difficult to measure the size of the composite material industry in the United States, because the Standard Industrial Classification (SIC) breakdowns do not include such a category.

This problem is not entirely solvable. There is value in some stability in categories, and quick changes may lead to short-lived, trendy categories before important changes become clear. Nevertheless, government data categories seem to inordinately lag changes in the economy that they purport to measure. Because technology policy normally deals with new developments, data to support analysis are wanting.

These general problems were exemplified in our attempts to define and measure the machine-tool industry. The traditional definition of the industry and the data available under that categorization are too restrictive, given the changes in the structure of the industry and the technology over the past few decades. Traditionally, the machine-tool industry is defined as firms engaged in the manufacture of metal-cutting machines[1] and metal-forming machines.[2] Our desire to go beyond this definition is not new. Recognizing the changing nature of the industry, the National Machine-tool Builder's Association (NMTBA) recently changed its focus and its name to the Association for Manufacturing Technology (AMT). Reflecting these changes, the AMT's directory of products (Machine Tools, Manufacturing Machinery & Related Products Built by Members of the Association for Manufacturing Technology) includes several categories beyond the traditional cutting and forming tools. These categories include electric action machines (EDM, ECM, laser, and plasma-arc machines), inspection and measuring machines and equipment, special purpose machines and equipment (including assembly machines, welding machines, and plastic-working machines), auxiliary equipment (including cad/cam systems, industrial robots, etc.), tools for machine tools, and software and services.

Our reliance on SIC codes for many categories of data put major limits on how far we could expand the definition of the industry. Furthermore, our expanded definition had to remain focused on establishments *primarily* engaged in manufacturing or assembling entire machine tools. Thus, we chose to exclude firms engaged in manufacturing accessories for such machine tools as industrial patterns, dies and tools, jigs and fixtures, industrial molds, machine-tool accessories, power-driven hand tools, and rolling-mill machinery and equipment. However, recognizing the major and increasing role of industrial controls in the industry, we felt it imperative to include firms engaged in such endeavors in our expanded definition of the industry.

Thus, our expanded definition of the machine-tool industry includes the traditional metal-cutting and metal-forming firms, but also includes electric and gas welding and soldering equipment manufacturers (SIC 3548); metalworking machinery, not elsewhere classified (SIC 3549) firms; and firms engaged in manufacturing relays and industrial controls (SIC 3625). Although we would

---

[1] Metal-cutting machines are included in SIC 3541, which is defined as "establishments primarily engaged in manufacturing metal cutting type machine tools, not supported in the hands of an operator when in use, that shape metal by cutting or use of electrical techniques; the rebuilding of such machine tools, and the manufacture of replacement parts for them." Also included in this industry are metalworking machine tools designed primarily for home workshops.

[2] Metal-forming machines are covered by SIC 3542, which is defined as "establishments primarily engaged in manufacturing metal forming machine tools, not supported in the hands of an operator while in use, for pressing, hammering, extruding, shearing, die-casting, or otherwise forming metal into shape. This industry also includes the rebuilding of such machine tools and the manufacture of repair parts for them."

have preferred to include establishments engaged in manufacturing tools for forming and shaping advanced materials, these establishments are included in an SIC code too broad to warrant their inclusion (they are included in SIC 3559, special industrial machinery, not elsewhere classified, which also includes industrial sewing machines, ammunition machines, and nuclear control rods).

This expanded definition of the machine-tool industry may lead to additional insights into the true nature of the industry and the changes it is undergoing. Unfortunately, most of our quantitative analysis has had to rely on the traditional definition. This traditional analysis allows us to compare our results to those found in previous studies that have focused on the traditional definition, use accessible data, and compare data from different nations. We have used our expanded definition where we have focused on the firm level instead of the national level and in our projections of future technologies. Thus, our analysis of the distribution of machine-tool firms and our focus groups have utilized our expanded definition. In any case, we are careful to point out the particular definitions of the machine-tool industry we use throughout the report.

Firm Data

In general, firm-level data are unavailable from government sources because of concerns about confidentiality. What government sources exist are focused on Securities and Exchange Commission (SEC) 10-K disclosures. SEC 10-K data cover only a sample of public firms and thus exclude the large number of private firms, which can seriously bias the data. Private sources that compile firm-level data and distribute such data electronically (on-line or CD-ROM) offer samples of firms that are biased by the criteria they use for firm inclusion. However, such sources often capture a larger sample than even the industry-level data provided by the Census of Manufactures. For example, while the Census provides information on over 6,000,000 establishments in the United States, private databases list over 10,000,000 U.S. establishments. Although their coverage is obviously larger than public sources, questions have been raised about the quality of such private databases.

Domestic Comparability

Data collected throughout the U.S. government are often not standardized and, therefore, are frequently difficult to compare. For example, the Department of Commerce's Input-Output Accounts are based on different industrial categories than the SIC codes used in many other reports. Furthermore, some data are too broad for industry-level analyses. For example, the NSF Science and Engineering

Indicators lists R&D spending by industry at the two-digit SIC-code level (i.e., Machinery-SIC 35 or Machinery, except electrical-SIC 35 without 357), which is too wide a category for analyzing R&D spending in the machine-tool industry (at the four-digit SIC-code level). Though increasing the specificity of such measures may raise concerns over disclosure, such an attempt should be made whenever possible to provide data of sufficient depth for meaningful analysis.

International Comparability

International comparative analysis multiplies the problems of comparability due to differences in categorizations across countries. Not only do data categorizations (i.e., product lines, corporate vs. government R&D) differ, but often the definition of industries differs. For example, Japanese data on machine-tool exports include hand-held sawing or cut-off machines that are not included in U.S. export data (or even in Japanese production data). Consequently, Japanese *production* of such machines is listed as 7,530 units in 1991, whereas Japanese *exports* of such machines are listed as 361,122 units in 1991. Clearly this change in categorization can significantly influence analytic results.

Reliance on Trade Associations

Many of the available data on machine tools come from trade associations (i.e., AMT, JMTBA, etc.). These data inevitably reflect the membership of these organizations, which do not represent the whole industry, and are therefore often biased against small firms. Furthermore, these associations have agendas and interests that naturally differ from the government or the nation as a whole. These interests may or may not bias reporting of statistics, may or may not lead to "shading" of data, and almost certainly lead, at least occasionally, to the selective release of data. The government and the policy community have come to rely on such data without a good idea of their accuracy or completeness. This reliance stems from the general inaccessibility of government data. Industry associations provide significant added value by collecting the scattered government data and providing them in a comprehensive and industry-specific format. Without such efforts, analysts would be hard pressed to determine what government data are available and relevant, let alone gather those data in a format that is conducive to effective analysis. Furthermore, though industry associations may provide significant data that are well-formatted, those associations may not be willing to provide such data electronically. Consequently, significant duplication of effort is required to re-code the data electronically. Efforts should be undertaken to increase the direct availability of

U.S. and foreign government data without the intervening associations in a format conducive to analysis and that is available electronically.

Accessibility

Data sources are numerous, scattered, and often hard to find. A directory of federal data sources (i.e., Census of Manufacturers; County Business Patterns; Science and Engineering Indicators; Directory of Federal Laboratory and Technology Resources; Clearinghouse for State & Local Government Initiatives in Productivity, Technology, and Innovation; Commerce MQ35W Reports; etc.) that is available on-line and is advertised appropriately would greatly foster the use of federal information resources. Such a directory could describe the resource, list the variables and time span covered, describe how to procure the resource, provide on-line/CD-ROM availability, and give a contact for questions. Providing and advertising a "data catalog" could reduce the search costs and increase the utility of government data.

On-Line Availability

Although most (if not all) federal data are accumulated through computerized databases, it is often possible to acquire such data only in hard-copy format. Lack of on-line availability greatly increases the costs and diminishes the utility of using federal data for analysis. Efforts should be undertaken to make federal data available on-line whenever possible. Furthermore, such data would be most accessible if available in a number of different formats (i.e., CD-ROM, Internet FTP, Direct-dial BBS) to take full advantage of the unstandardized nature of the U.S. information infrastructure.

Appendix I
Annotated Bibliography[1]

Carlsson, Bo, and Erol Taymaz, "Flexible Technology and Industrial Structure in the United States," *Small Business Economics*, 1992.

This article uses data from the *American Machinist* surveys of machine-tool capital stock in 1983 and 1989 to look at trends in firm size and usage of machine tools in the United States. The authors show that between 1983 and 1989, there was a 43.3-percent decline in the consumption of non-NC tools by U.S. firms employing more than 100 people, presumably the market in which U.S. suppliers were historically strongest. At the same time, these large buyers saw an increase in their stock of NC tools by 39.8 percent. Small employers, by contrast, increased their supply of both types of tools—non-NC by 75.5 percent, NC by 237.2 percent. The authors attribute these shifts to the changes in the relative costs of labor, NC tools, and non-NC tools, with the most popular NC tools (lathes, machining centers) seeing real declines in cost, while labor and non-NC tools both increased. For lathes, the cost ratio of NC versus non-NC dropped from 8.3 times more in 1983 to 2.9 times in 1989. The authors also demonstrate shifts in the organization of production, with big plants downsizing and replacing labor and old tools with new NC devices, while small plants picked up the production slack.

Carlsson, Bo, and Erol Taymaz, "Technological Capabilities and International Competitiveness in the Engineering Industries," *Review of Industrial Organization*, Vol. 8, No. 3, June 1993, pp. 293–313.

This article uses factor analysis and statistical regressions to argue that the decline in the competitiveness of the U.S. machine-tool industry has led to a decline in the competitiveness of machine-tool users. It demonstrates that the use of FMS among machine-tool users is significantly related to export success. The authors argue, but do not demonstrate, that there is a two-way relation between machine-tool users and suppliers and that the decline in the competitiveness of key U.S. engineering industries—particularly auto—and their failure to demand flexible technologies, may have led to the decline of U.S. machine-tool makers.

---

[1]This annotated bibliography contains brief descriptions of a number of studies that are useful in analyzing the changing competitive dynamics of the global machine-tool industry. It is not intended to be a comprehensive list of machine-tool-related research. As part of this project, we also compiled a separate, 90-page *Machine-Tool Industry Bibliography*, DRU-825-OSTP, Santa Monica: RAND, 1994.

Chakrabarti, Alok K., "Innovation and Productivity: An Analysis of the Chemical, Textiles and Machine-Tool Industries in the United States," *Research Policy,* Vol. 19, 1990, pp. 257–269.

Alok K. Chakrabarti, Dean of the School of Industrial Management at the New Jersey Institute of Technology, performed this analysis of the relationship between innovation and productivity during the 1967 to 1983 period by comparing the chemical, textile, and machine-tool industries.

Chakrabarti presents multifactor productivity estimates adjusting for capital utilization rates that were developed in previous research.[2] Multifactor productivity measures output per unit of multiple factors of production such as capital, labor, and materials. This research finds that the productivity growth rate in the machine-tool industry was 2.39 between 1967 and 1972, –0.33 between 1973 and 1979, and –2.26 between 1980 and 1983. Thus, Chakrabarti finds that the machine-tool industry has shown a consistent and accelerating decline in productivity since 1973.

To determine the number of innovations in each industry, Chakrabarti used published sources of technical information from trade and technical journals. Data on innovations in the machine-tool industry were obtained from issues of *Tool and Production.* To assist in the categorization of innovations, a model of innovation in the machine-tool industry was created (see Figure I.1).

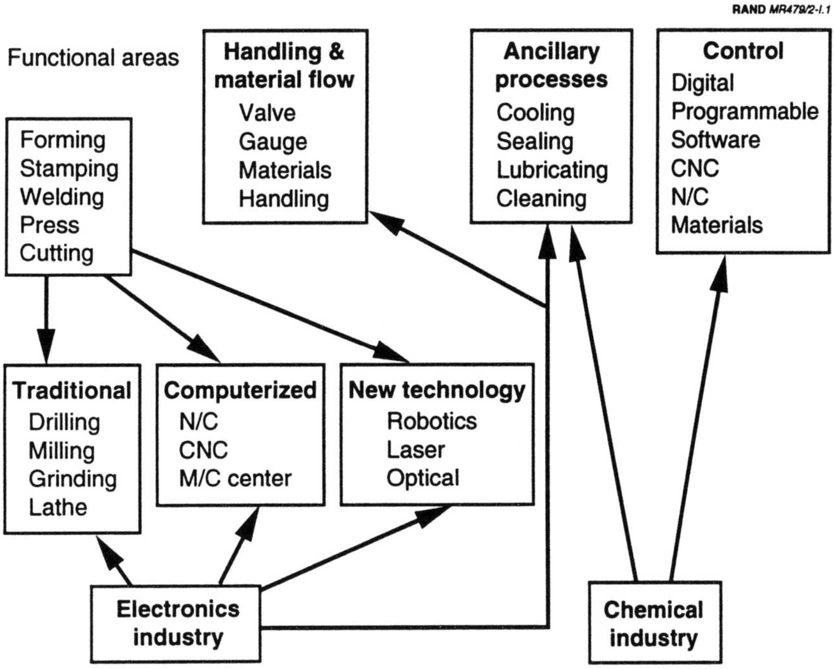

Figure I.1—A Model of Machine-Tool Innovation

[2]Baily and Chakrabarti, "Innovation and Productivity in United States Industry," Brookings Papers on Economic Activities 2, 1985, pp. 609–632.

The general conclusion of this analysis is that innovation increased in the machine-tool industry as a whole from 1967 to 1983. These findings support the hypothesis that the decline in U.S. competitiveness (defined here as multifactor productivity) is not a result of a lack of U.S. innovation.

Breaking down the findings on innovation into subcategories shows interesting trends in technology development. Traditional cutting tools experienced a slight decline in innovations from 1974 to 1979 versus 1967 to 1973, but rebounded in the 1980s. NC tools dominated innovation in computerized cutting tools from 1967 to 1973, but dropped significantly from 1974 to 1979 and became almost obsolete in the 1980s. CNC and machining center technologies both grew rapidly from 1974 to 1979 and from 1980 to 1982, but the rate of growth slowed in the latter period. Tools using new technologies declined from 1974 to 1979 over 1967 to 1973, predominantly as a result of the great decline in innovations using lasers. However, innovation in all technologies increased from 1980 to 1982, with lasers having quite an upsurge. Material handling and flow technologies had slight, though diminishing, growth in both periods, predominantly as a result of declining innovations in valve technologies. Control-for-machines innovations also had diminishing growth during both periods. All categories of control (except control software) had declining growth, with the greatest decline in control materials and digital readouts. No innovations in NC control technology were found for either 1974 to 1979 or 1980 to 1982. Growth in ancillary process technology also declined, led predominantly by a strong decline in cooling innovations. Growth in cutting-related functions increased over the two periods, led by a strong increase in cutting-equipment innovations.

Chakrabarti explains the coincidence of innovation growth and productivity loss with three hypotheses. First, most of the innovations in the industry were product innovations (such as microprocessors, robotics, and lasers), which added new performance features to products, rather than process innovations that would increase the efficiency of production. Manufacturers are supposed to benefit from these innovations through product differentiation leading to higher prices, but foreign manufacturers introduced similar technologies in their products, and U.S. firms thus failed to achieve a special advantage. Second, the dominance of small firms and the highly cyclical nature of demand in this industry led to a problem in labor productivity, because it was difficult to adjust the size of the labor force according to production requirements. Small companies often engage in making special-application machines in labor-intensive processes, leading to low productivity. Finally, the strong dollar of the 1980s made the United States less price competitive with manufacturers in Japan and Germany. Given the above-mentioned failure to gain advantage through product differentiation, these foreign manufacturers were able to realize a competitive advantage.

Although Chakrabarti does not provide any recommendations, his findings do point to several problems that the industry needs to address. First, machine-tool firms may be performing inappropriate innovation activity by focusing on product over process developments. This focus is exacerbated by fluctuations in exchange rates. This problem may be especially acute in small firms that focus on specialty items with their associated low labor productivity. Secondly, firms may fail to commercialize innovations successfully. The announcement of a new development in a trade journal does not necessarily imply that a firm will adopt that technology in its product line. Thirdly, there are shifts in the focus of innovations. Growth rates increased for traditional cutting tools, computerized cutting tools, tools using new technology, and cutting-related functions over the period studied, while growth rates declined for material handling and flow, control for machines, and ancillary process in metalworking.

Collis, D., "The Machine-Tool Industry and Industrial Policy 1955–82," in A. M. Spence and H. Hazard, *International Competitiveness*, Cambridge: Harper & Row, 1988.

This book provides a good overview of the industrial policies that have an impact on the machine-tool sectors in Japan, Germany, the United States, and the United Kingdom. The study shows the key role that developing standards can play in enabling small employers to compete successfully in this sector. Standards are linked to training, since users may be reluctant to invest in new, incompatible equipment if it requires the retraining of existing workers. The article provides a typology of the different types of market failure that government policies may attempt to address. The United States is shown to have a relatively weak industrial policy, with the main efforts coming from the Department of Defense (DoD); in 1970 DoD owned $1.5 billion worth of machine tools and loaned them out to its contractors.

The main weakness with the study is that it shows no causal links between policies and machine-tool performance, simply laying the two stories alongside each other. MITI is portrayed as largely successful, for example, although others' work (e.g., Friedman, 1988) suggests that most of its initiatives failed or were resisted by machine-tool firms. For example, the study does not show (1) the role of the Japanese government in ensuring that FANUC became the standard and (2) how successful MITI's flexible manufacturing systems cooperative research activity is seen to be by employers.

Council on Competitiveness, *A Competitive Profile of the Machine Tool Industry—Research Paper for Gaining New Ground: Technology Priorities for America's Future*, Washington, D.C., March 1991.

The machine-tool industry is one of nine industrial sectors included as part of the research for the Council on Competitiveness' book, *Gaining New Ground*. The study draws heavily from the working papers of the MIT Commission on Industrial Productivity and was supported by assistance from the NMTBA/The Association for Manufacturing Technology, the machine-tools' industry association. The study addresses the industries' structure, importance, international competitiveness, the role of technology, and the threats and factors supporting U.S. leadership in technological competitiveness.

The study states that U.S. users have shifted to foreign machine-tool companies because U.S. suppliers could not provide state-of-the-art equipment or could not meet foreign price or delivery schedules and that U.S. users do not have access to foreign machine tools in as timely a manner as their foreign competitors. Thus, increasing foreign supply could hamper U.S. competitiveness in other manufacturing sectors. The study discusses the leverage of the machine-tool industry across virtually all goods and services in the economy. Given this linkage, the study states that machine-tool builders must become more closely integrated with users to facilitate just-in-time production and total quality control to make their customers more competitive.

The study estimates that 25 percent of U.S. machine-tool consumption is directly or indirectly linked to defense requirements and that increasing import penetration means that the U.S. military mobilization base is increasingly dependent upon potentially unreliable foreign suppliers.

The most notable trend in the global machine-tool market has been the rise of Japan and the decline of the United States, while Germany and Switzerland maintained their share, the United Kingdom and France suffered major declines, and Italy increased its share. European firms are characterized as making high-performance, precision-engineered, customized machine tools and thus need a large share of the world market in their specialized areas to have sufficient volume to profit. The Japanese, on the other hand, focus on consistent, low-cost, standardized products usable by any number of firms, concentrating on a few types of general-purpose machines for high volume markets. To maintain economies of scale, they need large production runs and, therefore, also need to rely on exports.

The study states that R&D in the industry was about 1.6 percent of sales in the 1970s and declined to 1.3 percent in the 1980s and that this R&D has been concentrated in larger firms, since even a small R&D effort is prohibitively expensive for the typical machine-tool builder, with annual sales of about $7 million. The study claims that acquisition of machine-tool companies by conglomerates in the 1970s did little to change the historically low level of industry R&D, because profit opportunities were insufficient to justify investment in innovation or new technologies. Instead of developing new NC/CNC lines, the conglomerates invested in some controls and product upgrades, which could not offset Japanese advantages. Furthermore, user industries' focus on product innovation over process innovation failed to produce the market pull necessary to ignite innovation in the machine-tool industry. For instance, having developed the NC control through Air Force–funded studies at MIT and having fostered applications through Air Force procurements, the machine-tool industry developed less-sophisticated point-to-point machines that were suited to the bulk of U.S. applications. However, the industry was still confronted by user complacency and implementation doubts.

The study lists 11 technologies that are deemed critical to machine tools: metrology, metallurgy, physics of materials, dynamics of structures, advanced precision bearings, advanced material technology, electronic controls, software, artificial intelligence (AI), sensors, and lasers. These are deemed critical, because the capabilities of machine tools are determined by six factors: mechanical and physical design; materials used in construction; selection and application of bearings; controls directing motion, speed, and repeatability; the software commanding the controls; and sensors and measuring devices informing controls of operation and positions. The study provides detailed information on each of the 11 critical technologies, including descriptions, why it is critical, the U.S. position vis-à-vis the rest of the world, threats to the United States retaining or gaining prominence in the technology, and technological interdependencies.

The study cites a number of threats to U.S. leadership. First, the small size and family ownership of machine-tool firms have supported a fragmented industry structure based on slow product-line changes and limited resources for investment and research, few links to external technology sources, and difficulty sustaining systematic long-term R&D. Second, the extremely cyclical nature of demand, which results from the multiplier effects of users' business cycles, causes volatile cash flows, leading to unsystematic R&D and investment, problems in recruiting and retaining skilled technical people, and a tendency to backlog orders, delaying product delivery. Third, uneven interpretation, administration, and enforcement of export control policies vis-à-vis U.S. competitors have led to greater U.S. enforcement of COCOM, a 16-year gap since the machine-tool control list has been updated, and an inability of U.S. firms to take advantage of the large markets in Eastern Europe and the former Soviet Union. Fourth, U.S. tax laws are biased against investment and R&D, and provide inadequate capital cost recovery—increasing the cost of capital for the machine-tool industry and its users in comparison to competitors. Fifth, U.S. product liability, characterized by uncertainty, high transaction costs, and lack of uniformity, is a great burden to manufacturing firms (in 1988, machine-tool firms spent seven times more on liability than R&D). Sixth, the Japanese government aided its machine-tool industry by controlling licensing agreements, subsidizing it through tax breaks and direct aid, and sponsoring its technology development, including $60 million for FMS, financial assistance for FMS installation, and a commitment to underwrite $400 million of a $1 billion R&D effort on intelligent manufacturing systems. Similarly, the European Union (EU) provides direct R&D support to firms through cooperative initiatives, such as BRITE, EUREKA, and ESPRIT. The German government encourages cooperative R&D and standard setting, offers sales and service support in foreign markets, and channels bank funds to specialist producers for investment. Eight major technical institutes provide R&D that small companies cannot provide themselves, and funding for firm R&D is available if results are published within two years of completion. Finally, Canada, the United Kingdom, Italy, and Japan subsidize foreign buyer visits to their countries to foster exports.

The study states that a number of public policies have had some positive impact on the industry, but that U.S. support pales in comparison to that of Europe and Japan. First, the National Center for Manufacturing Sciences (NCMS), established in 1986, provides research support by sponsoring state-of-the-art R&D critical to advancing manufacturing technology. Second, the SBIR program, established in 1982, provides awards up to $50,000 for ideas of potential use to businesses having less than 500 employees. Third, the ManTech program has the potential for addressing some of the research needs of the machine-tool industry. Fourth, NIST has funded (with Navy assistance) work at the Advanced Manufacturing Research Facility (AMRF) to develop manufacturing standards applicable to the machine-tool industry. Fifth, NSF provides manufacturing technology research awards, which have been increasing in recent years. Sixth, the R&D tax credit was modified by Congress to be of greater use by small, slow-growth companies. Finally, the United States has the lead in AI and expert-system technologies applicable to machine-tool applications.

Daly, Anne, and Dan Jones, "The Machine-Tool Industry in Britain, Germany and the United States," ***National Institute Economic Review*****, No. 92, 1980, pp. 53–63.**

This study compares productivity levels in the UK, U.S., and German machine-tool industries from early this century through the late 1970s. This study is part of an on-going research effort by the London-based National Institute for Economic and Social Research to analyze the reasons for low UK productivity levels in a variety of sectors (ranging from metalworking to furniture manufacture to hotels) through international comparisons. Most of these studies draw on case studies of matched plants making a particular product, but this paper relies more heavily on analysis of aggregate productivity figures. One of the main themes of this research is the link between the available supply of skills, work organization, and productivity levels.

The authors find that British machine-tool firms' productivity levels in the 1970s were far behind those in Germany, which in turn were far behind those in the United States. This is based on comparisons of output per employee in 14 broad categories of machine tools. The data come from the industry associations in all three countries, along with the United States Census of Manufactures. Data were also drawn from *The International Statistics of Machine Tools*, 1974, which is published by the VDW, the German employers' organization for machine tools. The authors were unable to control for product quality, using gross measures of output and employment.

The authors explore the sources of the British machine-tool industry's decline. They dismiss such factors as firm size, cyclicality of demand, and, to a lesser extent, inadequate capital investment, because these factors do not vary greatly among the three countries. They conclude that a major source of British problems is the inadequate skill base.

Fransman, M., "International Competitiveness, Technical Change and the State: The Machine-Tool Industry in Taiwan and Japan," ***World Development*****, Vol. 14, No. 12, 1986, pp. 1375–1396.**

The article provides data from 1983 on the Japanese and Taiwan machine-tool industries, with more detailed information on four large Japanese machine-tool makers and ten Taiwan manufacturers of CNC machines. The key findings of the study still seem applicable, although the data are now a decade old:

Both countries cited customer demand (domestic and foreign) as a key driver of innovation. The Japanese appeared to have a clear edge over the United States, because they served auto manufacturers who wanted CNC to implement just-in-time production, while the U.S. firms concentrated on special-purpose, dedicated machines for aerospace, defense, and large U.S. auto plants. Japanese machine-tool makers have also gained an advantage in innovation by investing early in their own CNC machines and experimenting and refining them through continual use.

The introduction of CNC has dramatically altered the percentage of total value that is added in house by machine-tool makers; this in turn has decreased the importance of labor costs as a basis for competitive advantage in the sector. Taiwanese firms have received close assistance from the Japanese firm, FANUC, and state agencies to incorporate CNC technology in their relatively low-cost machines.

Friedman, David, *The Misunderstood Miracle: Industrial Development and Political Change in Japan*, Ithaca, New York: Cornell University Press, 1988.

The Misunderstood Miracle includes a study of the reasons for the success of the Japanese machine-tool industry. Friedman's argument is that the Japanese success stems from the early switch from mass production to flexible manufacturing, enabled by NC machine tools, as the dominant form of industrial organization. The bulk of this capacity is located in small and medium-sized firms. He traces the evolution of the organization of the Japanese machine-tool industry to the inability of Japanese firms to compete with U.S. mass production firms in the 1960s. Friedman argues that the policies of MITI and the Japanese national government had no positive role in promoting this evolution, and in fact, many of the policies were intended to promote consolidation of the machine-tool industry into larger firms better at mass production, which was resisted by employers.

He contrasts failed MITI efforts with the success of local regional development organizations, the *shokokai*—quasi-independent bureaucracies set up by local officials and funded about 50 percent by local government tax revenues and 50 percent by the national government. They provided capital and training on the use of NC tools to small firms. The flexible manufacturing system is also enabled by forms of cooperation among firms, including

- agreements among firms in a region where one firm can use the machine tools of another firm to complete an order; this allows small firms great flexibility in their effective capacity and assures customers that their order will be met on time
- what is in effect a small producers' union, in which all the firms in a region agree that none of them will accept an order from any large firm that attempts to start a price war among firms in the region.

Friedman's work raises important questions for machine-tool researchers: Is it true that the real problem with the U.S. machine-tool industry is that the Japanese adopted flexible manufacturing while the United States did not? If so, why did the U.S. machine-tool industry not adopt flexible manufacturing? The book also provides some metrics of use to examine the extent of flexible manufacturing in the U.S. machine-tool industry, for instance, the percentage of firms with NC tools, skill levels of employees in firms, number of different product lines per employee in firms, number of different customers per employee in firms. The higher these indices, the more a firm should be organized around the idea of flexible manufacturing. Furthermore, if sectors of the U.S. machine-tool industry that were more flexible than mass producers were performing better economically than the U.S. mass producers, this hypothesis would also be supported.

Gordon, Richard, Joel Krieger, Harley Shaiken, and Bernard Elbaum, *Technological Change, Production Organization and Skill Formation in the U.S. Machine Tool, Semiconductor and Auto Industries*, Washington, D.C.: U.S. Department of Labor, Office of Work-Based Learning, February 1993.

The Department of Labor commissioned a study to analyze how new technologies and changes in production were affecting skill requirements in several key industries, including machine tools. The following points are mong the contributions of this study for analysis of the machine-tool industry.

The authors conducted a survey of U.S. machine-tool makers that were members of NMTBA (now AMT), along with follow-up interviews. The study is strong in such areas as human resources, firm product markets, links with suppliers and customers, and work organization. There is little focus on new technologies, foreign firms operating in the United States, international comparisons, regional clustering and infrastructure, and perhaps surprisingly, given the sponsor, reasons for declining U.S. productivity.

In addition to analyzing the reasons for the decline of the U.S. machine-tool industry, the authors suggest there might be signs of resurgence in the U.S. industry in the last few years. This may be due to voluntary export restraints by Japan and Europe, foreign transplants production in the United States, and reorganization and improved performance of U.S. firms.

The authors show that the large decline in U.S. machine-tool shipments from 1981 to 1983 is not unique. A similar precipitous drop occurred from 1967 to 1971. Unlike the earlier period, the upswing following the decline in 1981 through 1983 was much weaker, but so were the subsequent downswings and upswings. The authors also show that the volatility in the traditional machine-tool industry is attributable to metal-cutting products and not to metal-forming products, which are much more stable. The authors do not analyze how much of the increase in import penetration in the U.S. is a result of increased demand in markets not served by U.S. firms.

The following are the main topics the survey covers: the customers of U.S. machine-tool firms; the regional distribution of principal suppliers to machine-tool firms; technology transfer from external sources; client-customer relationships; the output broken down by the specialized or customized nature of products and broken down by firm size and specialized or customized nature; the R&D decisionmaking process (who makes decisions and who has substantial, some, or no input in product development); the production planning process (who makes decisions and who has substantial, some, or no input in production planning, control, and schedule decisions); machine-tool operator skills in the United States, Germany, and Japan; product design influences (general information, client requirements, technical possibilities, etc.); the composition of machine-tool labor force (engineers, technicians, machinists, skilled, unskilled, trainees); the ways in which firms obtain new skills (hiring, in-house training, external training); workforce training history for recent hires; and educational level of production employees for different firm sizes. The authors also provide a brief overview of training and skill development in Germany and Japan.

The authors' policy recommendations focus on training and skill issues, including (1) a fundamental reassessment of the U.S. educational system, (2) expanding educational programs to enhance worker skills and ease entry of women and minorities into manufacturing, (3) establishing and coordinating work-based learning opportunities to apply elements of apprenticeship, (4) emphasizing work reorganization and continuous in-house training, and (5) establishing cluster-based regional innovation and training centers.

Guile, Bruce, *Investigation of a Transaction-Cost Approach to Market Failures in the Development and Diffusion of Manufacturing Technologies*, paper presented at the annual meeting of the Association for Public Policy Analysis and Management, National Academy of Engineering, Austin, Tex., October 30, 1986.

This unpublished paper focuses on two product types: programmable metalworking and handling equipment and microlithography. It adopts Williamson's transaction-cost economics framework to analyze why market failures may have arisen in the machine-tool industry as a result of changes from a relatively stable to a more rapidly changing, sophisticated CNC technology that requires increased system integration, particularly for large users.

In 1982, 77 percent of machine tools and parts were sold by wholesalers and commission sales operations. Most of these were tiny, with only 284 of 2,631 distributors employing more than 19 staff (data from Census of Wholesale Trade). At that time, most of the large machine-tool builders maintained just a few regional offices in areas of high demand—Los Angeles is cited as one of these.

Guile uses information from a survey conducted in 1985 by the American Machine Tool Distributor's Association (AMTDA) to rate the importance of the different sources of information buyers use to make machine-tool purchases. The survey rated trade journals at the top, then distributors, and builders' sales representatives at the bottom of the list. Paradoxically, respondents felt that builders' representatives had more technical knowledge than the distributors.

Guile's main argument is that, because the machine-tool industry has moved toward CNC and because of an increasing focus on system integration (particularly among large buyers), the burdens on distributors have increased dramatically. He cites five areas where distributors must increase capability: application engineering, service, technical training, flexible financing, and turnkey equipment. Failure to increase these leads to market failure. Most machine-tool distributors are not well equipped to deliver these services, but when they do start to add such capabilities, the structure of the industry prevents them from recapturing the added costs of engineers and support staff. For example, they have large costs in preparing bids for users which they cannot recover at the same time that builders appear to be passing more of these burdens on to them. The exceptions to this are those few builders who have established regional technology centers to offer enhanced services at the point of sale.

Three new sources of competition for machine-tool distributors are: (1) robot builders (e.g., GM/FANUC joint venture); (2) new engineering service groups; and (3) large capital-goods makers, especially those making controllers (e.g., HP, GE, Ingersoll Engineering) competing for the top end of the market.

The Japanese development of sophisticated but relatively standardized CNC product lines helped reduce transaction costs for distributors, thereby making it more attractive for them to push these products. This is on top of any economies of scale or scope advantages the Japanese gained through modular manufacturing.

Unfortunately, the report contains no comparative information on distributor networks. Thus, there is no sense of whether the U.S. distributor structure has made it easier for foreign entrants and whether it has contributed to the slowness of CNC diffusion in the United States by making it harder to educate users to the benefits of the new technology.

Holland, Max, *When the Machine Stopped: A Cautionary Tale from Industrial America*, Cambridge, Mass.: Harvard School of Business Press, 1989.

This book offers a detailed history of one U.S. machine-tool maker—Burg Tool—and the conditions in which it operated. Burg Tool provides an interesting microcosm of the fate of the U.S. machine-tool industry, from the start of the company as a family-run shop in the 1940s; through its growth in Los Angeles through the 1960s; its takeover by a conglomerate, Houdaille, in 1965; to the leveraged buyout of Houdaille in 1980; and to its high-profile unfair trade practices case against the Japanese in the early 1980s. The following are among the more general observations on the machine-tool industry Holland makes:

Defense orders were a large portion of total U.S. machine-tool sales in the postwar period, the result of conscious government policy following problems with the flooding of the market with low-cost, surplus tools post-1945. It is important to look at the indirect effect of government procurement—e.g., Burg Tool sold 5 percent directly to government but 30 percent to government contractors. Special orders help maintain innovation by forcing high R&D spending and testing new developments.

Imports accounted for only 5 percent of U.S. machine-tool purchases in 1960. This allowed U.S. firms to operate with large backorders; 70-plus U.S. firms set up export arrangements, often through wholly owned subsidiaries in Europe. Hughes avoided tariffs on German-made tools by simply rewiring those tools. In the 1960s, U.S. firms sought quick extra revenue and access to the Japanese market through licensing to Japanese firms (29 licenses between 1961 and 1964). MITI played a key role, preventing U.S. firms from setting up subsidiaries and insisting instead on licenses; licenses immediately cut U.S. exports to Japan (50 percent decrease in 1963; another 50 percent by 1965).

Introduction of a union at Burg resulted in the loss of its profit-sharing plan for blue-collar workers; at GM, machinists won the right to control NC technology in arbitration.

A key measure of machine-tool efficiency is downtime; thus, firms' focus is to minimize time for changing tools.

Acquisitions of U.S. machine-tool firms started in the early 1960s and increased in the latter half of the decade, fueled by Vietnam War buying (up to 50 percent of total sales). Mergers absorbed eight of the largest 24 U.S. machine-tool companies. Acquisitions slowed with the slump in 1969. In Burg's case, Houdaille's takeover of the firm resulted in problems due to financial management, rather than engineering management; increased bureaucracy and more confrontational labor-management relations; rigid accounting systems; and a lack of appreciation of the industry's cyclicality. The small conglomerates began to divest themselves of machine-tool firms in the recession of the early 1970s, while those with major machine-tool holdings (e.g., Textron, Litton) held on until the 1980s.

Burg abandoned its successful Econocenter tool targeted at the small buyer, because recession and inflation led to cuts in orders in this price-sensitive market. Thus, a vicious spiral began as lower product runs forced further increases in unit costs. This vicious spiral opened the market that Japanese firms later targeted.

Outsourcing is not a new phenomenon. At one time, Burg made only 7 percent of the final value of its machine tools in house, outsourcing the controller, motor, and most key parts and doing just the final assembly. Small, standardized products are among the most profitable, even though they are sold at low cost. Outsourcing was done to small "jobbers."

At a time of peak demand, Burg had $30 million in backlogs, compared to a monthly output of $0.9 million.

Poaching of trained workers was a problem, particularly in the Los Angeles area, where aerospace firms offer higher wages. A joint NMTBA-Department of Labor training program started in the 1960s, but poaching undermined it as Burg trained 15 machinists and then lost them right away to other area firms.

Capital was a problem, because even leading U.S. NC makers did not use NC machines in their factories.

MITI refused to protect the post–World War II Japanese domestic machine-tool market. The result was major imports (29 percent in 1950, 57 percent in 1955). Japan passed a law in 1956 to protect the machine-tool industry, which led to a 25 percent tariff on any products with a domestic equivalent. Japanese machine-tool firms got grants from MITI to buy foreign tools and study them (e.g., Mazak gets $140,000 for six tools). MITI was late to see the importance of NC—FANUC developed its first controller in Japan without MITI's help. A surge in Japanese imports of foreign machine tools from 1960 to 1962 led MITI to establish an $89-million fund for machine-tool firms to finance credit in 1962. The first Japanese inroads in the U.S. market occurred in the mid-1960s, when U.S. firms could not meet orders because of backlogs (Japanese imports increased from $2 million in 1964 to $26.2 million in 1967). The Japanese Diet passed a law in 1968 allowing joint ventures, which led to the second U.S. influx of agreements, including 12 licensing agreements for the latest NC technology (this argument would suggest that the law restricting direct U.S. investment in Japan is not the only reason for licensing). Yamazaki set up a wholly owned U.S. subsidiary (Mazak) in 1968, did its own marketing and service, and then began to ship NC lathes. They licensed Burg technology for all of Asia paying a fee equal to 10 percent of Burg's profits.

Magaziner, I., and M. Patinkin, *The Silent War*, New York: Random House, 1989.

This book, written in part by one of President Clinton's top policy advisors, includes a chapter on the German machine-tool industry, focusing on two firms: Traub (which specializes in grinding machines) and Scharmann (a small firm that has moved into machining cells and whole FMS plants). The book shows how the German firms began to worry about the Japanese in the 1970s, while U.S. managers remained complacent. German firms were not quick to react, however, because their markets were not immediately challenged by the Japanese (e.g., grinding is much harder to automate than lathes). Germany recognized that it could not compete on price and thus went for sophisticated machines that could reduce user costs in the long run. Germany made the transition by heavy investment in R&D and training, even during the recession of the early 1980s. German firms also elected to build in-house CNC expertise, rather than licensing Japanese technology or hiring computer programmers with no knowledge of the machine-tool industry. The German government helped through investments in the latest technologies (e.g., laser cutting), support for higher education and the training system, and grants to enable small companies to invest in CNC tools in-house.

Traub adapted U.S. innovations in computer diagnosis of machine-tool faults and improved relations with customers through satellite link-ups to users. Traub spent $3.5 million on a new training center that quickly (1984 to 1987) grew from 500 to 3,000 people trained annually. Traub also spends $1.5 million annually on apprentices. Scharmann became a leader in FMS by solving manufacturing bottlenecks for Caterpillar. Scharmann also recognized it was too small to compete, so it arranged a merger with a larger German company with the same investment philosophy.

This study criticizes the United States for a lack of awareness of foreign competition or markets; e.g., the United States lost its firm hold on the Swedish machine-tool market in the 1970s, when it focused on domestic orders in the post–oil-shock boom. When American companies returned during the next U.S. slump, the Germans had taken over the Swedish market. Managers in both German companies say the U.S. problem is a lack of worker skills needed to adopt and innovate with the latest technologies.

National Research Council, Commission on Engineering and Technical Systems, Manufacturing Studies Board, Committee on the Machine Tool Industry, *The U.S. Machine Tool Industry and the Defense Industrial Base*, Washington, D.C.: National Academy Press, 1983.

This 1983 study stemmed from a Department of Defense (DoD) request to the National Academy to study the defense readiness and international competitiveness of the U.S. machine-tool industry and recommend policies based on the DoD's needs. The 19-member committee, chaired by James Ashton of Rockwell, had heavy representation from DoD prime contractors, some machine-tool firms, and a handful of academics and bankers. The committee conducted written surveys of machine-tool users and suppliers, site visits, and interviews and augmented the data collection with the collective knowledge of the committee members. This study seems to have done a good job diagnosing the problems facing the U.S. machine-tool industry. The policy recommendations, however, suffer from a DoD focus and appear dated in comparison to more recent studies, which have the benefit of ten years of experience gleaned from state-level technology policy experiments during the 1980s.

The committee argues that the U.S. machine-tool industry is losing ground because of structural changes in the industry exacerbated by the severe recession in the early 1980s. In particular, it cites increased global competition, rapid technological change, and a change in the basic machine-tool business—from selling stand-alone metalworking tools to selling and maintaining manufacturing process improvement systems—as factors that made traditional practices in the U.S. machine-tool industry ill suited to the present day. The committee faults U.S. machine-tool suppliers for failing to invest and for practicing order-backlog management to cope with business cycles. It faults U.S. machine-tool users—particularly the auto industry—for failing to demand sophisticated manufacturing technology. The committee credited the Japanese success in penetrating the U.S. market to lower wages, lower interest rates, government-industry cooperation to promote exports, and better reliability and technical superiority of their product.

The committee's policy recommendations are divided into categories directed at DoD, major DoD contractors and other government agencies, and U.S. machine-tool builders. The most detailed are for DoD itself and include recommending that DoD (1) display greater commitment to increasing manufacturing productivity through existing programs (e.g., ManTech); (2) create incentives for productivity improvements that operate directly on machine-tool builders contracting with DoD or DoD prime contractors; (3) simplify contracting procedures so machine-tool builders can bid directly for government contracts; (4) establish industry-wide research centers to improve the flow of new technical information from universities and other laboratories to machine-tool firms; (5) require that contractors guarantee that they can maintain production for five years even if supply lines are disrupted to protect U.S. wartime production capabilities; and (6) study recent consolidations, acquisitions, and joint ventures within the machine-tool industry to determine their effects on domestic machine-tool firms and the ability of foreign firms to penetrate the U.S. market.

The committee argued that healthy macroeconomic policies that provide continuous growth over several years would be the most significant single contributor to a healthy machine-tool industry. It also recommended that Congress increase funding for existing DoD machine-tool programs, that the Department of Commerce promote U.S. machine-tool exports, and that the administration better coordinate the existing federal programs affecting the machine-tool industry. Finally, the committee encouraged the U.S. machine-tool industry to be more aggressive in applying new technology, invest more for the long-term, and conduct more joint R&D efforts. It also suggested that the industry association should mount an aggressive effort to educate machine-tool builders about the existing government programs designed to help them.

Parkinson, Stephen T., *New Product Development in Engineering: A Comparison of the British and West German Machine Tool Industries*, Cambridge, England: Cambridge University Press, 1984.

The study focused on the reasons for the relative failure of the British machine-tool industry by exploring the differences in the adoption of new technologies and the product development process in German and British firms. Parkinson's main interest was in the relationship between buyers and suppliers. He conducted surveys of machine-tool makers and users in the two countries. While the United States is not included in his sample, there are close parallels between the U.S. and British industry environments.

He found that the German machine-tool makers had greater direct involvement with customers in the design and development of new products. They took longer developing new machines and were more likely to test them in customer sites, as well as being more likely to customize machines to users' needs.

Among the factors that enabled Germans to develop technically superior machines were management with a technical rather than financial orientation and much closer links with research institutions.

He also attributed a large part of the British problem to machine-tool customers who are technologically unsophisticated, emphasize cost over quality, have a short-run investment timeframe, lack the skills necessary to utilize sophisticated machines, and fail to see the potential for the flexibility of the new technologies in reorganizing the work process.

He concluded that much closer, more cooperative relations between manufacturers and users are preferable to competitive market relations if a nation's machine-tool industry is to succeed in worldwide competition. He put the onus on both types of firms to restructure their organizations and approach to each other to build closer relationships. He conceded that differences in corporate and managerial culture between the United Kingdom and Germany may make this difficult.

Rees, J., R. Briggs, and D. Hicks, "New Technology in the United States' Machinery Industry: Trends and Implications," in Thwaites and Oakey, eds., *The Regional Impact of Technological Change*, London: Frances Pinter, 1985, p. 164.

This study demonstrates the rate of CNC and other technologies' diffusion in the U.S. machinery industry through a survey questionnaire sent to 4,000 U.S. plants with a 20-percent response rate. It finds that 50 to 60 percent of all machine-tool firms had some CNC technology in house in the early 1980s. It shows that the rate of adoption varied by region and was lower for small, independent companies. Surprisingly, older firms were found to be more likely to invest in the more recent technologies.

Taymaz, Erol, *Technological Capabilities and International Competitiveness: A Study on the Machine Tool Industry*, Ann Arbor, Mich.: Case Western Reserve University, UMI Dissertation Services, 1989.

The study attempts to quantify the importance of a domestic machine-tool industry to the health of a country's manufacturing base. While acknowledging that there is a two-way relationship between the health of makers and users of machine tools, Taymaz attempts to show that the declining competitiveness of the U.S. machine-tool industry in the early 1980s had an adverse impact on the U.S. engineering industry. The logic of the argument is as follows: Machine tools are a "nodal" industry—i.e. one that is crucial to regional development and continuous innovation. The importance of proximity between makers and users is essentially traced to decreases in transaction costs and the benefits attained by learning by doing. Many of these activities are also interdependent—e.g.

machine-tool innovations can be crucial to transforming the manufacturing process. The negative effects for users of declining machine-tool competitiveness, Taymaz argues, arise from inertia in the buyer-supplier relationship.

Taymaz makes some important breakdowns of the machine-tool sector: three types of parts are used in machine tools: (l) small, standard parts; (2) preassembled components (e.g., engines, in some cases controllers); and (3) machine-tool–specific components. The historical definition of machine-tool makers only includes the last of these. He also distinguishes between four groupings of machine-tool use: transfer lines, special-purpose machines (mass manufacturing), machining cells, and FMS (flexible production). He groups specific tools under these categories using factor analysis and shows that the United States is declining in competitiveness sharply in the flexible area. He argues that the United States' continued strength in transfer lines and special-purpose tools derives partly from the demands of U.S. users for these tools; the main reason, however, is that these tools are very difficult to trade internationally—e.g., one-off orders and close relations with the customer are difficult for foreign firms to establish. Despite these factors, he shows that the United States has also been losing competitiveness in this area, though at a slower rate. He shows that despite the general shift toward NC tools, that there has been no systematic decline in station-type machines. U.S. demand for these units, however, is highly cyclical—rising proportionately faster than total sales when machine-tool demand increases. This analysis, however, is based on data up to the mid-1980s and could miss recent trends that differ from historical practice.

The study provides detailed product breakdowns for the six largest machine-tool producing countries using *American Machinist* and trade data. Taymaz shows that the United States has a much lower export-output ratio than all other major machine-tool makers. The study defines competitiveness in a product segment as the net export ratio—on a scale of –1 (all imports) to +1 (all exports). It shows the United States relies more heavily on exports to developing countries than other leading machine-tool makers, linking this to demand from U.S. engineering firms who get their mass production tools from U.S. makers.